The
Vegetarian
Traveler

On the Cover—

Motrano, Societa Lila'aurora, Siena, Italy
see page 268

The Vegetarian Traveler

Where to Stay if You're—

Vegetarian

Vegan

Environmentally Sensitive

BY

JED & SUSAN CIVIC

Published for the Paul Brunton Philosophic Foundation by

LARSON PUBLICATIONS

International Standard Book Number: 0-943914-79-5
Library of Congress Catalog Card Number: 96-79707

Published for the Paul Brunton Philosophic Foundation by
Larson Publications
4936 NYS Route 414
Burdett, NY 14818 USA

03 02 01 00 99 98 97

10 9 8 7 6 5 4 3 2

Contents

Acknowledgments

CERTAIN PEOPLE deserve a special Thank-you for their contributions to this project:

Jonathan Back, proprietor of The Castle in St. John, Virgin Islands (page 125) for putting us in touch with Larson Publications and helping with a variety of tasks in the editorial process.

Paul Cash, Amy Cash, Kate Thomas, and Pamela Drix at Larson Publications for all their help in bringing the book to completion.

Dean Milan, artist, and Pam Teisler-Rice, founder of the Viva-Vegie Society. Pam and Dean take vegetarian advocacy to the streets of New York City, helping Mr. and Ms. Pedestrian get the facts about healthful, ethical, and environmentally conscious eating. For a copy of *101 Reasons Why I'm a Vegetarian*, send $1.00 and a self-addressed, stamped return envelope to the Viva-Vegie Society, Prince Street Station, P.O. Box 294, New York, NY 10012.

Martin Rowe, whose insightful contributions to the writing of this book came at the most opportune times. Martin is the managing editor of *Satya*, a magazine of vegetarianism, environmentalism, and animal advocacy. For information about subscribing, contact *Satya* at 212-674-0952.

Though they don't know it, Vegi Ventures from Norfolk, England (page 164) was one of the original inspirations for us to pursue vegetarian travel. It's no surprise to us that the British were the first to come up with the idea of actively promoting vegetarian travel.

We would also like to extend a Thank-you to Jean Thaler for encouraging us to charge for this book.

A special Thank-you goes to Patrick Smith from Veggies Catering Campaign in Nottingham, England, for his special work promoting vegetarianism and animal rights throughout the United Kingdom. Patrick is extremely knowledgeable and is a pleasure to work with. He is always quick to understand our needs and respond to them. Veggies Catering Campaign maintains an impressive library on vegetarianism, animal advocacy, and environmentalism which is open to the public. Write or visit them at 180 Mansfield Road, Nottingham, NG1 3HW England.

Introduction

WHY THIS BOOK?

Being strict vegetarians ourselves, we want to make it as easy as possible for other vegetarians to travel in a world where so many people prefer a meat-centered diet. We're a minority, but a growing one.

A recent Gallup poll reports, for example, that 20% of our population seeks vegetarian meals and a full third of our population will eat vegetarian meals when they are offered. Other surveys show that 12.4 million Americans consider themselves vegetarian and as many as 500,000 consider themselves vegan.

With this many people who can benefit from the service, it's time we had a book focusing on vegetarian lodging. Guidebooks oriented toward the general public help us research where to go, what to see, and things to do, but offer little or no information on how sympathetic or unsympathetic your host may be to vegetarian, vegan, or other special dietary needs. Other books, oriented toward vegetarians, provide mainly restaurants or are limited to specific regions.

The need became obvious, and we are responding. We hope that the work we've already done will be helpful to you. And we hope that you will help the whole vegetarian/vegan community by helping us improve this service in the many editions of this book we will bring forth in future years.

OUR JOURNEY

When the two of us met, we each had a sensitivity toward animals; but that sensitivity had not yet fully developed. Our awareness grew, and we started making donations to various nonprofit environmental and animal rights organizations. They in turn sent us all sorts of literature educating us about the ongoing devastation of animals throughout the world. This literature included an assortment of recipes, from appetizers to desserts.

Our early efforts in vegan cooking brought some surprise hits and some real disasters—making for many interesting experiences! Soon we learned what we liked best and developed a wide variety of breakfast, lunch, and dinner options. Now we have more variety in our diets than we did before we were vegetarians!

We've also been in the travel business since 1980, which has brought many opportunities to travel throughout the world. For the last five years, we have traveled as vegans and learned many things useful to other vegetarian travelers.

Thailand, for example, brought imaginative catering —but only after we learned to "just say no" to *nam pla* (fish sauce). India is excellent for lacto-vegetarians, but as vegans we had to repeat over and over again, "No dairy, no ghee, no cheese." After a while, it was "no problem."

Italy was easy: lots of pasta and pizza without cheese. In New Zealand we rented a camper and did most of our own cooking, but we found restaurants that were very happy to prepare imaginative vegan dishes not on their menus.

We found, in every country we visited, that we would not go hungry as long as we spoke up and insisted on being served vegan meals. This includes traveling to such widely varying places as Fiji, Singapore, Netherlands, England, St. Lucia, Costa Rica, Jamaica, and even New Jersey!

Our passion to discover new vegetarian locations soon became one of our main reasons for traveling. We feel as if we're pioneers discovering a new land. Finding a new restaurant or B&B or resort that caters thoughtfully to vegetarians gives us tremendous pleasure.

Each time we find a new travel destination worth telling about, we add their literature to our growing collection. With this material and more provided by vegetarian and animal rights organizations throughout the world, we now have a small library of information on vegetarian restaurants, hotels, motels, B&Bs, and local vegetarian organizations. We also enjoy meeting fellow vegetarians, with whom we usually find ourselves soon discussing, recommending, and sharing advice on planning trips.

One thing led to another, and soon we created a full-service travel agency, Environmental Travel, to cater to the needs of the vegetarian community. To assist our clients in vacation planning, we also self-published Environmental Travel's *Catalog of Worldwide Vegetarian and Vegan Vacation Spots.*

The response to the travel service and catalog was widespread and very enthusiastic. The next step was obvious: write the book you now hold in your hands!

YOUR ROLE

This book is just a beginning. It will no doubt help you a great deal already; but each edition should get better and better with more entries, more information, and more reports from people who visit the establishments we list.

You can help enormously in making these future editions more comprehensive and more useful. When you visit establishments we list, please give us your comments—both positive and negative. Was the staff helpful and courteous? Did they prepare meals to satisfy your requirements? Was the accommodation the way you imagined it to be from their description in the book or on the phone or in their brochure? Tell us about any unusual experiences you had—and not necessarily just food-related. Was there anything special en route to your destination, or nearby attractions, and so on? Have we left anything out of our listing that the vegetarian traveler needs or wants to know?

You can also help by telling us about good vegetarian accommodations not contained in this book. To help us better serve the vegetarian/vegan community in future editions, please photocopy and complete the "Your

Feedback" questionnaire at the back of the book and return it to us.

Restaurants and lodging establishments respond to the needs of their guests. If guests don't speak up, nothing changes. So don't hesitate to ask if an establishment will cater to your dietary needs and preferences. Many establishments whose menus don't include vegetarian fare can and will provide it on request.

One further note. Most of our research so far has been oriented primarily to locating good spots for vacations. We are particularly interested now in learning about good places you've found to stay at on business or other non-vacation travel. Establishments need not be entirely vegetarian; they simply need to be pleasant, courteous and thoughtfully accommodating to the needs of the vegetarian traveler.

INTERPRETING THE FORMAT OF THIS BOOK

We sent the following questionnaire to establishments that have shown themselves to be specially accommodating to vegetarians. We learned of them either through their own advertising, articles written about them, recommendations from other vegetarians, or our own visits.

1. Name of Establishment
  Address:
  Country:
  Telephone:
  Fax:
  Name of Proprietor:

2. What type of establishment are you?

○ Bed & Breakfast ○ Motel ○ Hotel ○ Spa
○ Resort ○ Cruise ○ Outdoor Adventure ○ Retreat
○ Other _____

3. Describe your location. Please mark all that apply.

○ Beachfront ○ Mountain ○ Desert ○ City Center
○ Quaint Village ○ Resort Town ○ Suburban
○ Lakefront ○ Other _____

4. Please mark all activities your establishment offers or that can be found nearby.

○ Indoor pool ○ Water sports ○ Massage
○ Outdoor pool ○ Cross-country skiing ○ Juice
fasting ○ Tennis ○ Downhill skiing ○ Weight loss
classes ○ Golf ○ Horseback riding ○ Educational
lectures ○ Bicycling ○ Nutrition classes
○ Sightseeing tours ○ Hiking ○ Camping
○ Nightclub ○ Canoeing/kayaking ○ Beach
○ Antique shops ○ Boating ○ Yoga ○ Museums
○ Snorkeling ○ Fitness ○ Scuba diving
○ Fitness classes ○ Exercise room ○ Other ____

5. Please mark the meals you offer.

○ Breakfast ○ Lunch ○ Dinner

What meals are normally included in your basic rates?

○ Breakfast ○ Lunch ○ Dinner

*What percentage of your meals do you estimate is
vegetarian* (including dairy/eggs/honey)?_____%

*What percentage of your meals do you estimate is vegan
(no animal products at all)?_____%*

*What percentage of your foods do you estimate is
organically grown?_____%*

Which of the following types of diets can you cater for?*
○ Wheat/soy free ○ Oil free ○ Sugar free
○ Low salt ○ Yeast free ○ Kosher

Are there restaurants nearby that accommodate vegans?
○ Yes ○ No

* A "yes" entry in our listings indicates that most or all these special diets are catered to on request. Contact the establishment directly for details.

6. Based on the type of establishment listed in question #2, please rate your overall price category:

○ Inexpensive ○ Moderate ○ Expensive

Do you offer specials or package deals? ○ Yes ○ No

7. What percentage of your rooms has private bath/shower? _____%

What percentage of your rooms is nonsmoking? _____%

Do you offer car parking facilities? ○ Yes ○ No

Do you supply non-animal tested toiletries in your rooms?
○ Yes ○ No

Are your facilities wheelchair accessible? ○ Yes ○ No

Do you spray the rooms with insecticide? ○ Yes ○ No

Do you offer child discounts? ○ Yes ○ No

Are pets welcome? ○ Yes ○ No

8. Which of the following can be found in your establishment?

○ Leather furniture ○ Wool rugs ○ Down comforters ○ Feather pillows ○ Dead/mounted/stuffed animals ○ Farm animals ○ Live caged animals/birds

9. Will you offer a discount for readers of this book?

Please describe (i.e., 10% discount for mentioning book, etc.)

10. Forms of payment accepted. Mark all applicable.

US Currency:

○ Cash ○ Travelers checks ○ Personal checks

Local Currency:

○ Cash ○ Travelers checks ○ Personal checks

Credit Cards:

○ American Express ○ Visa ○ MasterCard

○ Discover ○ Other _____

11. In 50 words or less, please give a colorful description of your establishment.

Our intent with these questions was to evoke a general feel for the establishment. Questions that asked for estimates (i.e., price category, % organic, etc.) required us (for now at least!) to rely on the respondents' honesty and judgment.

We also allowed flexibility in how proprietors interpreted these questions, which may result in some inconsistency. For example, when asked what percentage of their meals is vegetarian or vegan, some said 100% but only on request; we take this to mean that you can get an entirely vegetarian meal if you ask for it, but the person sitting next to you may be eating meat or fish. Others responded that while they don't regularly serve vegetarian or vegan meals, they are quite capable of providing good ones "on request."

All the information in our listings was provided by

the establishments themselves. We do not represent any of them and do not assume responsibility for misleading information. To avoid misunderstanding, we strongly advise that you verify items of concern and contact establishments well in advance when making reservations.

As mentioned in "Your Role" above, future editions of this resource will incorporate the feedback of those of you who use it.

Entries are arranged by geographic regions that fit conveniently into one map. Within the United States, listings within the region proceed alphabetically by state, and then by city or town within the state. Canada is arranged alphabetically by province, then by city or town within the province. Outside the United States and Canada, listings within a region are arranged alphabetically by country, then alphabetically by city or town.

MAKING RESERVATIONS

Our listings provide country codes for telephone and fax numbers outside the U.S. and Canada. These appear in parentheses at the beginning of the numbers. When calling from outside a given country, first access an international operator (dial 011 in the U.S.), then dial the country code. If the next number is a 0, it is usually omitted when dialing from outside that country: drop it and then dial the rest of the number. When inside that country, the country code is not needed but the 0 is.

Just as we in the U.S. are regularly adding new area codes, other countries are regularly adding digits to their city codes and main numbers and making other changes. Check with an operator if you have difficulty making connections.

When calling or faxing, be prepared with some of the local language when dialing a non-English-speaking country. (Your long-distance operator may be able to provide a translation service.) Also, times differ throughout the world: Make your call or fax at a time that is reasonable for the person on the other end.

As an alternative to contacting the establishment yourself, you can take this book to a travel agency and ask an agent to make the reservations. He or she should be willing to make these reservations as a courtesy for you in conjunction with your round-trip airline tickets, or for a small service fee to defray their costs.

JED AND SUSAN CIVIC
KEW GARDENS, NEW YORK
OCTOBER, 1996

United States
and Canada

MOUNTAIN TREK FITNESS RETREAT & HEALTH SPA

**P.O. Box 1352
Ainsworth Hot Springs, BC V0G 1A0
Canada
Phone: 800-661-5161 or
604-229-5636
Fax: 604 229-5636**

Proprietor: Wendy Pope

Category: Outdoor adventure

Location: Mountain, quaint village, lakefront

Open all year? Open Apr.–Nov.

Price: Moderate

Special packages: Yes

Reader discount: $100 off regular price of hiking vacations, $50 off fasting retreats

Child discount: No

MEALS

Included: B, L, D

Offered: B, L, D

% Vegetarian: 100%

% Vegan: 80%

% Organic: 75%

Special diets: Yes

Nearby restaurants: No

ROOMS

% Private bath/shower: 100%

% Non-smoking: 100%

% Air conditioned: 0%

Car parking: Yes

Wheelchair access: No

Non-animal tested toiletries: No

Insecticides used? No

Pets welcome? No

Of animal origin: Feather pillows, down comforters

Nearby activities: Outdoor pool, golf, bicycling, hiking, yoga, exercise room, massage, juice fasting, weight loss classes, educational lectures.

Description: Our deluxe mountain lodge is nestled in the spectacular Kootenay mountains of southern British Columbia, just a five-minute walk from

hot springs. Vigorous hiking vacations or restful supervised fasting retreats are offered. Wonderful vegetarian or vegan meals are part of the package, as well as massage, yoga, and spa amenities.

Forms of payment: *U.S. currency*—cash, travelers checks, personal checks; *Local currency*—cash, travelers checks; MC, VI

WESTERN CANADA

British Columbia .... ➤

HOLLYHOCK

Box 127
Mansons Landing
Cortes Island, BC V0P 1K0 Canada
Phone: 800-933-6339
Fax: 604-935-6424

Proprietor: N/A

Category: Resort, retreat

Location: Beachfront, rural wilderness

Open all year? Open mid-March to end of October

Price: Moderate

Special packages: Yes

Reader discount: No

Child discount: Yes

MEALS

Included: B, L, D

Offered: B, L, D

% Vegetarian: 70%

% Vegan: 30%

% Organic: 65%

Special diets: Yes

Nearby restaurants: No

ROOMS

% Private bath/shower: 5%

% Non-smoking: 100%

% Air conditioned: 0%

Car parking: Yes

Wheelchair access: Yes

Non-animal tested toiletries: Yes

Insecticides used? No

Pets welcome? No

Of animal origin: Feather pillows, wool rugs, down comforters

Nearby activities: Bicycling, hiking, canoeing/kayaking, boating, scuba diving, camping, beach, yoga, massage, educational lectures, sightseeing tours, star gazing, wilderness interpretation, meditation, craft & gift store, holistic learning

Description: Hollyhock is Canada's leading holistic learning and vacation center. Since 1982, Hollyhock has offered seminars, workshops, and holidays in the practical, creative, and healing arts. Spectacular west coast island wilderness environment. Enjoy nature interpretation, sailing and kayaking,

DEWITT JONES

ocean swimming, forest trails, organic gardens, and gourmet vegetarian meals.

Forms of payment: *U.S. currency*—cash, travelers checks, personal checks; *Local currency*—cash, travelers checks; MC, VI

YASODHARA ASHRAM SOCIETY

Box 9
Kootenay Bay, BC V0B 1X0 Canada
Phone: 604-227-9224
Fax: 604-227-9494

Proprietor: Non-profit organization
Category: Retreat
Location: Mountain, lakefront
Open all year? Yes
Price: Moderate
Special packages: Yes
Reader discount: No
Child discount: Yes

MEALS

Included: B, L, D
Offered: B, L, D
% Vegetarian: See comment
% Vegan: On request
% Organic: 20%
Special diets: None
Nearby restaurants: Yes
Comment: Vegetarian meals always; non-vegetarian also 3 days/wk

ROOMS

% Private bath/shower: 5%
% Non-smoking: 100%
% Air conditioned: 0%
Car parking: Yes
Wheelchair access: Yes
Non-animal tested toiletries: No
Insecticides used? No
Pets welcome? No
Of animal origin: Farm animals, wool rugs
Nearby activities: Tennis, golf, bicycling, hiking, canoeing/kayaking, boating, scuba diving, water sports, cross-country skiing, downhill skiing, horseback riding, camping, beach, yoga, educational lectures, sightseeing tours, antique shops, museums
Description: Experience the serene beauty of Yasodhara Ashram in the mountains of southeastern British Columbia. The Ashram is a vibrant spiritual community with an atmosphere conducive to reflection, study, and renewal. It is the home of the Temple of Divine Light, dedicated to all religions. Founded more than thirty years ago by Swami Sivananda Radha. A full range of courses, family and individual retreats.
Forms of payment: *U.S. currency*—cash, travelers checks, personal checks; *Local currency*—cash, travelers checks; MC, VI

KOOTENAY TAI CHI CENTRE

P.O. Box 566
Nelson, BC V1L 5R3 Canada
Phone/Fax: 604-352-3714

Proprietor: Rex Eastman

Category: Retreat

Location: Mountain, lakefront

Open all year? Open August only, for two weeks

Price: Inexpensive

Special packages: Yes

Reader discount: No

Child discount: Yes

MEALS

Included: B, L, D

Offered: B, L, D

% Vegetarian: 100%

% Vegan: On request

% Organic: 60%

Special diets: Yes

Nearby restaurants: Yes

ROOMS

% Private bath/shower: 0%

% Non-smoking: 100%

% Air conditioned: 0%

Car parking: Yes

Wheelchair access: Yes

Non-animal tested toiletries: No

Insecticides used? No

Pets welcome? No

Of animal origin: None

Nearby activities: Hiking, canoeing/kayaking, camping, beach, fitness classes, massage, tai chi instruction, qi gong meditation and philosophy

Description: Nestled between towering mountains on a beautiful lake, this is the perfect environment for experiencing a simple, natural lifestyle and getting away from the complexities of modern living. Join us in living and learning unique exercises for health and martial arts on the shores of beautiful Kootenay Lake. Week 1: Tai Chi—an oriental system of health maintenance, stress reduction, and self-defense. Week 2: Pakua—the sister art of Tai Chi, promoting flexibility and strength through graceful circular movements.

Forms of payment: *U.S. currency*—cash, travelers checks, personal checks; *Local currency*—cash, travelers checks, personal checks

GOLDEN DREAMS B&B

**6412 Easy St.
Whistler, BC V0N 1B6 Canada
Phone: 604-932-2667
Fax: 604-932-7055**

Proprietor: Ann Spence
Category: Bed & Breakfast
Location: Resort town
Open all year? Inquire directly
Price: Moderate
Special packages: No
Reader discount: No
Child discount: No

MEALS

Included: B
Offered: B
% Vegetarian: 10%
% Vegan: 10%
% Organic: 50%
Special diets: Yes
Nearby restaurants: Yes

ROOMS

% Private bath/shower: 25%
% Non-smoking: 100%
% Air conditioned: 0%

Car parking: Yes
Wheelchair access: No
Non-animal tested toiletries: No
Insecticides used? No
Pets welcome? No
Of animal origin: Wool rugs, down comforters
Nearby activities: Indoor pool, tennis, golf, bicycling, hiking, canoeing/kayaking, boating, water sports, cross-country skiing, downhill skiing, horseback riding, camping, beach, fitness classes, exercise room, massage, sightseeing tours, nightclub
Description: Be surrounded by nature's beauty and pampered with a wholesome breakfast! Located just one mile from the village express gondolas. Valley trail system and bus route at our doorstep. Three unique "theme" rooms with cozy duvets and sherry decanter. Relax in the private jacuzzi or family room with wood fireplace. Full guest kitchen.
Forms of payment: *U.S. currency*—cash; *Local currency*—cash

WESTERN U.S. & HAWAII

*Alaska
Arizona
California
Hawaii
Oregon
Utah
Washington*

RAINFOREST RETREAT

Box 8005
Port Alexander, AK 99836 USA
Phone: 907-568-2229

Proprietor: Paul & Gayle Young
Category: Bed & Breakfast
Location: Beachfront, quaint village
Open all year? Yes
Price: Moderate
Special packages: No
Reader discount: No
Child discount: Yes

MEALS

Included: B, L, D
Offered: B, L, D
% Vegetarian: 100%
% Vegan: 100%
% Organic: 50%
Special diets: Yes
Nearby restaurants: No
Comment: All meals
   included only if
   meal option chosen

ROOMS

% Private bath/shower: 100%
% Non-smoking: 100%
% Air conditioned: 0%
Car parking: No
Wheelchair access: No
Non-animal tested toiletries: No
Insecticides used? No
Pets welcome? No
Of animal origin: Feather pillows
Nearby activities: Hiking,
   canoeing/kayaking, boating,
   camping, beach

Description: Remote wilderness cabin
   situated on beach in southeast
   Alaska village of 100 residents.
   Wilderness at your doorstep.
   Hiking, ski trips, subsistence
   activities. Generous vegan
   meals and snacks or light
   cooking option available in
   the cabin. Fully modern.
   Enthusiastic Alaskan hosts.

Forms of payment: *U.S. currency*—cash,
   travelers checks, personal
   checks
Comment: No roads/cars here. Access
   by float plane only.

CANYON RANCH HEALTH & FITNESS RESORT

**8600 E. Rockcliff Road
Tucson, AZ 85750 USA
Phone: 520-749-9655
Fax: 520-749-1646**

Proprietor: Mel Zuckerman
Category: Spa
Location: Desert
Open all year? Yes
Price: Expensive
Special packages: Yes
Reader discount: No
Child discount: Yes

MEALS

Included: B, L, D
Offered: B, L, D
% Vegetarian: 37%
% Vegan: 35%
% Organic: Varies
Special diets: Yes
Nearby restaurants: Yes

ROOMS

% Private bath/shower: 100%
% Non-smoking: 100%
% Air conditioned: 100%
Car parking: Yes
Wheelchair access: Yes
Non-animal tested toiletries: No
Insecticides used? No
Pets welcome? Varies
Of animal origin: None
Nearby activities: Indoor pool, outdoor pool, tennis, bicycling, hiking, nutrition classes, yoga, fitness classes, exercise room, massage, educational lectures, sightseeing tours, antique shops, museums

Description: Internationally renowned health and fitness resort. Lifestyle vacations focus on a person's goals whether fitness, relaxation, spiritual, mind-body connection, or just a total escape. Five-time *Conde Nast Traveler* "Best Spa" award winner. Invest in yourself and experience the best.

Forms of payment: *U.S. currency*— cash, travelers checks, personal checks; AX, MC, VI, Discover

Comment: Discount for children over 14 during certain months

NATURAL BED AND BREAKFAST

**3150 East Presidio Road
Tuscon, AZ 85716 USA
Phone: 520-881-4582
Fax: 520-326-1385**

Proprietor: L. Marc Haberman

Category: Bed & Breakfast

Location: City center, mountain, desert

Open all year? Yes

Price: Inexpensive

Special packages: Yes

Reader discount: $5

Child discount: Yes

MEALS

Included: B

Offered: B, D

% Vegetarian: 100%

% Vegan: 90%

% Organic: 50%

Special diets: Yes

Nearby restaurants: No

ROOMS

% Private bath/shower: 60%

% Non-smoking: 100%

% Air conditioned: 30%

Car parking: No

Wheelchair access: Yes

Non-animal tested toiletries: No

Insecticides used? No

Pets welcome? No

Of animal origin: Wool rugs, down comforters, feather pillows

Nearby activities: Outdoor pool, tennis, bicycling, hiking, horseback riding, nutrition classes, camping, massage, juice fasting, educational lectures, sightseeing tours, nightclub, antique shops, museums

Description: At Natural B&B, the word "natural" is true in all senses of the word. Attention is paid to a natural, non-toxic, non-allergenic environment. My home is water-cooled. Only natural foods are served. Excellent professional massage is available at a discount. I invite you to share the very special atmosphere of my natural healing home environment.

Forms of payment: *U.S. currency*—cash, travelers checks, personal checks

WE CARE HEALTH CENTER

**18000 Long Canyon Rd
Desert Hot Springs, CA 92241 USA
Phone: 800-888-2523 or
619-251-2261
Fax: 619-251-5399**

Proprietor: Susana Lombardi
Category: Retreat
Location: Desert
Open all year? Yes
Price: Inexpensive
Special packages: Yes
Reader discount: 10%
Child discount: No

MEALS

Included: See comments
Offered: See comments
% Vegetarian: 100%
% Vegan: 100%
% Organic: 80%
Special diets: None
Nearby restaurants: Yes
Comment: 13 liquid meals per day, all freshly prepared. Fasting only.

ROOMS

% Private bath/shower: 80%
% Non-smoking: 100%
% Air conditioned: 90%
Car parking: Yes
Wheelchair access: No
Non-animal tested toiletries: Yes
Insecticides used? No
Pets welcome? No
Of animal origin: None
Nearby activities: Outdoor pool, hiking, nutrition classes, yoga, massage, juice fasting, weight loss classes, educational lectures, vegetarian cooking classes

Description: Enjoy, relax, learn, while cleansing and revitalizing your body, mind, and spirit. Fasting, yoga, colonics, massage, vegetarian cooking demonstration. Just 12 rooms. California warm desert, mineral waters. Operating since 1986.

Forms of payment: *U.S. currency*—cash, travelers checks, personal checks; AX, MC, VI

HEARTWOOD INSTITUTE

**220 Harmony Lane
Garberville, CA 95542 USA
Phone: 707-923-5004
Fax: 707-923-5010**

Proprietor: Robert Fasic
Category: Retreat, healing arts school
Location: Mountain
Open all year? Yes
Price: Moderate
Special packages: Yes
Reader discount: No
Child discount: No

MEALS

Included: B, L, D
Offered: B, L, D
% Vegetarian: 95%
% Vegan: 55%
% Organic: 95%
Special diets: Yes
Nearby restaurants: No

ROOMS

% Private bath/shower: 0%
% Non-smoking: 100%
% Air conditioned: 0%
Car parking: Yes
Wheelchair access: No

Non-animal tested toiletries:
No

Insecticides used? No

Pets welcome? No

Of animal origin: None

Nearby activities:
Outdoor pool, hiking, yoga, tai chi, massage, other therapeutic sessions

HEARTWOOD INSTITUTE

Description: Heartwood Institute, located on the side of a pristine mountain wilderness area, is a healing arts school with year-round classes and retreat facilities. Our kitchen prepares delicious vegetarian meals, primarily organic. Some of the produce comes directly from our extensive garden. We also have an outdoor hot tub, a sauna, and in summer a large, clothing-optional pool for our students and guests.

Forms of payment: *U.S. currency*—cash, travelers checks, personal checks; MC, VI

OPTIMUM HEALTH INSTITUTE OF SAN DIEGO

**6970 Central Avenue
Lemon Grove, CA 91945 USA
Phone: 619-464-3346
Fax: 619-589-4098**

Proprietor: Non-profit organization

Category: Wellness center

Location: Suburban

Open all year? Yes

Price: Inexpensive

Special packages: No

Reader discount: No

Child discount: Yes

MEALS

Included: B, L, D

Offered: B, L, D

% Vegetarian: 100%

% Vegan: 100%

% Organic: 75%

Special diets: Yes

Nearby restaurants: Yes

ROOMS

% Private bath/shower: 100%

% Non-smoking: 100%

% Air conditioned: 40%

Car parking: Yes

Wheelchair access: Yes

Non-animal tested toiletries: No

Insecticides used? No

Pets welcome? No

Of animal origin: None

Nearby activities: Outdoor pool, golf, bicycling, hiking, nutrition classes, fitness classes, exercise room, massage, juice fasting, educational lectures, antique shops, museums

Description: Since our founding in
1976, more than 35,000 people
from throughout the world
have attended and benefited
from our program. It is our
belief, shared by more and
more health-conscious people,
that the natural state of the
person is vibrant and optimal
health: Given the proper tools,
the body will find its perfect
health and balance. At OHI we
teach you what those tools are
and how to use them effectively. Our program is based on the
whole person, including the
mental, physical, and emotional aspects of the person. We
encourage our guests to come
for a three-week stay in order
to achieve the full benefit of
our program, but shorter stays
of at least one week are
allowed.

Forms of payment: *U.S. currency*—cash,
travelers checks, personal
checks; AX, MC, VI, Discover

HARBIN HOT SPRINGS & STONEFRONT RESTAURANT

P.O. Box 782
Middletown, CA 95461 USA
Phone: 707-987-2477
Fax: 707-987-0616

Proprietor: Collectively owned
Category: Retreat
Location: Mountain
Open all year? Yes
Price: Moderate
Special packages: Yes
Reader discount: No
Child discount: No

MEALS

Included: None
Offered: B, D
% Vegetarian: 100%
% Vegan: 75%
% Organic: 85%
Special diets: Yes
Nearby restaurants: No

ROOMS

% Private bath/shower: 10%
% Non-smoking: 100%
% Air conditioned: 0%
Car parking: Yes
Wheelchair access: Yes
Non-animal tested toiletries: Yes
Insecticides used? No
Pets welcome? No
Of animal origin: Down comforters

Nearby activities: Outdoor pool, bicycling, hiking, camping, yoga,
massage, educational lectures,
hot springs, sauna, clay, clothing-
optional sunbathing

Description: We are a non-profit
retreat and workshop center
nestled on 1160 acres of
secluded woodland above the
northern California wine
country. Our community of
150 residents and volunteers

welcomes visitors from around the world to relax, renew, and revitalize. Call for our free catalog or visit our web site at http://www.harbin.org.

Forms of payment: *U.S. currency*—cash, travelers checks, personal checks; VI, MC, Discover

LA MAIDA HOUSE

11159 La Maida Street
North Hollywood, CA 91601 USA
Phone: 818-769-3857
Fax: 818-753-9363

Proprietor: Megan Timothy
Category: Bed & Breakfast
Location: Suburban
Open all year? Yes
Price: Moderate
Special packages: No
Reader discount: No
Child discount: No

MEALS

Included: B
Offered: B, D
% Vegetarian: 100%
% Vegan: On request
% Organic: 50%
Special diets: Yes
Nearby restaurants: Yes

ROOMS

% Private bath/shower: 100%
% Non-smoking: 100%
% Air conditioned: 100%
Car parking: Yes
Wheelchair access: No
Non-animal tested toiletries: Yes
Insecticides used? No

Pets welcome? Call
Of animal origin: Wool rugs, down comforters
Nearby activities: Outdoor pool, tennis, golf, bicycling, hiking, canoeing/kayaking, boating, snorkeling, scuba diving, water sports, horseback riding, camping, beach, yoga, fitness classes, exercise room, sightseeing tours, nightclub, antique shops, museums, motion picture studios, theater, music center, Hollywood Bowl

Description: The serene atmosphere of La Maida House and its gardens with tinkly fountains have won the inn renown as an urban oasis. Two-story 1926 Italian villa, lofty ceilings, pool, exercise room, 2 dining rooms plus outdoor breakfast patio, den, plant room, living room, 4 bedrooms with bath, 2 also with dressing rooms. Fresh-baked bread and vegetarian continental breakfast. Also offer 3 small Spanish homes with rooms and suites, private bath, some with jacuzzi. TV on request.

Forms of payment: *U.S. currency*—cash, travelers checks, personal checks; AX, MC, VI

SHENOA RETREAT & LEARNING CENTER

P.O. Box 43
Philo, CA 95466 USA
Phone: 707-895-3156
Fax: 707-895-3236

Proprietor: Susan Stowens
Category: Retreat, learning center
Location: Quaint village, wine country

Open all year? Open May 1–Nov. 30
Price: Moderate
Special packages: Yes
Reader discount: 10%
Child discount: Yes

MEALS

Included: B, L, D
Offered: B, L, D
% Vegetarian: 100%
% Vegan: On request
% Organic: Varies
Special diets: Kitchen available
Nearby restaurants: No

ROOMS

% Private bath/shower: 100%
% Non-smoking: 100%
% Air conditioned: 0%
Car parking: Yes
Wheelchair access: Yes
Non-animal tested toiletries: Yes
Insecticides used? No
Pets welcome? No
Of animal origin: None
Nearby activities: Outdoor pool, tennis, bicycling, hiking, canoeing/kayaking, boating, snorkeling, scuba diving, water sports, horseback riding, camping, beach, yoga, massage, educational lectures, sightseeing tours, antique shops
Description: For groups, families, and individuals. Rustic cabins, contemporary cottages, camping, and vegetarian cuisine 2.5 hours north of San Francisco near the Mendocino coast. Workshops/conferences on inner and outer ecology for up to 100.

Forms of payment: *U.S. currency*—cash, travelers checks, personal checks; MC, VI, Discover

WELLSPRING RENEWAL CENTER

P.O. Box 332
Philo, CA 95466 USA
Phone: 707-895-3893
Fax: 707-895-2291

Proprietor: Ron Davis, Director
Category: Retreat
Location: Redwood coast in valley along river
Open all year? Yes
Price: Inexpensive
Special packages: Yes
Reader discount: No
Child discount: Yes

MEALS

Included: None
Offered: B, L, D
% Vegetarian: 100%
% Vegan: On request
% Organic: 20%
Special diets: Yes
Nearby restaurants: No

ROOMS

% Private bath/shower: 70%
% Non-smoking: 100%
% Air conditioned: 0%
Car parking: Yes
Wheelchair access: No
Non-animal tested toiletries: No
Insecticides used? No
Pets welcome? No
Of animal origin: Feather pillows, wool rugs

Nearby activities: Bicycling, hiking, canoeing/kayaking, boating, snorkeling, scuba diving, horseback riding, camping, beach, massage, sightseeing tours, museums

Description: Wellspring Renewal Center is a spiritual retreat and conference center. Surrounded by the majestic Redwood forest and graced with the flowing movements of the Navarro River, it is a place of great natural beauty. A non-profit, interdenominational organization, it addresses the need for deepening spirituality, personal renewal, self-discovery, nurturing the creative arts, and positive social and environmental change. Known for our sumptuous vegetarian cuisine, we provide meals for groups of 10 or more. Guests have the option of renting the kitchen, or smaller groups may cook for themselves in the lodges at no extra cost. Smaller groups or individuals may also have meals upon special request or may use the farmhouse kitchen if we are not serving meals.

Forms of payment: *U.S. currency*—cash, travelers checks, personal checks; MC, VI

Comment: Meals provided only to groups of 10 or more. Kitchen facilities available. Discounts for groups.

THE ABIGAIL HOTEL & MILLENNIUM RESTAURANT

246 Mc Allister St.
San Francisco, CA 94102 USA
Phone: 800-243-6510
Fax: 415-861-5848

Proprietor: Jim Diskin
Category: Hotel
Location: City center
Open all year? Yes
Price: Moderate
Special packages: Yes
Reader discount: No
Child discount: Yes

MEALS

Included: B
Offered: B, L, D
% Vegetarian: 100%
% Vegan: 100%
% Organic: 90%
Special diets: Yes
Nearby restaurants: Yes

ROOMS

% Private bath/shower: 100%
% Non-smoking: 0%

ABIGAIL HOTEL

U.S. AND CANADA

% Air conditioned: 0%

Car parking: Yes

Wheelchair access: Yes

Non-animal tested toiletries: No

Insecticides used? No

Pets welcome? No

Of animal origin: Down comforters

Nearby activities: Indoor pool, bicycling, boating, nutrition classes, beach, yoga, fitness classes, massage, nightclub, antique shops, museums

Description: A secret charmer in the Civic Center within a short walk of the opera, ballet, and symphony, Union Square and cable cars, Civic Auditorium, Brooks Hall, and all major government offices. Our rooms are furnished with exquisite antiques. Our own Millenium Restaurant is nationally recognized as one of the premier gourmet organic restaurants in the country.

Forms of payment: *U.S. currency*—cash, travelers checks; AX, VI, MC, Discover

GREEN TORTOISE ADVENTURE TRAVEL

494 Broadway
San Francisco, CA 94133 USA
Phone: 800-867-8647 or
**   415-956-7500**
Fax: 415-956-4900

Proprietor: Gardner Kent

Category: Outdoor adventure

Location: Varies

Open all year? Inquire directly

Price: Moderate

Special packages: Inquire

Reader discount: No

Child discount: Inquire

MEALS

Included: B, D

Offered: B, D

% Vegetarian: 100%

% Vegan: See comment

% Organic: Varies

Special diets: See comment

Nearby restaurants: Varies

Comment: Vegans and others with

special diets must be present at the preparation of every meal in order to extract a portion for themselves before the dairy products are added.

ROOMS

% Private bath/shower: N/A

% Non-smoking: N/A

% Air conditioned: N/A

Car parking: N/A

Wheelchair access: N/A

Non-animal tested toiletries: N/A

Insecticides used? N/A

Pets welcome? Yes

Of animal origin: N/A

Nearby activities: Varies

Description: Why Green Tortoise? Because there's nothing else like it. Our buses are beautiful, with names and literally millions of miles of character. Our passengers are happy. They don't sit up all night with their heads against the window, nor are they crashed in a heap on dirty mattresses on the floor of an old school bus. They sleep lying down on fitted sheets over thick foam on raised platforms and bunks—listening to beautiful music as they doze off. They sleep for hours and in the morning they are usually somewhere incredibly beautiful. By day we swim, cook breakfast, explore caves, climb mountains, raft down streams, stand under waterfalls, walk through the forest, cook dinner, build campfires, visit towns, meet people, and generally take it easy. Some days we travel and some nights we camp. Even a short ride on the Tortoise is a vacation. Longer trips become life-long memories.

Forms of payment: *U.S. currency*—cash, travelers checks

THE RED VICTORIAN PEACE CENTER B&B

**1665 Haight Street
San Francisco, CA 94117 USA
Phone: 415-864-1978
Fax: 415-863-3293**

Proprietor: Sami Sunchild

Category: Bed & Breakfast

Location: City center

Open all year? Yes

Price: Inexpensive

Special packages: Yes

Reader discount: Yes; inquire directly

Child discount: Yes

MEALS

Included: B

Offered: B

% Vegetarian: 100%

% Vegan: 80%

% Organic: 50%

Special diets: Yes

Nearby restaurants: Yes

ROOMS

% Private bath/shower: 30%

% Non-smoking: 100%

% Air conditioned: 0%

Car parking: Yes

Wheelchair access: No

Non-animal tested toiletries: Yes

Insecticides used? No

Pets welcome? No

Of animal origin: Feather pillows, down comforters

Nearby activities: Tennis, golf, bicycling, hiking, horseback riding, nutrition classes, beach, yoga, fitness classes, educational lectures, sightseeing tours, nightclub, museums, meditation, wellness counseling, peace pilgrim center

Description: The Red Victorian is the "San Francisco Connection" of friendly, creative people from throughout the world. Located in the geographic heart of San Francisco, two blocks from beautiful Golden Gate Park. Walk, run, bike, or roller skate to museums, the Conservatory of Flowers, Japanese Tea Garden, Rose Garden, tennis courts, and the Ocean Beach. Casual, artistic, friendly atmosphere with 18 rooms, each

celebrating the summer of love and Golden Gate Park with its own name and personality. Breakfast is one of the best parts of the day, where you can join people from a variety of cultures, lifestyles, and professions at one of the family-style tables for a nutritious continental buffet breakfast. Art gallery for meditation and purchases.

Forms of payment: *U.S. currency*—cash, travelers checks; AX, MC, VI

ROYAL GORGE CROSS COUNTRY SKI RESORT

P.O. Box 1100
Soda Springs, CA 95728 USA
Phone: 916-426-3871
Fax: 916-426-9221

Proprietor: John Slouber

Category: B&B, resort, retreat

Location: Mountain

Open all year? Yes. Wilderness Lodge open mid-Dec.–mid-Apr. only

Price: Moderate

Special packages: Yes

Reader discount: No

Child discount: Yes

MEALS

Included: B, L, D

Offered: B, L, D

% Vegetarian: 30%

% Vegan: 5%

% Organic: Varies

Special diets: Yes

Nearby restaurants: No

Comment: Rainbow Lodge serves breakfast only. Wilderness Lodge serves breakfast, lunch, and dinner.

ROOMS

% Private bath/shower: Rainbow Lodge 35%; Wilderness Lodge 0%

% Non-smoking: 100%

% Air conditioned: 0%

Car parking: Yes

Wheelchair access: Yes

Non-animal tested toiletries: No

Insecticides used? No

Pets welcome? No

Of animal origin: Wool rugs, down comforters

Nearby activities: Indoor pool, tennis, golf, bicycling, hiking, boating, water sports, cross-country skiing, downhill skiing, horseback riding, camping, beach, sightseeing tours, nightclub, sauna/hot tub, museums

Description: Located on the Donner Summit near Lake Tahoe. The 328 km groomed track system features 88 trails of beginner, intermediate, and advanced levels along gentle rolling and hilly terrain. Four surface lifts help skiers negotiate the steeper inclines and practice downhill techniques, while ten warming huts and four trailside cafes keep them refreshed and ready for more. At the summit station day lodge, you'll find rental and retail shop, cafe and bar, restrooms, phones, ski school, and ski patrol. For those with the desire to stay and explore—

mountain retreat nestled in the heart of the track system.

Forms of payment: *U.S. currency*—cash, travelers checks, personal checks; MC, VI

LAND OF MEDICINE BUDDHA

5800 Prescott Road
Soquel, CA 95073 USA
Phone: 408-462-8383
Fax: 408-462-8380

Proprietor: Foundation for the Preservation of the Mahayana Tradition

Category: Retreat, hotel, conference center

Location: Suburban, forest, meadowland

Open all year? Yes

Price: Moderate

Special packages: No

Reader discount: 10%

Child discount: Yes

MEALS

Included: B, L

Offered: B, L, D

% Vegetarian: 100%

% Vegan: 80%

% Organic: 85-90%

Special diets: Yes

Nearby restaurants: Yes

ROOMS

% Private bath/shower: 100%

% Non-smoking: 100%

% Air conditioned: 0%

Car parking: Yes

Wheelchair access: Yes

Non-animal tested toiletries: No

DAVID MADISON/ROYAL GORGE

and an appetite for fine food, fresh-baked breads, and homemade soups—there are two lodges: Rainbow Lodge, a historic bed and breakfast inn, and Wilderness Lodge, a

Insecticides used? No

Pets welcome? No

Of animal origin: Wool rugs

Nearby activities: Outdoor pool, tennis, golf, bicycling, hiking, canoeing/kayaking, water sports, camping, beach, massage, juice fasting, educational lectures, sightseeing tours, antique shops, workshops in healing body and mind and environment, classes in chi gong, meditation

Description: Nestled between the Pacific Ocean and the California redwoods on 55 acres of forest and meadowland just a few miles south of Santa Cruz. Walking trails, a pool, sauna, bookstore, and audiovisual library complement your stay. Join us in an environment that refreshes, recharges, and gladdens the heart.

Forms of payment: *U.S. currency*—cash, travelers checks, personal checks; MC, VI

MANZANITA VILLAGE

P.O. Box 62
Warner Springs, CA 92086 USA
Phone/Fax: 619-782-9223

Proprietor: Christopher Reed

Category: Retreat

Location: Back country

Open all year? Yes

Price: Inexpensive

Special packages: No

Reader discount: No

Child discount: No

MEALS

Included: B, L, D

Offered: B, L, D

% Vegetarian: 100%

% Vegan: 50%

% Organic: 50%

Special diets: Yes

Nearby restaurants: No

ROOMS

% Private bath/shower: 0%

% Non-smoking: 100%

% Air conditioned: 0%

Car parking: Yes

Wheelchair access: No

Non-animal tested toiletries: Yes

Insecticides used? No

Pets welcome? No

Of animal origin: Wool rugs

Nearby activities: Hiking, meditation instruction, participation in community work—gardening and other

Description: Manzanita Village is the country retreat center for Ordinary Dharma. Situated in a quiet and unspoiled valley in the hills, it borders several thousand acres of National forest: walk and revive yourself in a natural setting. Just a few miles from the spectacular Anza Borrego desert. Enjoy homemade food and plenty of time for your own personal meditation, rest, or study. Visit for your own personal retreat, participate in our ongoing schedule of morning and evening meditation, and help with communal work. We also have a solitary hermitage for private meditation retreats.

Forms of payment: *U.S. currency*—cash, travelers checks, personal checks

MOUNT MADONNA CENTER

445 Summit Road
Watsonville, CA 95076 USA
Phone: 408-847-0406
Fax: 408-847-2683

Proprietor: Non-profit organization
Category: Retreat, conference center
Location: Mountain
Open all year? Yes
Price: Moderate
Special packages: No
Reader discount: 10%
Child discount: Yes

MEALS

Included: B, L, D
Offered: B, L, D
% Vegetarian: 100%
% Vegan: 85%
% Organic: 55%
Special diets: Yes
Nearby restaurants: Yes

ROOMS

% Private bath/shower: 2%
% Non-smoking: 100%
% Air conditioned: 0%
Car parking: Yes
Wheelchair access: Yes
Non-animal tested toiletries: Yes
Insecticides used? No
Pets welcome? No
Of animal origin: None
Nearby activities: Tennis, camping, yoga, massage, herbal steam box, swimming

Description: Personal retreat and conference center set on 350 acres overlooking Monterey Bay. The Center offers yoga, massage, hiking trails, volleyball, tennis, basketball, hot tub, and a small lake for swimming.

Forms of payment: *U.S. currency*—cash, travelers checks, personal checks

WEIMAR INSTITUTE

P.O. Box 486
20601 W. Paoli Lane
Weimar, CA 95736 USA
Phone: 916-637-4111
Fax: 916-637-4408

Proprietor: Henry Martin
Category: Retreat
Location: Mountain
Open all year? Yes
Price: Moderate
Special packages: Yes
Reader discount: Inquire directly
Child discount: Yes

MEALS

Included: B, L, D

Offered: B, L, D

% Vegetarian: 100%

% Vegan: 100%

% Organic: Varies

Special diets: Yes

Nearby restaurants: Yes

ROOMS

% Private bath/shower: 100%

% Non-smoking: 100%

% Air conditioned: 100%

Car parking: Yes

Wheelchair access: Yes

Non-animal tested toiletries: No

Insecticides used? No

Pets welcome? No

Nearby activities: Bicycling, hiking, canoeing/kayaking, boating, water sports, cross-country skiing, downhill skiing, horseback riding, nutrition classes, fitness classes, massage, weight loss classes, sightseeing tours, antique shops, museums

Description: Weimar Institute is a non-profit wellness center in the Sierra foothills on I-80 between Lake Tahoe and Sacramento, California. Secluded on a 500-acre campus, it has twelve miles of pine shaded trails frequented year round by sport walkers. Home of physician-directed NEW-START Lifestyle Center, it is renowned for reversal of heart disease, diabetes, high blood pressure, obesity, arthritis, and allergies using natural methods. Treat yourself to the bountiful, heart-healthy vegan buffet in our country cafeteria. Comfortable lodging is available on-campus in the Weimar Inn.

Forms of payment: *U.S. currency*—cash, travelers checks; AX, MC, VI, Discover

WEIMAR INSTITUTE

LAUGHING HEART ADVENTURES

**P.O. Box 669
3003 Highway 96
Willow Creek, CA 95573 USA
Phone/Fax: 916-629-3516**

Proprietor: Dezh Pagen

Category: Outdoor adventure

Location: Mountain, wild and scenic river

Open all year? Open May–October

Price: Moderate

Special packages: Yes

Reader discount: No

Child discount: Yes

MEALS

Included: B, L, D
Offered: B, L, D
% Vegetarian: 95%
% Vegan: 50%
% Organic: 50%
Special diets: Yes
Nearby restaurants: No

ROOMS

% Private bath/shower: N/A
% Non-smoking: N/A
% Air conditioned: N/A
Car parking: Yes
Wheelchair access: No
Non-animal tested toiletries: No
Insecticides used? No
Pets welcome? No
Of animal origin: None

Nearby activities: Outdoor pool, tennis, golf, bicycling, hiking, canoeing/kayaking, boating, snorkeling, water sports, cross-country skiing, horseback riding, camping, beach, yoga, fitness classes, massage, sightseeing tours, antique shops, museums

Description: Canoe, kayak, and raft trips on wild and scenic northern California rivers: Trinity, Klamath, Smith, Eel. Also desert trips on the Colorado and Green Rivers in Utah and Arizona. Also totally tropical explorations in Belize: includes islands, mountains, and rivers. Winter trips to Baja, Mexico.

Forms of payment: *U.S. currency*—cash, travelers checks, personal checks; MC, VI

HAWAII

KALANI OCEANSIDE ECO-RESORT

RR2, Box 4500
Kehena Beach, HI 96778 USA
Phone: 800-800-6886 or
  808-965-7828
Fax: Call first

Proprietor: Richard Koob
Category: Resort
Location: Beachfront
Open all year? Yes
Price: Inexpensive
Special packages: Yes
Reader discount: 10%
Child discount: Yes

MEALS

Included: B, L, D
Offered: B, L, D
% Vegetarian: 100%
% Vegan: On request
% Organic: 50%
Special diets: Yes
Nearby restaurants: Yes

ROOMS

% Private bath/shower: 50%
% Non-smoking: 100%
% Air conditioned: 0%
Car parking: Yes
Wheelchair access: Yes
Non-animal tested toiletries: Yes
Insecticides used? No
Pets welcome? No
Of animal origin: None
Nearby activities: Outdoor pool, tennis, bicycling, hiking, canoeing/kayaking, snorkeling, scuba diving, water sports, nutrition classes, camping, beach, yoga, fitness classes, exercise room, massage, juice fasting, weight loss classes, educational lectures, sightseeing tours, museums, volcanoes, national park, natural steam baths, thermal springs
Description: Kalani Eco-Resort is the only coastal lodging facility within Hawaii's largest conservation area—treating you to healthful cuisine, thermal springs, a dolphin beach, spectacular Volcanoes National Park, and traditional culture. We're non-profit and educational, fun and affordable. Our international and native staff welcome you with Aloha!

Our Internet color brochure can be downloaded from http://www.randm.com/kh. html or http://www.randm. com/kh2.html
Forms of payment: *U.S. currency*—cash, travelers checks; AX, MC, VI, Diners Club

DR. DEAL'S HAWAIIAN WELLNESS HOLIDAY

Box 279
Koloa, HI 96756 USA
Phone: 800-338-6977

Proprietor: Dr. Grady Deal
Category: Health, metaphysical vacation program
Location: Beachfront
Open all year? Yes
Price: Moderate
Special packages: No
Reader discount: No
Child discount: Yes

MEALS

Included: B, L, D
Offered: B, L, D
% Vegetarian: On request
% Vegan: On request
% Organic: 85%
Special diets: Yes
Nearby restaurants: No

ROOMS

% Private bath/shower: 100%
% Non-smoking: 100%
% Air conditioned: 0%
Car parking: Yes
Wheelchair access: No
Non-animal tested toiletries: No

Insecticides used? No

Pets welcome? No

Of animal origin: None

Nearby activities: Outdoor pool, tennis, golf, bicycling, hiking, canoeing/kayaking, boating, snorkeling, scuba diving, water sports, horseback riding, nutrition classes, camping, beach, yoga, fitness classes, exercise room, massage, juice fasting, educational lectures, sightseeing tours, museums

Description: Hawaiian Wellness Holiday is a back-to-nature health vacation program on the garden island of Kauai. Enjoy nature walks, waterfalls, energy vortex, sacred lava pool, ancient Hawaiian temples and myths, seasonal whale watch boat rides, yoga, exercise, natural therapies, wellness and weight loss programs, personal transformation, astro-numerology readings, and delicious vegetarian meals on request. Individualized programs and lots of tender loving care.

Forms of payment: *U.S. currency*—cash, travelers checks, personal checks; MC, VI

STRONG, STRETCHED & CENTERED MIND/BODY INSTITUTE

P.O. Box 758
Paia, HI 96779 USA
Phone: 808-575-2178
Fax: 808-575-2275

Proprietor: Gloria Keeling

Category: Fitness instructor training

Location: Beachfront, resort town

Open all year? 4 training sessions—winter, spring, summer, and fall, each six weeks long.

Price: Inexpensive

Special packages: No

Reader discount: No

Child discount: No

MEALS

Included: B, L, D

Offered: B, L, D

% Vegetarian: 25%

% Vegan: 75%

% Organic: 40%

Special diets: Yes

Nearby restaurants: Yes

ROOMS

% Private bath/shower: 10%

% Non-smoking: 100%

% Air conditioned: 0%

Car parking: Yes

Wheelchair access: No

Non-animal tested toiletries: No

Insecticides used? No

Pets welcome? No

Of animal origin: Leather furniture, feather pillows

Nearby activities: Outdoor pool, tennis, golf, bicycling, hiking, canoeing/kayaking, boating, snorkeling, scuba diving, water sports, horseback riding, nutrition classes, beach, yoga, fitness classes, exercise room, massage, weight loss classes, educational lectures, sightseeing tours, nightclub, antique shops

Description: Strong, Stretched & Centered is a vocational training school that prepares you to be a personal trainer and aerobics instructor. Our six-week residential training is located on Maui's sunny south shore. Clients participate in the program for their own knowledge, not only to become instructors.

Forms of payment: *U.S. currency*—cash, travelers checks, personal checks

OREGON

AESCULAPIA

Box 301
Wilderville, OR 97543 USA
Phone: 541-476-0492

Proprietor: Graywolf Swinney

Category: Retreat

Location: Countryside, valley

Open all year? Yes

Price: Moderate

Special packages: Yes

Reader discount: Yes; inquire directly

Child discount: Yes

MEALS

Included: L, D

Offered: B, L, D

% Vegetarian: 100%

% Vegan: On request

% Organic: Varies

Special diets: Yes

Nearby restaurants: Yes

ROOMS

% Private bath/shower: 0%

% Non-smoking: 100%

% Air conditioned: 0%

Car parking: Yes

Wheelchair access: No

Non-animal tested toiletries: Yes

Insecticides used? No

Pets welcome? No

Of animal origin: Feather pillows

Nearby activities: Bicycling, hiking, canoeing/ kayaking, cross-country skiing, camping, massage, juice fasting, weight loss classes, educational lectures, sight- seeing tours, dream journeys

Description: Aesculapia is a wilderness and dream sanctuary in nature's cathedral, a safe nurturing haven for self-enrichment, healing, and evolution. Whatever your reason for seeking retreat—recreation, healing, stress reduction, spiritual quest, personal evolution, or just a need to escape from the city— you will find what you need here. We are located in 80 acres of secluded forest in the beautiful Blue Glen on the edge of the mystical Siskiyou Mountains in southwest Oregon. Miles of hiking trails lead to our cave, old gold mine, and majestic vistas. Our air is clean, our water pure and we provide delicious and nutritious vegetarian food.

Forms of payment: *U.S. currency*—cash, travelers checks, personal checks

UTAH

PAH TEMPE HOT SPRINGS

**825 North 800 East 35-4
Hurricane, UT 84737 USA
Phone: 801-635-2879
Fax: 801-635-2553**

Proprietor: Ken Anderson
Category: Bed & Breakfast
Location: Desert
Open all year? Yes
Price: Moderate
Special packages: Yes
Reader discount: No
Child discount: Yes

MEALS

Included: B
Offered: B
% Vegetarian: 100%
% Vegan: 50%
% Organic: 70%
Special diets: Yes
Nearby restaurants: Yes

ROOMS

% Private bath/shower: 20%
% Non-smoking: 100%
% Air conditioned: 100%
Car parking: Yes
Wheelchair access: No
Non-animal tested toiletries: No
Insecticides used? No
Pets welcome? No
Of animal origin: None

Nearby activities: Outdoor pool, tennis, golf, bicycling, hiking, boating, water sports, cross-country skiing, downhill skiing, horseback riding, camping, massage, antique shops, museums, Zion Park, Bryce Canyon, Grand Canyon

Description: Located in the spectacular Virgin River Canyon, Pah Tempe Hot Springs has been dedicated to uplift and heal all who visit this ancient Native American sanctuary. Our natural non-treated mineral pools offer rest and relaxation for travelers from around the world. Professional massage available by appointment.

Forms of payment: *U.S. currency*—cash, travelers checks, personal checks; MC, VI

FRANKLIN QUEST INSTITUTE OF FITNESS

202 N. Snow Canyon Road
Ivins, UT 84738 USA
Phone: 801-673-4905
Fax: 801-673-1363

Proprietors: Mark Sorenson, Dave Beck

Category: Spa, resort

Location: Desert

Open all year? Closed 2 weeks during Christmas/New Year

Price: Inexpensive/Expensive

Special packages: No

Reader discount: No

Child discount: No

MEALS

Included: B, L, D

Offered: B, L, D

% Vegetarian: See comment

% Vegan: See comment

% Organic: 100%

Special diets: Yes

Nearby restaurants: No

Comment: Two low-fat options at each meal: vegan, or some meat

ROOMS

% Private bath/shower: 20%

% Non-smoking: 100%

% Air conditioned: 100%

Car parking: No

Wheelchair access: Yes

Non-animal tested toiletries: No

Insecticides used? Yes

Pets welcome? No

Of animal origin: Leather furniture

Nearby activities: Indoor pool, tennis, bicycling, hiking, horseback riding, nutrition classes, yoga, fitness classes, exercise room, massage, weight loss classes,

educational lectures, sight-seeing tours

Description: Nestled in one of nature's most stunning creations, near St. George with Snow Canyon State Park in its backyard. Surrounded by desert wilderness, red rock canyons, and lava flows. Guests are introduced to the natural beauty of life, fitness, and well-being and often enjoy an increase in muscle tone and strength as they hike or bike through the desert. They experience improvements in diabetic conditions, arthritis, and cholesterol levels through the healthful diet and relaxing atmosphere of our program.

Forms of payment: *U.S. currency*—cash, travelers checks, personal checks; AX, MC, VI, Discover

Comment: Not for anyone under 18

SNOWBIRD SKI & SUMMER RESORT

**Snowbird Resort
Snowbird, UT 84092 USA
Phone: 800-453-3000 or
   801-742-2222
Fax: 801-742-3300**

Proprietor: Dick Bass
Category: Resort
Location: Mountain
Open all year? Yes
Price: Moderate
Special packages: Yes
Reader discount: Yes; inquire directly
Child discount: Yes

MEALS

Included: None
Offered: B, L, D
% Vegetarian: 20%
% Vegan: 10%
% Organic: 10%
Special diets: Yes
Nearby restaurants: Yes

ROOMS

% Private bath/shower: 100%
% Non-smoking: 90%

% Air conditioned: 0%
Car parking: Yes
Wheelchair access: Yes
Non-animal tested toiletries: No
Insecticides used? No
Pets welcome? No
Of animal origin: Leather furniture, wool rugs
Nearby activities: Outdoor pool, tennis, bicycling, hiking, cross-country

skiing, downhill skiing, camping, fitness classes, exercise room, massage, sightseeing tours, nightclub, tram

Description: Snowbird is blessed with beautiful summer, fall, and ski seasons and facilities that can put you on top of the world. Choose from full-service Cliff Spa located atop The Cliff Lodge, our activities center for on-site tennis, mountain biking, and guided hikes, or the nearby

Snowbird Canyon Racquet Club. The mountain will appeal to skiers who like rolling cruise runs, steep and deep, and every kind of terrain in between. Our food and beverage director has been a strict vegetarian for over twenty-five years and easily caters to any dietary requirement.

Forms of payment: *U.S. currency*—cash, travelers checks; AX, MC, VI, Discover

WASHINGTON

CARSON HOT MINERAL SPRINGS RESORT

Box 370
Carson, WA 98610 USA
Phone: 800-607-3678 or
509-427-8292
Fax: 509-427-7242

Proprietor: William Sim & Sally Daggy
Category: Resort
Location: Rural, forest
Open all year? Yes
Price: Moderate
Special packages: Inquire
Reader discount: No
Child discount: No

MEALS

Included: B, L, D
Offered: B, L, D
% Vegetarian: 30%
% Vegan: 10%
% Organic: As available
Special diets: Yes
Nearby restaurants: No

1880S SETTING–CARSON HOT MINERAL SPRINGS RESORT

ROOMS

% Private bath/shower: 0%
% Non-smoking: 100%
% Air conditioned: 0%
Car parking: Yes
Wheelchair access: Yes
Non-animal tested toiletries: No
Insecticides used? No
Pets welcome? Yes
Of animal origin: Feather pillows
Nearby activities: Tennis, golf, bicycling, hiking, canoeing/kayaking, boating, water sports, cross-country skiing, downhill

skiing, horseback riding, camping, fitness classes, antique shops

Description: Step back in time to our original 1880s buildings, iron bedsteads, and rustic setting. Also 18-hole golf course, RV park with full hook-ups, restaurant, licensed massage therapists, hot mineral baths, cabins (some with kitchenettes), hot tub suite, and hotel rooms.

Forms of payment: *U.S. currency*—cash, travelers checks; MC, VI

SEA QUEST EXPEDITIONS ZOETIC RESEARCH

P.O. Box 2424
Friday Harbor, WA 98250 USA
Phone: 360-378-5767
Fax: 360-378-5768

Proprietor: Mark Lewis
Category: Outdoor adventure
Location: Beachfront, desert, rain-forest
Open all year? Yes
Price: Moderate
Special packages: Yes
Reader discount: No
Child discount: No

MEALS
Included: B, L, D
Offered: B, L, D
% Vegetarian: 100%
% Vegan: 90%
% Organic: 30%
Special diets: Yes
Nearby restaurants: Yes

ROOMS
% Private bath/shower: N/A
% Non-smoking: N/A
% Air conditioned: N/A
Car parking: N/A
Wheelchair access: N/A
Non-animal tested toiletries: N/A
Insecticides used? N/A
Pets welcome? No
Of animal origin: None
Nearby activities: Hiking, canoeing/kayaking, snorkeling, camping, beach, natural history, wildlife and whale watching

Description: Our kayak expeditions offer all the fun and excitement of outdoor adventure, plus something more: Every Sea Quest trip is an adventure in learning as our guides are biologists and professional educators. Expeditions visit areas rich in marine wildlife and emphasize encountering whales. No previous experience is necessary.

Forms of payment: *U.S. currency*—cash, travelers checks, personal checks

TOWERHOUSE BED & BREAKFAST

1230 Little Road
Friday Harbor, WA 98250 USA
Phone: 360-378-5464

Proprietor: Chris and Joe Luma
Category: Bed & Breakfast
Location: Island
Open all year? Yes
Price: Moderate
Special packages: No
Reader discount: No
Child discount: No

MEALS

Included: B
Offered: B
% Vegetarian: 100%
% Vegan: On request
% Organic: Varies
Special diets: Yes
Nearby restaurants: Yes

ROOMS

% Private bath/shower: 100%
% Non-smoking: 100%
% Air conditioned: 0%
Car parking: Yes
Wheelchair access: No
Non-animal tested toiletries: No
Insecticides used? No
Pets welcome? No
Of animal origin: None
Nearby activities: Golf, bicycling, hiking, canoeing/kayaking, boating, camping, beach, sightseeing tours, antique shops, museums
Description: Queen Anne style home on ten acres overlooks the San Juan Valley. The Towerhouse

features two suites with queen-size beds and private baths. Chris and Joe pride themselves on their breakfast cuisine and assure that even people on special diets such as vegan or gluten-free can enjoy a full

breakfast served on china with crystal, silver, and antique linens.

Forms of payment: *U.S. currency*—cash, travelers checks; AX, MC, VI, Discover

DOE BAY VILLAGE AND CAFE

Star Route 86
Orcus Island, WA 98279 USA
Phone: 360-376-2291
Fax: 360-376-5809

Proprietor: Ish Cowan
Category: Retreat, resort
Location: Beachfront, island
Open all year? Yes
Price: Moderate
Special packages: Yes
Reader discount: 5% on rooms
Child discount: Yes

MEALS

Included: None

Offered: B, D

% Vegetarian: 85%

% Vegan: 35%

% Organic: 50%

Special diets: None

Nearby restaurants: No

ROOMS

% Private bath/shower: 50%

% Non-smoking: 100%

% Air conditioned: 0%

Car parking: Yes

Wheelchair access: Yes

Non-animal tested toiletries: No

Insecticides used? No

Pets welcome? Yes

DOE BAY VILLAGE

Of animal origin: None

Nearby activities: Bicycling, hiking, canoeing/kayaking, boating, scuba diving, water sports, camping, beach, yoga, massage, sightseeing cruises

Description: This gracefully aging rustic waterfront island retreat resort is intentionally under-developed in celebration of Mother Nature. Facilities include sauna, hot tubs, kayak trips, massage, camping, tent cabins and housekeeping cabins and hostel, small natural foods boutique, and cafe serving vegetarian fare, fish, and organic coffee. Under the same vegetarian ownership for 15 years. The ferry trip to the island is stunning.

Forms of payment: *U.S. currency*—cash, travelers checks; AX, MC, VI, Discover

SOL DUC HOT SPRINGS

Box 2169
Port Angeles, WA 98362 USA
Phone: 360-327-3583
Fax: 360-327-3593

Proprietor: Connie Pons and Steve Olson

Category: Spa, resort

Location: Mountain

Open all year? Open daily May 14–Sept. 21; weekends Apr. 1–May 14, Sept. 22–Oct. 30

Price: Moderate

Special packages: No

Reader discount: No

Child discount: Yes

MEALS

Included: None

Offered: B, L, D

% Vegetarian: 25%

% Vegan: On request

% Organic: 10%

Special diets: Yes

Nearby restaurants: No

ROOMS

% Private bath/shower: 100%

% Non-smoking: 100%

% Air conditioned: 0%

Car parking: Yes

Wheelchair access: Yes

Non-animal tested toiletries: Yes

Insecticides used? No

Pets welcome? Yes

Of animal origin: None

Nearby activities: Outdoor pool, bicycling, hiking, boating, camping, massage, museums, environmentally friendly gift shop

Description: The Quileute Indians called it Sol Duc—a land of sparkling water. When the first resort was built in 1912, ten thousand visitors a year came to take the waters. Today, the tradition continues. Sol Duc Hot Springs offers guests of all ages an experience unique in all the world. Nestled amid the breathtaking vistas of Olympic National Park, Sol Duc Hot Springs is a place of enchanting beauty and delightful discoveries. Relax in the invigorating mineral pools. Pause in a flowered mountain meadow surrounded by lofty alpine peaks. Enjoy the captivating campfire-side talks given under the stars by park naturalists.

Forms of payment: *U.S. currency*—cash, travelers checks; MC, VI, Discover

THE ANNAPURNA INN

538 Adams St.
Port Townsend, WA 98368 USA
Phone: 800-868-2662 or 360-385-2909

Proprietor: Robin Shoulberg and Tim Swanson

Category: B&B, retreat, spa

Location: Beachfront, quaint village, resort town

Open all year? Yes

Price: Moderate

Special packages: Yes

Reader discount: See comments

Child discount: Yes

MEALS

Included: B

Offered: B, D

% Vegetarian: 100%

% Vegan: 99%

% Organic: 90%

Special diets: Yes

SOL DUC HOT SPRINGS POOL

Nearby restaurants: Yes

Comment: We have honey.
10% reader discount on
weekdays and from 11/1-6/1;
5% discount on weekends.

ROOMS

% Private bath/shower: 50%

% Non-smoking: 100%

% Air conditioned: 0%

Car parking: Yes

Wheelchair access: Yes

Non-animal tested toiletries: Yes

Insecticides used? No

Pets welcome? Yes

Of animal origin: Feather   pillows,
wool rugs, down comforters

Nearby activities: Tennis, golf,
bicycling, hiking, canoeing/
kayaking, boating, beach, yoga,
fitness classes, exercise room,
massage, juice fasting, weight
loss classes, educational lectures, sightseeing tours, antique
shops, museums

Description: Our spa retreat center
provides the atmosphere neces-
sary to regain balance and

peace of mind through delicious vegan cuisine, therapeutic massage, yoga, steam bath,
sauna, and the quiet beautiful
setting of the Victorian seaport
of Port Townsend. Only two
hours from Seattle. Our three-
day retreat package, which has
gotten rave reviews, is $250 +
tax per person.

Forms of payment: *U.S. currency*—cash,
travelers checks, personal
checks; MC, VI

Comment: Parking on street. We use
Dr. Bronner's soap. Proprietors
in transitional period from
vegetarian to vegan.

MIDWEST AND ROCKIES

Colorado
Iowa
Michigan
Minnesota
Missouri
New Mexico
South Dakota
Texas
Wisconsin

SKY DANCER AYURVEDA
HEALTH RETREAT

**P.O. Box 2146
Durango, CO 81301 USA
Phone/Fax: 970-385-5549**

Proprietor: Mara Legrand
Category: Retreat
Location: Mountain
Open all year? Yes
Price: Moderate
Special packages: Yes
Reader discount: 10%
Child discount: No

MEALS

Included: L, D
Offered: B, L, D
% Vegetarian: On request
% Vegan: On request
% Organic: 90%
Special diets: Yes
Nearby restaurants: No

ROOMS

% Private bath/shower: 100%
% Non-smoking: 100%
% Air conditioned: 0%
Car parking: Yes
Wheelchair access: Yes
Non-animal tested toiletries: Yes
Insecticides used? No
Pets welcome? No
Of animal origin: Feather pillows, wool rugs, down comforters
Nearby activities: Bicycling, hiking, canoeing/kayaking, boating, downhill skiing, horseback riding, nutrition classes, yoga, massage, weight loss classes, educational lectures, sightseeing tours, natural hot springs

Description: Sky Dancer Ayurveda Retreat is a picturesque hideaway in Colorado's Rocky Mountains. We offer a customized health detox and rejuvenation program to our guests which includes a health

assessment, hands-on body therapies, massage, outdoor steam box, nutritious meals, therapeutic yoga, meditation, relaxation training and—for those interested—many outdoor activities.

Forms of payment: *U.S. currency*—cash, travelers checks, personal checks; MC, VI

EDEN VALLEY LIFESTYLE CENTER

**6263 N. County Rd. #29
Loveland, CO 80538 USA
Phone: 970-669-7730
Fax: 970-667-1742**

Proprietor: Daniel D. McKibben
Category: Retreat, lifestyle center
Location: Mountain
Open all year? Yes
Price: Inexpensive
Special packages: Yes
Reader discount: No
Child discount: No

MEALS

Included: B, L, D
Offered: B, L, D
% Vegetarian: 5%
% Vegan: 95%
% Organic: 40%
Special diets: Yes
Nearby restaurants: No

ROOMS

% Private bath/shower: 50%
% Non-smoking: 100%
% Air conditioned: 0%
Car parking: Yes
Wheelchair access: Yes
Non-animal tested toiletries: No
Insecticides used? No
Pets welcome? No
Of animal origin: Farm animals
Nearby activities: Indoor pool, outdoor pool, bicycling, hiking, water sports, cross-country skiing, downhill skiing, horseback riding, nutrition classes, camping, massage, juice fasting, weight loss classes, educational

lectures, sightseeing tours

Description: Eden Valley Lifestyle Treatment Center is located in a peaceful valley in the foothills of the Rocky Mountains. It provides neat rooms, a healthy vegetarian diet, hydrotherapy and massage treatments, educational classes on health and natural remedies, and beautiful surroundings that give plenty of opportunity for enjoyable walks and extended, guided hikes.

Forms of payment: *U.S. currency*—cash, travelers checks, personal checks; MC, VI

THE PEAKS AT TELLURIDE

P.O. Box 2702
Telluride, CO 81435 USA
Phone: 800-789-2220 or
970-728-6800
Fax: 970-728-6175

Proprietor: Gayle Moeller
Category: Spa, resort
Location: Mountain
Open all year? Open May 16–Apr. 14
Price: Expensive
Special packages: Yes
Reader discount: Yes; inquire directly
Child discount: Yes

MEALS

Included: B
Offered: B, L, D
% Vegetarian: 25%
% Vegan: 10%
% Organic: Varies
Special diets: Yes
Nearby restaurants: Yes

ROOMS

% Private bath/shower: 100%
% Non-smoking: 75%
% Air conditioned: 0%
Car parking: Yes
Wheelchair access: Yes
Non-animal tested toiletries: Yes
Insecticides used? No
Pets welcome? Yes
Of animal origin: Leather furniture, feather pillows, wool rugs, down comforters
Nearby activities: Indoor pool, outdoor pool, tennis, golf, bicycling, hiking, canoeing/kayaking, boating, water sports, cross-country skiing, downhill skiing, horseback riding, nutrition classes, camping, yoga, fitness classes, exercise room, massage, weight loss classes, educational lectures, sightseeing tours, nightclub, antique shops

Description: There's nothing remotely like it. Reminiscent of the great Alpine resorts of Europe with an Old World attitude about service. Also a uniquely Western experience with historic Telluride's quaint Victorian charm. Off the beaten path on the far slopes of the magnificent Colorado Rockies. New adventures every season of the year. The Peaks at Telluride offers a tempting assortment of 181 luxury rooms, suites, and penthouse condominiums with sweeping panoramic views of 14,000 foot Mt. Wilson and the San Juan Mountains. Step out your door and onto the slopes in a spectacular setting known for its short lift lines. There's also hiking through the mountains in springtime, golfing against the backdrop of summer wildflowers, and biking past brilliant fall foliage.

Forms of payment: *U.S. currency*—cash, travelers checks; AX, MC, VI, Diners Club

GOLD LAKE MOUNTAIN RESORT

**3371 Gold Lake Road
Ward, CO 80481 USA
Phone: 303-459-3544
Fax: 303-459-9080**

Proprietor: Linda

Category: Spa, resort, retreat

Location: Mountain, lakefront

Open all year? Yes

Price: Moderate/Expensive

Special packages: Yes

Reader discount: Yes; inquire directly

Child discount: Yes

MEALS

Included: B

Offered: B, L, D

% Vegetarian: 50%

% Vegan: On request

% Organic: 100%

Special diets: Yes

Nearby restaurants: No

ROOMS

% Private bath/shower:
  100%

% Non-smoking: 100%

% Air conditioned: 0%

Car parking: Yes

Wheelchair access: Yes

Non-animal tested toiletries:
  Yes

Insecticides used? No

Pets welcome? No

Of animal origin: Leather furniture, feather pillows, dead mounted/stuffed animals, down comforters

Nearby activities: Bicycling, hiking, canoeing/ kayaking, boating, cross-country skiing, horseback riding, yoga, massage

Description: Come visit a place of olde. A place which once served as the summer retreat of Chief Niwot, a Southern Arapahoe hero and peacemaker of the late 1800s. A place of pristine mountains, woodlands, meadows, and wetlands. Dine in our rustic log lodge and try our delicious gourmet vegetarian dishes. Start with organic whole grain breads and finish off fireside with a fresh baked dessert and an aperitif or cappuccino.

What lies between Heaven and Earth is easily found here at Gold Lake—just bring the desire to find it.

Forms of payment: *U.S. currency*—cash, travelers checks, personal checks; MC, VI

U.S. AND CANADA

LALLEY HOUSE BED AND BREAKFAST

**701 5th St.
Adair, IA 50002 USA
Phone: 515-742-5541**

Proprietor: Kay Faga

Category: Bed & Breakfast

Location: Small town, farming, scenic area

Open all year? Yes

Price: Moderate

Special packages: Yes

Reader discount: No

Child discount: No

MEALS

Included: B

Offered: B

% Vegetarian: 100%

% Vegan: 10%

% Organic: 20%

Special diets: Yes

Nearby restaurants: No

ROOMS

% Private bath/shower: 100%

% Non-smoking: 100%

% Air conditioned: 100%

Car parking: Yes

Wheelchair access: Yes

Non-animal tested toiletries: No

Insecticides used? No

Pets welcome? No

Of animal origin: Wool rugs

Nearby activities: Tennis, golf, bicycling, hiking, canoeing/kayaking, boating, camping, antique shops

Description: Lalley House is a warm, beautifully decorated retreat. Antique lovers marvel at all the large and small collectibles. People from all over the world have found this surprising spot just five blocks from busy I-80. A bonus for guests: a log cabin built circa 1840, furnished with primitives, but luxurious.

Forms of payment: *U.S. currency*—cash, travelers checks, personal checks; MC, VI, Discover

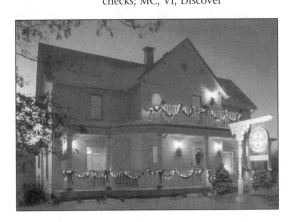

THE RAJ MAHARISHI AYUR-VEDA HEALTH CENTER

**1734 Jasmine Ave.
Fairfield, IA 52256 USA
Phone: 800-248-9050 or
    515-472-9580
Fax: 515-472-2496**

Proprietor: Roger & Candace Badgett

Category: Health center

Location: Rural

Open all year? Yes

Price: Expensive

Special packages: Yes

Reader discount: No

Child discount: No

MEALS

Included: B, L, D

Offered: B, L, D

% Vegetarian: 100%

% Vegan: 50%

% Organic: See comments

Special diets: Yes

Nearby restaurants: Yes

Comment: Restaurant is open to public lunch Sun–Fri. 90% organic produce in summer, 20–40% rest of year. Special vegan meals can be made if requested in advance.

ROOMS

% Private bath/shower: 100%

% Non-smoking: 100%

% Air conditioned: 100%

Car parking: Yes

Wheelchair access: Yes

Non-animal tested toiletries: No

Insecticides used? No

Pets welcome? No

Of animal origin: Wool rugs

Nearby activities: Golf, horseback riding, yoga, exercise room, massage, educational lectures, ayurvedic rejuvenation and beauty treatments, weekend seminars on ayur-veda, ayurvedic consultations

Description: Ayurveda at its best! Maharishi Ayur-veda consultations and rejuvenation treatments are offered at this four-star health center. Once reserved for the royal families of India, these rejuvenation treatments help remove stress and toxins to promote health and longevity. Packages include classes in diet, exercise, and ayurvedic knowledge. Phone consultations also available.

Forms of payment: *U.S. currency*—cash, travelers checks, personal checks; AX, MC, VI, Discover

MICHIGAN

CIRCLE PINES CENTER

**8650 Mullen Road
Delton, MI 49046 USA
Phone: 616-623-5555
Fax: 616-623-9054**

Proprietor: Amy Ryan and Tim Dwyer

Category: Cooperative

Location: Lakefront, country

Open all year? Yes

Price: Moderate

Special packages: Yes

Reader discount: 10%

Child discount: Yes

MEALS

Included: B, L, D

Offered: B, L, D

% Vegetarian: 25-30%

% Vegan: 10-15%

% Organic: 75-80%

Special diets: Yes

Nearby restaurants: No

Comment: Meals served weekends only. Always a vegan option.

ROOMS

% Private bath/shower: 0%

% Non-smoking: 100%

% Air conditioned: 0%

Car parking: Yes

Wheelchair access: No

Non-animal tested toiletries: No

Insecticides used? No

Pets welcome? No

Of animal origin: Farm animals

Nearby activities: Bicycling, hiking, canoeing/kayaking, boating, water sports, cross-country skiing, horseback riding, camping, beach sightseeing tours, antique shops, museums

Description: For over 50 years, Circle Pines has served people from all walks of life. Founded by a group of cooperative individuals, we remain an independent membership-based non-profit organization. Our mission is to teach cooperation and to support groups of a kindred spirit. Open year round with seasonal programs for all ages, the Center's rustic facilities are used for retreats and conferences. We also offer an accredited summer camp for families and youths, and an elder camp.

Forms of payment: *U.S. currency*—cash, travelers checks, personal checks

MICHIGAN BICYCLE TOURING

**3512 Red School Rd.
Kingsley, MI 49649 USA
Phone: 616-263-5885**

Proprietor: Michael & Libby Robold

Category: Outdoor adventure

Location: Beachfront, mountain, quaint village, lakefront, resort town

Open all year? May to October only

Price: Moderate

Special packages: Yes

Reader discount: No

Child discount: Yes

MEALS

Included: B, D

Offered: B, L, D

% Vegetarian: 25%

% Vegan: 5%

% Organic: 5%

Special diets: Yes

Nearby restaurants: Yes

ROOMS

% Private bath/shower: 90%

% Non-smoking: 75%

% Air conditioned: 75%

Car parking: Yes

Wheelchair access: N/A

Non-animal tested toiletries: No

Insecticides used? Varies

Pets welcome? No

Of animal origin: Varies

Nearby activities: Indoor pool, outdoor pool, tennis, golf, bicycling, hiking, canoeing/kayaking, scuba diving, water sports, horseback riding, beach, yoga, massage, sightseeing tours, antique shops, museums

Description: Experience the undiscovered and spectacular beauty of Northern Michigan on a biking or hiking trip. Stay in comfort at a charming inn, a delightful B&B, or even a lighthouse on Lake Superior. Enjoy sharing wonderful vegetarian meals and companionship with like-minded individuals. We are an environmentally conscious company offering a very personable vacation.

Forms of payment: *U.S. currency*—cash, travelers checks, personal checks; MC, VI

SPIRAL PATHWAYS

5375 W. Deerfield
Remus, MI 49340 USA
Phone: 517-773-7884

Proprietor: Gary Greenan

Category: B&B, retreat

Location: Forest

Open all year? Yes, except when workshops are going on. Call at least 40 days ahead.

Price: Inexpensive

Special packages: Yes

Reader discount: 10%

Child discount: No

MEALS

Included: L

Offered: L

% Vegetarian: 100%

% Vegan: On request

% Organic: 90%

Special diets: Yes

Nearby restaurants: Yes

ROOMS

% Private bath/shower: 0%

% Non-smoking: 100%

% Air conditioned: 100%

Car parking: Yes

Wheelchair access: Yes

Non-animal tested toiletries: Yes

Insecticides used? No

Pets welcome? No

Of animal origin: Farm animals

Nearby activities: Golf, bicycling, hiking, canoeing/kayaking, boating, snorkeling, cross-country and downhill skiing, nutrition classes, horseback riding, camping, beach, yoga, fitness classes, exercise room, massage, juice fasting, weight loss classes, educational lectures, sightseeing tours, nightclub, antique shops, museums

Description: We are located 3/4 mile back into the forest. The nearest house is 3/8 mile through the woods. On site we have a 26' x 26' open (dance, meditation) area, 2 fireplaces, fire circle, medicine wheel, 16 person sauna, commercial kitchen, greenhouse, massage, colon therapy, cross-country skiing, mushroom hunting, and a bunk house for private workshops.

Forms of payment: *U.S. currency*—cash, travelers checks

MINNESOTA

WOODSWOMEN INC.

25 West Diamond Lake Road
Minneapolis, MN 55419 USA
Phone: 612-822-3809
Fax: 612-822-3814

Proprietor: Denise Mitten/Contact: Peggy Willens
Category: Outdoor adventure
Location: Beachfront, mountain, desert
Open all year? Yes
Price: Moderate
Special packages: No
Reader discount: No
Child discount: Yes

MEALS
Included: B, L, D
Offered: B, L, D
% Vegetarian: 80%
% Vegan: 20%
% Organic: 50%
Special diets: Yes
Nearby restaurants: Yes

ROOMS
% Private bath/shower: 90%

% Non-smoking: 100%
% Air conditioned: Varies
Car parking: Yes
Wheelchair access: No
Non-animal tested toiletries: No
Insecticides used? No
Pets welcome? No
Of animal origin: None
Nearby activities: Bicycling, hiking, canoeing/kayaking, snorkeling, scuba diving, cross-country skiing, horseback riding, camping, rafting, back packing
Description: Woodswomen is an adventure travel company dedicated to providing fun, safe, and educational adventures for women in some of the most beautiful places on earth. We have special trips for women and kids. Our well-trained, highly experienced guides enjoy people and love to teach. Some trips each year include: cruise through Galapagos, bicycling in Tuscany, canoeing in northern Minnesota.

Forms of payment: *U.S. currency*—cash, travelers checks, personal checks; MC, VI

CHATSWORTH B&B

**984 Ashland Avenue
St. Paul, MN 55104 USA
Phone: 612-227-4288
Fax: 612-225-8217**

Proprietor: Donna Gustafson
Category: Bed & Breakfast
Location: City center
Open all year? Yes
Price: Moderate
Special packages: Yes
Reader discount: No
Child discount: Yes

MEALS

Included: B
Offered: B
% Vegetarian: 100%
% Vegan: 0%
% Organic: 60%
Special diets: Yes
Nearby restaurants: Yes

ROOMS

% Private bath/shower: 60%
% Non-smoking: 100%
% Air conditioned: 20%
Car parking: No
Wheelchair access: No
Non-animal tested toiletries: Yes
Insecticides used? No
Pets welcome? No
Of animal origin: Feather pillows, wool rugs, down comforters
Nearby activities: Indoor pool, outdoor pool, tennis, golf, bicycling, hiking, canoeing/kayaking, cross-country skiing, downhill skiing, horseback riding, nutrition classes, beach, yoga, fitness classes, exercise room, massage, juice fasting, weight loss classes, educational lectures, sightseeing tours, nightclub, antique shops, museums

Description: Discover Chatsworth Bed & Breakfast, a spacious 1902 Victorian home on a large corner lot with maple and basswood trees. Choose a room

with a four-poster bed and private double whirlpool bath; one with African-Asian decor and an adjoining porch. Or, if you prefer, select a room with Victorian, Oriental, or antique Scandinavian decor. Enjoy a leisurely breakfast in a beautifully paneled dining room and take time to read or relax by the fireplace in the lace-curtained living room.

Forms of payment: *U.S. currency*—cash, travelers checks, personal checks

WHOLISTIC LIFE CENTER

Route 1, Box 1783
Washburn, MO 65772 USA
Phone: 417-435-2212
Fax: 417-435-2211

Proprietor: Non-profit organization

Category: Retreat, health & educational center

Location: Mountain

Open all year? Yes

Price: Inexpensive

Special packages: Yes

Reader discount: 10%

Child discount: Yes

MEALS

Included: B, L, D

Offered: B, L, D

% Vegetarian: 100%

% Vegan: 100%

% Organic: 50%

Special diets: Yes

Nearby restaurants: No

ROOMS

% Private bath/shower: 0%

% Non-smoking: 100%

% Air conditioned: 50%

Car parking: Yes

Wheelchair access: No

Non-animal tested toiletries: No

Insecticides used? No

Pets welcome? No

Of animal origin: None

Nearby activities: Outdoor pool, tennis, bicycling, hiking, canoeing/kayaking, boating, horseback riding, nutrition classes, camping, fitness classes, exercise room, massage, educational lectures, weight loss classes, juice fasting, indoor swim spa

Description: The Wholistic Life Center is a non-profit health and educational center, located on 900 beautiful acres filled with wildlife, wooded trails, streams, and lakes in the heart of the Ozark Mountains. We help people discover their potential and let go of undesirable patterns in an atmosphere of learning and love.

Forms of payment: *U.S. currency*—cash, travelers checks, personal checks; MC, VI

THE RANCHETTE B&B

2329 Lakeview Rd. SW
Albuquerque, NM 87105 USA
Phone: 505-877-5140
Fax: 505-873-8274

Proprietor: Rev. Janis Hildebrand

Category: Bed & Breakfast

Location: Suburban, high desert

Open all year? Yes

Price: Moderate

Special packages: Yes

Reader discount: 10%

Child discount: Yes

MEALS

Included: B

Offered: B, L, D

% Vegetarian: 100%

% Vegan: On request

% Organic: 90%

Special diets: Yes

Nearby restaurants: Yes

ROOMS

% Private bath/shower: 50%

% Non-smoking: 100%

% Air conditioned: 100%

Car parking: Yes

Wheelchair access: No

Non-animal tested toiletries: No

Insecticides used? No

Pets welcome? Yes

Of animal origin: Feather pillows, farm animals, down comforters

Nearby activities: Outdoor pool, tennis, golf, bicycling, hiking, cross-country skiing, downhill skiing, horseback riding, nutrition classes, camping, yoga, massage, juice fasting, weight loss classes, educational lectures, sightseeing tours, nightclub, antique shops, museums

Description: Enjoy vistas of mountains at sunrise and sunset in the restful spiritual surroundings of an adobe-style home with Arabian horses outside. Lovely indoor and outdoor living areas include cozy fireplace, grand piano, hot tub, swings, and walking paths. Gourmet vegetarian meals, dinner on request. Smoke and alcohol free environment. Refrigerated air. Licensed and approved by the Albuquerque Bed & Breakfast Association.

Forms of payment: *U.S. currency*—cash, travelers checks, personal checks; MC, VI, Discover

THE GALISTEO INN

HC75—Box 4
Galisteo, NM 87540 USA
Phone: 505-466-4000
Fax: 505-466-4008

Proprietor: Joanna & Wayne Aarniokoski
Category: Bed & Breakfast
Location: Quaint village, rural
Open all year? Yes, except early January to early February
Price: Moderate
Special packages: No
Reader discount: No
Child discount: No

DONALD WOODMAN

MEALS

Included: B
Offered: B, L, D
% Vegetarian: 25%
% Vegan: 25%
% Organic: 25%
Special diets: Yes
Nearby restaurants: Yes

ROOMS

% Private bath/shower: 75%
% Non-smoking: 100%
% Air conditioned: 0%
Car parking: Yes
Wheelchair access: Yes
Non-animal tested toiletries: No
Insecticides used? No
Pets welcome? No
Of animal origin: Feather pillows, farm animals, wool rugs, down comforters
Nearby activities: Indoor pool, outdoor pool, tennis, bicycling, hiking, cross-country skiing, downhill skiing, horseback riding, fitness classes, exercise room, massage, sauna, hot tub, facials
Description: Magical 250-year-old adobe Spanish hacienda on 8 acres of grounds and pastures, bordered by stone walls and the Galisteo Creek. Towering cottonwoods, duck pond, hammocks. Gourmet dinners and breakfasts. Guided horseback rides, massage, 50' lap pool, sauna, spa, and mountain bikes all available on premises. Serene and retreat-like.
Forms of payment: *U.S. currency*—cash, travelers checks, personal checks; MC, VI, Discover

HAWK, I'M YOUR SISTER

**Box 9109
Santa Fe, NM 87504 USA
Phone: 505-984-2268**

Proprietor: Beverly Antaeus

Category: Outdoor adventure

Location: Beachfront, mountain, lakefront, desert, rivers

Open all year? Various months: Call

Price: Expensive

Special packages: No

Reader discount: $25

Child discount: Yes

MEALS

Included: B, L, D

Offered: B, L, D

% Vegetarian: 85%

% Vegan: 50%

% Organic: 50%

Special diets: Yes

Nearby restaurants: No

Comment: Can accommodate most requests.

ROOMS

% Private bath/shower: N/A

% Non-smoking: N/A

% Air conditioned: N/A

Car parking: N/A

Wheelchair access: N/A

Non-animal tested toiletries: N/A

Insecticides used? N/A

Pets welcome? No

Of animal origin: None

Nearby activities: Hiking, canoeing/kayaking, boating, snorkeling, scuba diving, camping, beach, wilderness seminars, writing retreats, river journeys

Description: On wilderness canoe trips, Hawk, I'm Your Sister aims to teach you the language of forests, canyons, deserts, rivers, lakes, and the sea. In a safe, supportive atmosphere, without competition, women of all ages and degrees of experience are encouraged to recognize and appreciate their own

physical and inner strengths and abilities. We offer wilderness seminars, writing retreats, and river journeys within the United States and to the Bahamas, Russia, and Peru. Most trips are for women only but some are co-ed.

Forms of payment: *U.S. currency*—cash, travelers checks, personal checks

Comment: We live outdoors in tents.

THE MABEL DODGE LUHAN HOUSE

**240 Morada Lane
P.O. Box 3400
Taos, NM 87571 USA
Phone: 800-84MABEL or
505-758-9456**

Proprietor: N/A

Category: B&B, retreat, conference center

Location: Quaint village, desert, resort town

Open all year? Yes

Price: Moderate

Special packages: No

Reader discount: No

Child discount: No

MEALS

Included: B

Offered: B

% Vegetarian: 60%

% Vegan: On request

% Organic: 10%

Special diets: Yes

Nearby restaurants: Yes

ROOMS

% Private bath/shower: 50%

% Non-smoking: 100%

% Air conditioned: 0%

Car parking: Yes

Wheelchair access: No

Non-animal tested toiletries: No

Insecticides used? No

Pets welcome? No

Of animal origin: Wool rugs

Nearby activities: Indoor pool, outdoor pool, tennis, golf, bicycling, hiking, canoeing/kayaking, cross-country skiing, downhill skiing, horseback riding, camping, yoga, fitness classes, exercise room, massage, educational lectures, sightseeing tours, antique shops, museums, art galleries, writing, painting

Description: The Mabel Dodge Luhan House offers you supportive solitude for creative reflection at an unusual sanctuary within the heart of Taos. From colorful bathroom windows painted by D.H. Lawrence to carefully crafted traditional breakfasts, we offer lodgings unparalleled in northern New Mexico. Let our experienced staff offer you all the amenities you deserve when you visit our quintessential Southwestern bed and breakfast.

Forms of payment: *U.S. currency*—cash, travelers checks, personal checks; MC, VI

BLACK HILLS HEALTH & EDUCATION CENTER

P.O. Box 19
Hermosa, SD 57744 USA
Phone: 605-255-4101
Fax: 605-255-4687

Proprietor: Bob Willard
Category: Wellness center
Location: Mountain
Open all year? Yes
Price: Moderate
Special packages: Yes
Reader discount: 5%
Child discount: No

MEALS

Included: B, L, D
Offered: B, L, D
% Vegetarian: 100%
% Vegan: 100%
% Organic: 30%
Special diets: Yes
Nearby restaurants: Yes

ROOMS

% Private bath/shower: 90%
% Non-smoking: 100%
% Air conditioned: 0%
Car parking: Yes
Wheelchair access: Yes
Non-animal tested toiletries: No
Insecticides used? No
Pets welcome? No
Of animal origin: None

Nearby activities: Indoor pool, hiking, nutrition classes, fitness classes, exercise room, massage, weight loss classes, educational lectures

Description: Leave tight schedules and tired habits behind and walk a mountaintop—where the air is clean and the spirit is strong. Be inspired and renewed as you experience the wonderful and natural way your body can achieve radiant health and abundant energy. Besides great meals, exercise sessions, classes on health, nutrition, and stress management, you can include a massage, water therapy, a cooking class, an individual consultation with a doctor, swimming, or a picnic outing to one of the nearby attractions.

Forms of payment: *U.S. currency*—cash, travelers checks, personal checks

LAKE AUSTIN SPA RESORT

1705 Quinlan Park Rd.
Austin, TX 78732 USA
Phone: 800-847-5637
Fax: 512-266-4386

Proprietor: Jeff Wall, Director
Category: Spa, resort
Location: Lakefront, countryside
Open all year? Yes
Price: Moderate
Special packages: Yes
Reader discount: Inquire directly
Child discount: No

MEALS

Included: B, L, D
Offered: B, L, D
% Vegetarian: 60%
% Vegan: On request
% Organic: 75%
Special diets: Yes
Nearby restaurants: No

ROOMS

% Private bath/shower: 100%
% Non-smoking: 95%
% Air conditioned: 100%
Car parking: Yes
Wheelchair access: No
Non-animal tested toiletries: Yes
Insecticides used? Yes

Pets welcome? Yes

Of animal origin: Feather pillows, farm animals, wool rugs, down comforters

Nearby activities: Indoor pool, outdoor pool, tennis, bicycling, hiking, canoeing/kayaking, nutrition classes, horseback riding, camping, yoga, exercise room, fitness classes, massage, juice fasting, weight loss classes, educational lectures, sightseeing tours, nightclub, antique shop

Description: Surrounded by rolling hills and snuggled along the shore of Lake Austin is an ideal environment to discover your personal best. Innovators in the health and fitness community, we focus on the whole person and total wellness of each guest, which allows you to do as little or as much as you like. Balance your day with a full range of European spa services, insight programs, fitness activities, and periods of quiet meditation. Relax in charming bed and breakfast style cottages with panoramic views of the lake and hills. Dine in the lakeside dining room and enjoy all natural and organic foods directly from the spa's own gardens. Work out, stretch, or meditate in the Studio, Atrium, or Training Room with incredible views of the lake and hill country. Find peace and tranquillity on lakeside swings, hammocks, deck, and dock retreats deep in the heart of Texas.

Forms of payment: *U.S. currency*—cash, travelers checks, personal checks; MC, VI

ARBOR HOUSE,
AN ENVIRONMENTAL INN

3402 Monroe Street
Madison, WI 53711 USA
Phone: 608-238-2981
Fax: 608-238-1175

Proprietor: Cathie Imes
Category: Bed & Breakfast
Location: City center
Open all year? Yes
Price: Moderate
Special packages: Yes
Reader discount: No
Child discount: No

MEALS

Included: B
Offered: B
% Vegetarian: On request
% Vegan: On request
% Organic: 20%
Special diets: Yes
Nearby restaurants: Yes

ROOMS

% Private bath/shower: 100%
% Non-smoking: 100%
% Air conditioned: 65%
Car parking: Yes
Wheelchair access: Yes
Non-animal tested toiletries: Yes
Insecticides used? No
Pets welcome? No
Of animal origin: Feather pillows, wool rugs, down comforters
Nearby activities: Tennis, golf, bicycling, hiking, canoeing/kayaking, boating, water sports, cross-country skiing, beach, massage, nightclub, antique shops, museums

Description: One of Madison's oldest existing homes is also one of the city's most charming and unique inns. While preserving the charm of this nationally registered home, Arbor House is evolving into a model for urban ecology in the areas of architecture, landscaping, interior design, energy and water use, and inn operations. All five guest rooms have distinct personalities and our award-winning Annex has three rooms named after prominent leaders from Madison's past who have worked to preserve and protect our natural environment. We are within

walking distance of Lake Wingra, just a few blocks from Edgewood College, and one mile from Camp Randall Stadium.

Forms of payment: *U.S. currency*—cash, travelers checks, personal checks; AX, MC, VI

AKALA POINT

**Box 1627, RR 1
Tantallon, Nova Scotia, B0J 3J0
 Canada
Phone: 902-823-2160**

Proprietor: Barbara Jannasch
Category: Retreat
Location: Beachfront
Open all year? Yes
Price: Inexpensive
Special packages: Yes
Reader discount: No
Child discount: Yes

MEALS

Included: B, L, D
Offered: B, L, D
% Vegetarian: 100%
% Vegan: 0%
% Organic: 50%
Special diets: Yes
Nearby restaurants: No

ROOMS

% Private bath/shower: 0%
% Non-smoking: 100%
% Air conditioned: 0%
Car parking: Yes

Wheelchair access: Yes
Non-animal tested toiletries: No
Insecticides used? No
Pets welcome? No
Of animal origin: Wool rugs
Nearby activities: Beach, yoga

Description: Akala Point is a hostel-style retreat at the Atlantic Ocean that helps open all our senses to nature and the gifts of simplicity. You will discover an organic garden, meditation and yoga, and practice of awareness and eco-psychology near Peggy's Cove about 30 miles from Halifax.

Forms of payment: *U.S. currency*—cash, travelers checks; *Local currency* —cash, travelers checks

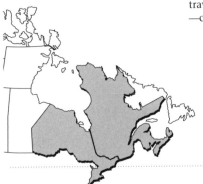

EASTERN CANADA

*Nova Scotia
Ontario
Quebec*

U.S. AND CANADA

MACROBIOTICS CANADA

RR 3
Almonte, ON K0A 1A0 Canada
Phone: 613-256-2665

Proprietor: Wayne Diotte
Category: Retreat
Location: Quaint village
Open all year? Yes
Price: Moderate
Special packages: Yes
Reader discount: 10%
Child discount: Yes

MEALS

Included: B, L, D
Offered: B, L, D
% Vegetarian: 100%
% Vegan: 100%
% Organic: 80%
Special diets: Yes
Nearby restaurants: Yes

ROOMS

% Private bath/shower: 0%
% Non-smoking: 100%
% Air conditioned: 0%
Car parking: Yes
Wheelchair access: Yes
Non-animal tested toiletries: No
Insecticides used? No
Pets welcome? No
Of animal origin: Wool rugs
Nearby activities: Tennis, golf, bicycling, hiking, boating, cross-country skiing, downhill skiing, horseback riding, nutrition classes, yoga, fitness classes, massage, weight loss classes, educational lectures, sightseeing tours, nightclub, antique shops, consultation, cooking classes, shiatsu, counselling, macrobiotic education, compresses

Description: Macrobiotics Canada is internationally renowned. Educational services include consultations, cooking instruction, residential programs, seminars, 9-star-ki analysis, business and organization consulting, meditation, and spiritual life programs. Personal support services include shiatsu, compresses, private yoga classes, breathwork, palm healing, and facials. Food services include macrobiotic, vegan food including jam, fruit from our trees, pickles, etc. Catering (large scale) throughout North America, kitchen consulting services (home and commercial). We are enthusiastic, energetic, sincere, very skilled and very focused on our clients' endeavors to create a healthy life!

Forms of payment: *U.S. currency*—cash, travelers checks; *Local currency* —cash, travelers checks, personal checks; MC, VI

KING VIEW FARM

P.O. Box 217
Aurora, ON L4G 3H3 Canada
Phone: 905-727-1013
Fax: 905-727-7031

Proprietor: Maureen Mooney
Category: Retreat
Location: Countryside
Open all year? Varies; inquire directly
Price: Inexpensive

KING VIEW FARM

Special packages: No
Reader discount: No
Child discount: Yes

MEALS

Included: None
Offered: B, L, D
% Vegetarian: On request
% Vegan: On request
% Organic: 80%
Special diets: Yes
Nearby restaurants: No

ROOMS

% Private bath/shower: 5%
% Non-smoking: 100%
% Air conditioned: 0%
Car parking: Yes
Wheelchair access: No
Non-animal tested toiletries: No
Insecticides used? No
Pets welcome? No
Of animal origin: Leather furniture, farm animals
Nearby activities: Outdoor pool, golf, bicycling, hiking, cross-country skiing, horseback riding, massage, art gallery, shopping

Description: Beautiful country setting 30 minutes north of Toronto with 86 acres of rolling hills, maple forest, marked trails, all chemical-free for 20+ years. Resident spiritual community: Society of Emissaries of Divine Light. Ideal for individual, couple, and family retreats or attending events.

Forms of payment: *U.S. currency*—cash, travelers checks, personal checks; *Local currency*—cash, personal checks, travelers checks; VI

HIDDEN VALLEY FARM

RR 2
Chatsworth, ON N0H 1G0 Canada
Phone: 519-794-3727
Fax: 519-794-4220

Proprietor: W. and E. Bruggemann
Category: Bed & Breakfast
Location: Rural
Open all year? Yes
Price: Moderate
Special packages: Yes
Reader discount: No
Child discount: Yes

MEALS

Included: B, L, D
Offered: B, L, D
% Vegetarian: 100%
% Vegan: On request
% Organic: 95%
Special diets: Yes
Nearby restaurants: No

ROOMS

% Private bath/shower: 0%
% Non-smoking: 100%
% Air conditioned: 0%
Car parking: Yes

Wheelchair access: No
Non-animal tested toiletries: Yes
Insecticides used? No
Pets welcome? No
Of animal origin: Down comforters, feather pillows, farm animals
Nearby activities: Golf, bicycling, hiking, canoeing/kayaking, cross-country skiing, downhill skiing, horseback riding, nutrition classes, antique shops, museums
Description: Member of Ontario Farm and Country Accommodations. Secluded, wonderfully peaceful 120 acres of certified organic land. Delicious vegan or lacto-ovo vegetarian meals offered as required. Warm hospitality. Cozy, smoke and alcohol free home. Clean and unspoiled tourist area. Hiking on world-famous Bruce Trail. Biking on quiet country roads. Two hours NW of Toronto airport. Easy to reach by major bus lines.
Forms of payment: *U.S. currency*—cash, travelers checks, personal checks; *Local currency*—cash, personal checks, travelers checks

STILL POINT BED & BREAKFAST

Village of Northpoint
RR #2
Picton, ON K0K 2T0 Canada
Phone: 613-476-8061

Proprietor: Glenn Mifsud
Category: Bed & Breakfast, retreat
Location: Beachfront, quaint village, lakefront
Open all year? Yes

Price: Inexpensive
Special packages: No
Reader discount: No
Child discount: No

MEALS

Included: B
Offered: B, D
% Vegetarian: 100%
% Vegan: On request
% Organic: 70%
Special diets: Yes
Nearby restaurants: No

ROOMS

% Private bath/shower: 20%
% Non-smoking: 100%
% Air conditioned: 0%
Car parking: Yes
Wheelchair access: No
Non-animal tested toiletries: No
Insecticides used? No
Pets welcome? No
Of animal origin: Leather furniture, feather pillows, wool rugs
Nearby activities: Golf, bicycling, canoeing/kayaking, boating, snorkeling, water sports, cross-country skiing, horseback riding, camping, beach, yoga, fitness classes, exercise room, massage, educational lectures, antique shops
Description: Still Point is a quiet waterfront property with wonderful energy on the Bay of Quinte. Relax and enjoy scheduled yoga retreats or create your own retreat.
Forms of payment: *U.S. currency*—cash, personal checks; *Local currency*—cash, personal checks

SIVANANDA ASHRAM YOGA CAMP

673 8th Avenue
Val Morin, Quebec J0T 2R0 Canada
Phone: 819-322-3226
Fax: 819-322-5876

Proprietor: S.W. Kartikeya
Category: Yoga ashram
Location: Mountain, forest
Open all year? Yes
Price: Inexpensive
Special packages: Yes
Reader discount: No
Child discount: Yes

MEALS

Included: B, D
Offered: B, D
% Vegetarian: 100%
% Vegan: 50%
% Organic: 20%
Special diets: None
Nearby restaurants: No

ROOMS

% Private bath/shower: 40%
% Non-smoking: 100%
% Air conditioned: 0%
Car parking: Yes

Wheelchair access: Yes
Non-animal tested toiletries: No
Insecticides used? No
Pets welcome? No
Of animal origin: None
Nearby activities: Outdoor pool, tennis, golf, bicycling, hiking, canoeing/kayaking, boating, cross-country skiing, downhill skiing, horseback riding, camping, yoga, educational lectures, meditation and temple

Description: In the heart of the Laurentian Mountains, the Sivananda Yoga Camp offers year-round yoga vacations, summer teacher-training courses, and a children's yoga camp. The daily schedule includes morning and evening meditation, two yoga classes, workshops, and plenty of time to relax and enjoy the beautiful natural surroundings.

Forms of payment: *U.S. currency*—cash, travelers checks, certified personal checks; *Local currency*—cash, travelers checks; AX, VI

NORTHEASTERN U.S.

Connecticut
Maine
Maryland
Massachusetts
New Jersey
New York
Pennsylvania
Vermont

BUTTERBROOKE BED & BREAKFAST

**78 Barry Road
Oxford, CT 06478 USA
Phone: 203-888-2000**

Proprietor: Tom Butterworth

Category: Bed & Breakfast

Location: Mountain, rural

Open all year? Open Apr. 1–Dec.

Price: Moderate

Special packages: Yes

Reader discount: Yes; inquire directly

Child discount: Yes

MEALS

Included: B

Offered: B, D

% Vegetarian: On request

% Vegan: On request

% Organic: 100%

Special diets: Yes

Nearby restaurants: Yes

ROOMS

% Private bath/shower: 100%

% Non-smoking: 0%

% Air conditioned: 0%

Car parking: Yes

Wheelchair access: No

Non-animal tested toiletries: No

Insecticides used? No

Pets welcome? Yes

Of animal origin: Feather pillows, wool rugs

Nearby activities: Tennis, golf, bicycling, hiking, canoeing/kayaking, boating, water sports, cross-country skiing, downhill skiing, horseback riding, nutrition classes, camping, fitness classes, nightclub, antique shops, private pond

Description: Butterbrooke is an authentically restored 1711 Saltbox Colonial house in the historic Quaker Farms section of Oxford. Four beautifully landscaped acres provide a pond with a dock for swimming, a babbling brook for swimming, and over one hundred different flowers, fruits, vegetables, and herbs, with most of the varieties similar to those grown here in the 1700s. Several dozen species of birds are in residence at the site.

Forms of payment: *U.S. currency*—cash, travelers checks, personal checks

HER WILD SONG

**P.O. Box 515
Brunswick, ME 04011 USA
Phone: 207-721-9005
Fax: 207-721-0235**

Proprietor: Anne Dellenbaugh

Category: Outdoor adventure

Location: Beachfront, mountain, river lakefront, desert, resort town,

Open all year? Yes

Price: Moderate

Special packages: No

Reader discount: No

Child discount: No

MEALS

Included: B, L, D

Offered: B, L, D

% Vegetarian: 100%

% Vegan: 75%

% Organic: 70%

Special diets: Yes

Nearby restaurants: No

ROOMS

% Private bath/shower: N/A

% Non-smoking: N/A

% Air conditioned: N/A

Car parking: Yes

Wheelchair access: No

Non-animal tested toiletries: N/A

Insecticides used? N/A

Pets welcome? No

Of animal origin: None

Nearby activities: Hiking, canoeing/kayaking, snowshoeing, meditation, camping, beach, educational lectures

Description: Contemplative wilderness journeys for women offered in the American southwest, southeast, and northeast,

as well as eastern Canada. We travel by canoe, sea-kayak, or on foot. Instruction is offered on all trips as needed. Travel with a company that encourages deepening of our intimacy with the Earth.

Forms of payment: *U.S. currency*—cash, travelers checks, personal checks; MC, VI

POLAND SPRING HEALTH INSTITUTE

**226 Schellinger Road
Poland Spring, ME 04274 USA
Phone: 207-998-2894
Fax: 207-998-2164**

Proprietor: Richard A. Hansen, M.D.

Category: Retreat

Location: Lakefront, resort town

Open all year? Yes

Price: Moderate

Special packages: Yes

Reader discount: No

Child discount: No

MEALS

Included: B, L, D

Offered: B, L, D

% Vegetarian: 100%

% Vegan: 100%
% Organic: 20%
Special diets: Yes
Nearby restaurants: Yes

ROOMS

% Private bath/shower: 40%
% Non-smoking: 100%
% Air conditioned: 0%
Car parking: Yes
Wheelchair access: No
Non-animal tested toiletries: No
Insecticides used? No
Pets welcome? No
Of animal origin: Farm animals, wool rugs
Nearby activities: Tennis, golf, bicycling, hiking, canoeing/kayaking, cross-country skiing, downhill skiing, horseback riding, nutrition classes, beach, fitness classes, massage, weight loss classes, educational lectures, sightseeing tours, antique shops, museums
Description: We offer several health enhancement programs for a wide variety of medical problems, including heart disease, cancer, emphysema, arthritis, chronic fatigue, diabetes, depression, chronic pain, and nerve disorders. We are available year round with individualized counseling, complete medical and diagnostic evaluations, nutrition instruction, hydrotherapy, and exercises carefully prescribed by your assigned physician. The atmosphere is relaxed and restful, for the best help with stress. Our vegetarian cuisine is served family style.

Forms of payment: *U.S. currency*—cash, travelers checks, personal checks

NORTHERN PINES

559 Rt. 85
Raymond, ME 04071-6248 USA
Phone: 207-655-7624
Fax: 207-655-3321

Proprietor: Marlee Turner
Category: Resort
Location: Rural, lakefront
Open all year? Inquire directly
Price: Moderate
Special packages: Yes
Reader discount: 10%
Child discount: Yes

MEALS

Included: B, L, D
Offered: B, L, D
% Vegetarian: 100%
% Vegan: 67%
% Organic: 25%
Special diets: Yes
Nearby restaurants: No

ROOMS

% Private bath/shower: 50%

% Non-smoking: 100%

% Air conditioned: 0%

Car parking: Yes

Wheelchair access: Yes

Non-animal tested toiletries: No

Insecticides used? No

Pets welcome? No

Of animal origin: None

Nearby activities: Tennis, golf, bicycling, hiking, canoeing/ kayaking, boating, water sports, cross-country skiing, downhill skiing, nutrition classes, camping, yoga, fitness classes, exercise room, massage, juice fasting, weight loss classes, educational lectures, sightseeing tours, antique shops, paddleboat steamer, hot tub, sauna, floatation tank

Description: Come to a special, relaxing, and caring environment where the air is clear, the water pure, and the food wholesome. Our beautiful lakeside retreat is in 70 acres of pine forest with 1/2 mile waterfront. A tranquil place for transitions, letting go of stress and toxins, and taking time for you!

Forms of payment: *U.S. currency*—cash, travelers checks, personal checks; MC, VI, Discover

WEST OF EDEN

**P.O. Box 114
Route 102 & Kelleytown Road
Seal Cove, ME 04674 USA
Phone: 207-244-9695**

Proprietor: Connie Pappas

Category: Bed & Breakfast

Location: Rural

Open all year? Inquire directly

Price: Inexpensive

Special packages: No

Reader discount: No

Child discount: No

MEALS

Included: B

Offered: B, D

% Vegetarian: 100%

% Vegan: 100%

% Organic: 90%

Special diets: Yes

Nearby restaurants: Yes

Comments: Dinner served a few times per week

ROOMS

% Private bath/shower: 0%

% Non-smoking: 100%

% Air conditioned: 0%

Car parking: Yes

Wheelchair access: No

Non-animal tested toiletries: Yes

Insecticides used? No

Pets welcome? No

Of animal origin: Leather furniture, wool rugs

Nearby activities: Golf, bicycling, hiking, canoeing/kayaking, boating, cross-country skiing, camping, beach, yoga, fitness classes, massage, sightseeing tours, antique shops, museums

Description: Quiet rural setting yet close to all island and park amenities. Lovingly prepared whole foods served in intimate, friendly atmosphere. Serene and simple Maine style house calms and restores. From guests: "Neat house, delicious breakfasts, good conversations." "Wonderful whole food." "Maravilloso!" "What a peaceful, beautiful spot!" "Nice discovery. We'll be back."

Forms of payment: *U.S. currency*—cash, travelers checks

THE ROARING LION BED & BREAKFAST

**995 Main Street
P.O. Box 756
Waldoboro, ME 04572 USA
Phone: 207-832-4038
Fax: 207-832-7892**

Proprietor: Robin & Bill Branigan
Category: Bed & Breakfast
Location: Quaint village
Open all year? Yes
Price: Moderate
Special packages: No
Reader discount: No
Child discount: No

MEALS

Included: B
Offered: B
% Vegetarian: 50%
% Vegan: 20%
% Organic: 50%
Special diets: Yes
Nearby restaurants: Yes

ROOMS

% Private bath/shower: 25%
% Non-smoking: 100%
% Air conditioned: 0%

Car parking: Yes
Wheelchair access: No
Non-animal tested toiletries: No
Insecticides used? No
Pets welcome? No
Of animal origin: Wool rugs, feather pillows
Nearby activities: Tennis, golf, bicycling, hiking, canoeing/kayaking, boating, snorkeling, scuba diving, water sports, cross-country skiing, downhill skiing, horseback riding, camping, beach, exercise room, massage, antique shops, museums

Description: Four rooms, one with private bath. 1905 Victorian with fireplaces, tin ceilings, wood paneling, two acres near village center. Stroll through flower and vegetable gardens. Full breakfast, in-room flowers, afternoon tea, special year-end holiday dinners. We accommodate special and vegetarian diets. Gallery and gift shop on premises.

Forms of payment: *U.S. currency*—cash, travelers checks, personal checks

GRAMERCY MANSION

1400 Greenspring Valley Rd.
Box 119
Stevenson, MD 21153 USA
Phone: 410-486-2405
Fax: 410-486-1765

Proprietor: Anne P.
Category: Bed & Breakfast
Location: Suburban
Open all year? Yes
Price: Moderate
Special packages: No
Reader discount: No
Child discount: No

MEALS

Included: B
Offered: B
% Vegetarian: 50%
% Vegan: 50%
% Organic: Varies
Special diets: Yes
Nearby restaurants: Yes

ROOMS

% Private bath/shower: 50%
% Non-smoking: Smoking outdoors
   only
% Air conditioned: All 10 bedrooms
Car parking: Yes
Wheelchair access: No
Non-animal tested toiletries: No
Insecticides used? No
Pets welcome? No
Of animal origin: Leather furniture,
   wool rugs, feather pillows,
   dead mounted/stuffed animals,
   down comforters
Nearby activities: Outdoor pool,
   tennis, bicycling, hiking,
   massage

Description: English Tudor Mansion
built in 1902 on a 45 acre
estate by Alexander Cassatt as a
wedding gift to his daughter.
The brother of famous impres-
sionist painter Mary Cassatt,
he was also president of the
Pennsylvania Railroad. 20
minutes from Baltimore Inner
Harbour. Three bedrooms with

fireplaces, one with whirlpool,
one with double jacuzzi.
Certified organic farm on
property.

Forms of payment: *U.S. currency*—cash,
travelers checks; AX, MC, VI,
Discover

KUSHI INSTITUTE

Leland Rd.
P.O. Box 7
Becket, MA 01223 USA
Phone: 413-623-5741
Fax: 413-623-8827

Proprietor: Chris Lefevre
Category: Retreat
Location: Mountain, quaint village
Open all year? Yes
Price: Moderate
Special packages: Inquire
Reader discount: No
Child discount: No

MEALS

Included: B, L, D
Offered: B, L, D
% Vegetarian: 100%
% Vegan: 100%
% Organic: 50–75%
Special diets: Yes
Nearby restaurants: No

ROOMS

% Private bath/shower: 15%
% Non-smoking: 100%
% Air conditioned: 0%
Car parking: Yes
Wheelchair access: Yes
Non-animal tested toiletries: No
Insecticides used? No
Pets welcome? No
Of animal origin: Feather pillows, wool rugs
Nearby activities: Bicycling, hiking, canoeing/kayaking, cross-country skiing, downhill skiing, nutrition classes, camping, beach, yoga, massage, weight loss classes, educational lec-

tures, antique shops, museums

Description: The Kushi Institute is an ideal setting in the Berkshire Mountains of western Massachusetts, for self-reflection and exploring local mountain scenery, art, and culture. Renowned for macrobiotic education, cooking classes, and publications, the Kushi Institute offers a "relax and

renew" program for short term visitors, including accommodations, delicious whole food meals, and exercise.

Forms of payment: *U.S. currency*—cash, travelers checks, personal checks; AX, MC, VI, Discover

TURNING POINT INN

3 Lake Buel Road
Great Barrington, MA 01230 USA
Phone: 413-528-4777

Proprietor: Irving G. Yost
Category: Bed & Breakfast
Location: Mountain, resort town
Open all year? Yes
Price: Moderate
Special packages: Yes

Reader discount: No
Child discount: Yes

MEALS

Included: B
Offered: B
% Vegetarian: 100%
% Vegan: 70%
% Organic: 50%
Special diets: Yes
Nearby restaurants: Yes

ROOMS

% Private bath/shower: 66%
% Non-smoking: 100%
% Air conditioned: 0%
Car parking: Yes
Wheelchair access: No
Non-animal tested toiletries: No
Insecticides used? No
Pets welcome? No
Of animal origin: None

Nearby activities: Indoor pool, tennis, golf, hiking, bicycling, canoeing/kayaking, boating, water sports, cross-country skiing, downhill skiing, horseback riding, nutrition classes, camping, beach, yoga, fitness classes, exercise room, massage, juice fasting, weight loss classes, educational lectures, sightseeing tours, nightclub, antique shops, museums

Description: We are an 18th century former stagecoach stop. In the heart of the Berkshire hills next to music, art, theater, hiking, skiing, sitting rooms with Rumford fireplaces, piano, cable TV in TV room only. A warm friendly atmosphere where families and groups are welcome.

Forms of payment: *U.S. currency*—cash, travelers checks, personal checks; AX, MC, VI

CANYON RANCH
IN THE BERKSHIRES

**165 Kemble Street
Lenox, MA 01240 USA
Phone: 800-726-9900 or
413-637-4100
Fax: 413-637-0057**

Proprietor: Mel Zuckerman
Category: Spa
Location: Mountain
Open all year?: Yes
Price: Expensive
Special packages: Yes
Reader Discount: No
Child discount: No

MEALS

Included: B, L, D
Offered: B, L, D
% Vegetarian: 50%
% Vegan: On request
% Organic: Varies
Special diets: Yes
Nearby restaurants: No

ROOMS

% Private bath/shower: 100%
% Non-smoking: 100%
% Air conditioned: 100%
Car parking: Yes
Wheelchair access: Yes
Non-animal tested toiletries: Yes

Insecticides used?: No

Pets welcome? No

Of animal origin: Leather furniture, Wool rugs

Nearby activities: Indoor
pool, outdoor pool,
tennis, golf, bicycling,
hiking,
canoeing/kayaking,
cross-country skiing,
downhill skiing, nutri-
tion classes, yoga, fit-
ness classes, exercise
room, massage, educational
lectures, antique shops

Description: See page 26 for description of Canyon Ranch facilities

Forms of payment: *U.S. currency*—cash,
travelers checks; AX, MC, VI,
Discover

KRIPALU CENTER
FOR YOGA AND HEALTH

Box 793
Lenox, MA 02140 USA
Phone: 413-448-3400
Fax: 413-448-3685

Proprietor: Non-profit organization

Category: Retreat

Location: Mountain, lakefront,
woods, hills

Open all year? Yes

Price: Inexpensive

Special packages: Yes

Reader discount: Yes; inquire directly

Child discount: No

MEALS

Included: B, L, D

Offered: B, L, D

% Vegetarian: 100%

% Vegan: 80%

% Organic: 25%

Special diets: Yes

Nearby restaurants: No

ROOMS

% Private bath/shower: 10%

% Non-smoking rooms: 100%

% Air conditioned: 0%

Car parking: Yes

Wheelchair access: Yes

Non-animal tested toiletries: Yes

Insecticides used? No

Pets welcome? No

Of animal origin: None

Nearby activities: Indoor pool, tennis, golf, bicycling, hiking, canoeing/kayaking, boating, cross-country skiing, downhill skiing, horseback riding, yoga, fitness classes, exercise room, massage, juice fasting, educational lectures, sightseeing tours, nightclub, antique shops, whirlpool, sauna

Description: Our retreat and renewal program offers a rich, flexible schedule of self-discovery workshops each morning, lunch hour meditations, and afternoon yoga. Open year-round. Two-night minimum for overnight stays.

Forms of payment: *U.S. currency*—cash, travelers checks; MC, VI

ROWE CAMP & CONFERENCE CENTER

King's Highway Road
Rowe, MA 01307 USA
Phone: 413-339-4954
Fax: 413-339-5728

Proprietor: N/A

Category: Retreat

Location: Mountain, woods

Open all year? Yes

Price: Inexpensive/Moderate

Special packages: Yes

Reader discount: Inquire directly

Child discount: No

MEALS

Included: None

Offered: D; see comment

% Vegetarian: 100%

% Vegan: On request

% Organic: 50%

Special diets: On request

Nearby restaurants: No

Comment: Dinner prepared for $10 extra; food supplied for self-catering B and L also

ROOMS

% Private bath/shower: 0%

% Non-smoking: 100%

% Air conditioned: 0%

Car parking: Yes

Wheelchair access: No

Non-animal tested toiletries: No

Insecticides used?

Pets welcome? No

Of animal origin: Feather pillows

Nearby activities: Sauna, bicycling, hiking, boating, snorkeling, cross-country skiing, downhill skiing, camping, beach, educational lectures (on weekends), antique shops, museums

Description: Unitarian Universalist retreat community in the Berkshires just a few miles from Vermont. Miles of hiking, meditation house, garden in the woods, stone chapel, waterfall, mill pond, lake, single and double rooms. 1-1/2 hrs from Albany and Hartford, 2-1/2 from Boston and Burlington.

Forms of payment: *U.S. currency*—travelers checks, personal checks; MC, VI

THE OPTION INSTITUTE

2080 South Undermountain
Sheffield, MA 01257-9643 USA
Phone: 413-229-2100
Fax: 413-229-8931

Proprietor: Barry Neil Kaufman

Category: Learning center

Location: Berkshire Mountains

Open all year? Yes, except
Christmas week

Price: Moderate

Special packages: No

Reader discount: No

Child discount: No

MEALS

Included: None

Offered: B, L, D

% Vegetarian: 100%

% Vegan: See comments

% Organic: See comments

Special diets: Inquire directly

Nearby restaurants: Yes

Comments: Vegan options at
every meal. Grains and
beans are organic.

ROOMS

% Private bath/shower: 20%

% Non-smoking: 100%

% Air conditioned: 0%

Car parking: Yes

Wheelchair access: Yes

Non-animal tested toiletries: Yes

Insecticides used? No

Pets welcome? No

Of animal origin: None

Nearby activities: Indoor pool, outdoor
pool, tennis, golf, hiking, boating,
snorkeling, scuba diving, water

sports, cross-country skiing,
downhill skiing, nutrition
classes, horseback riding, camping, yoga, fitness classes, exercise room, massage, educational
lectures, antique shops

Description: Set on a wooded mountainside with magnificent views
of the surrounding Berkshires,
this 85-acre property includes
ponds and meadows, sweeping
lawns and forests, streams and
waterfalls. Easy access to a variety of seasonal sports as listed
above.

Forms of payment: *U.S. currency*—cash,
travelers checks, personal
checks; AX, MC, VI

GENESIS FARM

**41A Silver Lake Road
Blairstown, NJ 07825 USA
Phone: 908-362-6735
Fax: 908-362-9387**

Proprietor: Maureen Wild
Category: Ecological learning center
Location: Quaint village
Open all year? Yes
Price: Moderate
Special packages: No
Reader discount: No
Child discount: No

MEALS

Included: B, L, D
Offered: B, L, D
% Vegetarian: 100%
% Vegan: 5%
% Organic: 90%
Special diets: Yes
Nearby restaurants: No

ROOMS

% Private bath/shower: 0%
% Non-smoking: 100%
% Air conditioned: 0%
Car parking: Yes
Wheelchair access: No
Non-animal tested toiletries: Yes
Insecticides used? No
Pets welcome? No
Of animal origin: Wool rugs, farm animals
Nearby activities: Bicycling, hiking, nutrition classes, educational lectures, programs about the new cosmology
Description: Genesis Farm is a learning center for Earth studies. It welcomes all people of good will to attend courses, workshops, and celebrations which help in the search for alternative ways to achieve true human and ecological well-being. It is rooted in a spirituality that reverences the Earth as a primary revelation of the divine.

Forms of payment: *U.S. currency*—cash, personal checks

APPEL FARM ARTS & MUSIC CENTER

**457 Shirley Road
Elmer, NJ 08318 USA
Phone: 609-358-2472
Fax: 609-358-6513**

Proprietor: Mark Packer, Executive Director
Category: Retreat
Location: Rural farming area
Open all year? Closed Sept.– May
Price: Moderate
Special packages: No
Reader discount: No
Child discount: No

MEALS

Included: B, L, D
Offered: B, L, D
% Vegetarian: 50%
% Vegan: 10%
% Organic: 100%
Special diets: Yes
Nearby restaurants: No
Comments: Meals for groups only

ROOMS

% Private bath/shower: None
% Non-smoking: 100%
% Air conditioned: 0%

Car parking: No

Wheelchair access: Yes

Non-animal tested toiletries: No

Insecticides used? No

Pets welcome? No

Of animal origin: None

Nearby activities: Outdoor pool, tennis, bicycling, camping, antique shops, museums

Description: The Appel Farm Conference Center is in rural Salem County in South Jersey. Conference facilities are comfortable, meals are planned according to retreat groups needs. Our grounds are spacious (176 acres), sunsets are spectacular, and the air is fresh!

Forms of payment: *U.S. currency*—cash, travelers checks, personal checks; MC, VI, Discover

SERENDIPITY BED AND BRUNCH

712 Ninth Street
Ocean City, NJ 08226-3554 USA
Phone: 800-842-8544 or
609-399-1554

Proprietor: Clara and Bill Plowfield

Category: Bed & Breakfast

Location: Beachfront

Open all year? Yes

Price: Moderate

Special packages: Yes

Reader discount: No

Child discount: No

MEALS

Included: B

Offered: B, D

% Vegetarian: 95%

% Vegan: 95%

% Organic: 75%

Special diets: Yes

Nearby restaurants: Yes

ROOMS

% Private bath/shower: 33%

% Non-smoking: 100%

% Air conditioned: 100%

Car parking: Yes

Wheelchair access: No

Non-animal tested toiletries: No

Insecticides used? No

Pets welcome? No

Of animal origin: None

Nearby activities: Tennis, golf, bicycling, boating, water sports, beach, yoga, fitness classes, exercise room, massage, nightclub, antique shops, museums, casinos

Description: Serendipity is an immaculately maintained and beautifully renovated 1912 seashore inn where privacy, hospitality, and delicious, healthy vegetarian breakfasts and dinners are tastefully blended for your get-away! One-half block to the island's beaches and boardwalk, within walking distance of restaurants, shops, and the Music Pier, and 8 miles from the shows and casinos of Atlantic City.

Forms of payment: *U.S. currency*—cash, travelers checks, personal checks; AX, MC, VI, Discover

New York State is especially accommodating to vegetarians and vegans and merits high recommendations as a place for veggie vacations. The southern Cayuga Lake/Seneca Lake area of Finger Lakes wine country, with its local veggie/vegan/whole food population, rates particularly high for variety and quality. The listings in this edition are just those who responded to our questionnaire in time to be included. We plan to list many more in future editions.

—S. & J. Civic

CHALET LEON

3835 Rt 414
Burdett, NY 14818 USA
Phone: 607-546-7171
Fax: 607-546-4091

Proprietor: George Eisman
Category: Motel
Location: Lakefront, resort town, waterfall
Open all year? Open Apr. 28–Nov. 1
Price: Moderate
Special packages: Yes
Reader discount: 10%
Child discount: Yes

MEALS

Included: B
Offered: B
% Vegetarian: 100%
% Vegan: 100%
% Organic: 60%
Special diets: None
Nearby restaurants: Yes

ROOMS

% Private bath/shower: 100%

% Non-smoking: 60%
% Air conditioned: 0%
Car parking: Yes
Wheelchair access: No
Non-animal tested toiletries: Yes
Insecticides used? See comments
Pets welcome? Yes
Of animal origin: None
Nearby activities: Hiking, canoeing/kayaking, nutrition classes, waterfall bathing, Farm Sanctuary, wineries
Description: Eleven motel rooms and eight cabins nestled on a hillside overlooking Seneca Lake. Hector Falls, a 160-foot waterfall in three tiers runs through

the property owned by and operated by vegans.

Forms of payment: *U.S. currency*—cash, travelers checks; MC, VI

Comments: Only spray insecticide if dog has been quartered there

RED HOUSE COUNTRY INN

Finger Lakes National Forest
4586 Picnic Area Road
Burdett, NY 14818
Phone: 607-546-8566
Fax: 607-546-4105

Proprietor: Sandy Schmanke

Category: Bed & Breakfast

Location: Finger Lakes National Forest

Open all year? Yes

Price: Moderate

Special packages: No

Reader discount: No

Child discount: No

MEALS

Included: B

Offered: B, See comment

% Vegetarian: On request

% Vegan: On request

% Organic: 0%

Special diets: Low salt, sugar free

Nearby restaurants: Yes

Comments: Dinner by request Nov–Apr.

ROOMS

% Private bath/shower: 0%

% Non-smoking: 100%

% Air conditioned: 0%

Car parking: Yes

Wheelchair access: No

Non-animal tested toiletries: No

Insecticides used? No

Pets welcome? No

Of animal origin: Leather furniture, wool rugs, down comforters, feather pillows, farm animals

Nearby activities: Outdoor pool, tennis, golf, bicycling, hiking, canoeing/kayaking, boating, cross-country and downhill skiing, camping, massage, sightseeing tours, antique shops, museums, wineries

Description: Originally a farmstead built in the mid-1800s, this classy inn is nestled in the beautiful 16,000 acre Finger Lakes National Forest. Warm, comfortable rooms furnished with turn-of-the-century

antiques. Public room, large verandah, lawns, in-ground pool, lush flower beds, picnic areas, fully-equipped guest kitchen for making lunch or snacks, immediate access to over 30 miles of maintained trails and ponds. Website www.fingerlakes.net/ redhouse; E-mail redhsinn@aol. com

Forms of payment: *U.S. currency*—cash, travelers checks, personal checks; AX, MC, VI, Discover

RUSTIC LOG CABINS

**5685 Route 414
P.O. Box 18
Hector, NY 14841 USA
Phone: 607-546-8489**

Proprietor: J.K. Leidenfrost
Category: Log cabins, self-catering
Location: Country, lakefront
Open all year? Open May 15–Oct. 15
Price: Moderate
Special packages: No
Reader discount: 10%
Child discount: No

MEALS

Included: None
Offered: Self-catering
% Vegetarian: N/A
% Vegan: N/A
% Organic: N/A
Special diets: N/A
Nearby restaurants: Yes

ROOMS

% Private bath/shower: 0%
% Non-smoking: 50%
% Air conditioned: 0%
Car parking: Yes
Wheelchair access: Yes
Non-animal tested toiletries: No
Insecticides used? No
Pets welcome? Yes
Of animal origin: None
Nearby activities: Hiking, boating,
   cross-country skiing, horseback
   riding, camping, beach,
   antique shops, estate wineries,
   Wisdom's Goldenrod Center
   for Philosophic Studies
Description: Quaint, one-room cabins

with large porches and fireplaces furnished for light
housekeeping. Will accommodate 4-6 persons. Central bath
house with hot and cold run-
ning water. Beautiful grounds
with apple orchard, vineyards,
all sloping towards Seneca
Lake. Spectacular sunsets.
Swimming and boating 5 minutes by car.

Forms of payment: *U.S. currency*—cash,
   travelers checks, personal checks

VATRA MOUNTAIN VALLEY LODGE & SPA

**Route 214
Hunter, NY 12442 USA
Phone: 800-232-2772 or
   518-263-4919
Fax: 518-263-4994**

Proprietor: George Borkacki
Category: Spa
Location: Mountain, quaint village,
   resort town
Open all year? Yes
Price: Inexpensive/Moderate
Special packages: Yes
Reader discount: 5%

Child discount: No

MEALS

Included: B, L, D

Offered: B, L, D

% Vegetarian: 100%

% Vegan: 50%

% Organic: 50%

Special diets: Yes

Nearby restaurants: Yes

ROOMS

% Private bath/shower: 100%

% Non-smoking: 90%

% Air conditioned: 100%

Car parking: Yes

Wheelchair access: Yes

Non-animal tested toiletries: No

Insecticides used? No

Pets welcome? No

Of animal origin: None

Nearby activities: Indoor pool, outdoor pool, tennis, golf, bicycling, hiking, canoeing/kayaking, cross-country skiing, downhill skiing, horseback riding, nutrition classes, camping, beach, yoga, fitness classes, exercise room, massage, juice fasting, weight loss classes, educational lectures, sightseeing tours, nightclub, antique shops, museums, shiatsu, reflexology, beauty treatments, body composition analysis

Description: Our 15 acre resort at the base of Hunter Mountain in the majestic Northern Catskills magnifies the beauty of all seasons. We have trails for hiking and cross country skiing right here on our Catskill State Park location. Our healthy and heal-ing environment supports los-ing weight and reducing stress. Expert fitness and aquatic trainers guide you through classes that move at your own pace. Your fat weight goes down as your heart rate goes up. At Vatra Mountain Valley Lodge and Spa wellness is not just a concept, it's a commitment.

VATRA MOUNTAIN VALLEY LODGE & SPA

Forms of payment: *U.S. currency*—cash, travelers checks, personal checks; AX, MC, VI

GURNEY'S INN RESORT & SPA

290 Old Montauk Hwy.
Montauk, NY 11954 USA
Phone: 516-668-2345
Fax: 516-668-3576

Proprietor: Nick Monte

Category: Spa, resort

Location: Beachfront, quaint village, resort town

Open all year? Yes

Price: Moderate

Special packages: Yes

Reader discount: See comments

Child discount: Yes; inquire directly

MEALS

Included: B, D
Offered: B, L, D
% Vegetarian: 25%
% Vegan: 10%
% Organic: Varies
Special diets: Yes
Nearby restaurants: Yes
Comments: 10% reader discount on food at the Caffe Monte only

ROOMS

% Private bath/shower: 100%
% Non-smoking: 100%
% Air conditioned: 100%
Car parking: Yes
Wheelchair access: Yes
Non-animal tested toiletries: No
Insecticides used? Yes
Pets welcome? No
Of animal origin: None
Nearby activities: Indoor pool, outdoor pool, tennis, golf, bicycling, hiking, canoeing/kayaking, boating, water sports, horseback riding, nutrition classes, camping, beach, yoga, fitness classes, exercise room, massage, juice fasting, weight loss classes, educational lectures, sightseeing tours, nightclub, antique shops, museums
Description: We are a full service resort and international health spa located approximately 125 miles from Manhattan (2-1/2 hours). We are situated on 1000 feet of a private ocean beach with a full service bar and grille operating July and August on the beach. Our spa menu is creative and caters to vegetarians with the emphasis on wholesome locally grown foods. We have an on-premises bake shop and coffee bar known as Caffe Monte serving light fare and specializing in organically grown Native American gourmet coffees and teas.

Forms of payment: *U.S. currency*—cash, travelers checks, personal checks; AX, MC, VI, Discover

NEW AGE HEALTH SPA

**Route 55
Neversink, NY 12765 USA
Phone: 800-682-4348 or
914-985-7600
Fax: 914-985-2467**

Proprietor: Werner Mendel
Category: Spa
Location: Mountain, quaint village
Open all year? Yes
Price: Inexpensive
Special packages: Yes
Reader discount: 10%
Child discount: No

MEALS

Included: B, L, D
Offered: B, L, D
% Vegetarian: 100%
% Vegan: On request
% Organic: 15%
Special diets: Yes
Nearby restaurants: No

ROOMS

% Private bath/shower: 100%
% Non-smoking: 100%
% Air conditioned: 25%
Car parking: Yes
Wheelchair access: No

Non-animal tested toiletries: Yes
Insecticides used? No
Pets welcome? No
Of animal origin: None
Nearby activities: Indoor pool, outdoor pool, tennis, hiking, water sports, cross-country skiing, nutrition classes, yoga, fitness classes, exercise room, massage, juice fasting, weight loss classes, educational lectures, alpine climbing tower
Description: Welcome to a retreat that offers endless possibilities —a haven that provides every-

thing for the perfect vacation. By participating in our programs for proper nutrition and exercise, you will discover health's threefold benefits: feeling good, looking good, and living well. New Age Health Spa offers quiet intimacy and personalized service. We're nestled in 155 acres of beautiful rolling hills and forest in the majestic Catskill Mountains of Sullivan County.

Forms of payment: *U.S. currency*—cash, travelers checks, personal checks; AX, MC, VI, Discover

THE PHOENICIA PATHWORK CENTER

P.O. Box 66
Phoenicia, NY 12464 USA
Phone: 914-688-2211
Fax: 914-688-2007

Proprietor: Regan McCarthy, Director
Category: Spa, retreat
Location: Mountain
Open all year? Yes, but inquire
Price: Inexpensive
Special packages: Yes
Reader discount: No
Child discount: Yes

MEALS

Included: B, L, D
Offered: B, L, D
% Vegetarian: On request
% Vegan: On request
% Organic: 25%
Special diets: Inquire directly
Nearby restaurants: Yes

ROOMS

% Private bath/shower: 40%
% Non-smoking: 100%
% Air conditioned: 0%
Car parking: Yes
Wheelchair access: Yes
Non-animal tested toiletries: Yes

Insecticides used? No
Pets welcome? No
Of animal origin: None
Nearby activities: Indoor pool, outdoor

pool, tennis, golf, bicycling, hiking, canoeing/kayaking, snorkeling, scuba diving, cross-country skiing, downhill skiing, horseback riding, nutrition classes, camping, beach, fitness classes, exercise room, massage, juice fasting, weight loss classes, educational lectures, nightclub, antique shops, tubing

Description: Not-for-profit educational institution on 300 acres in the heart of the Catskills. Two Native American sweat lodges, sanctuary, spa, library, boutique, bookstore, meeting rooms. Stone and wood buildings house 10 to 200+ people in single, double, and dormitory rooms. Tenting in season.

Forms of payment: *U.S. currency*—cash, travelers checks; MC, VI

LIVING SPRINGS LIFESTYLE CENTER

**12 Living Springs Lane
Putnam Valley, NY 10579 USA
Phone: 800-SAY-WELL or
914-526-2800
Fax: 914-528-9171**

Proprietor: Wes Rozell
Category: Retreat
Location: Lakefront, rural
Open all year? Yes
Price: Moderate
Special packages: Yes
Reader discount: No
Child discount: No

MEALS

Included: B, L, D
Offered: B, L, D
% Vegetarian: 33%
% Vegan: 66%
% Organic: 5%
Special diets: Yes
Nearby restaurants: No

ROOMS

% Private bath/shower: 100%
% Non-smoking: 100%
% Air conditioned: 13%
Car parking: Yes
Wheelchair access: Yes
Non-animal tested toiletries: No
Insecticides used? No
Pets welcome? No
Of animal origin: None
Nearby activities: Hiking, cross-country skiing, nutrition classes, fitness classes, exercise room, massage, educational lectures, weight loss classes, museums

Description: Located one hour north of Manhattan, Living Springs Retreat offers live-in programs for people who want to change or improve their health habits. Guests come for structured programs of one or more weeks or just a healthy getaway. Our most popular programs include smoking cessation, weight loss, and fatigue reduction.

Forms of payment: *U.S. currency*—cash, travelers checks, personal checks; MC, VI

OUR HOUSE RETREAT

**422 Bostock Road
Shokan, NY 12481 USA
Phone/Fax: 914-657-2864**

Proprietor: Claudia & Lester
Category: Retreat
Location: Mountain

Open all year? Yes
Price: Inexpensive
Special packages: Yes
Reader discount: 10%
Child discount: No

MEALS

Included: B, D
Offered: B, D
% Vegetarian: 95%
% Vegan: On request
% Organic: 80%
Special diets: Yes
Nearby restaurants: Yes

ROOMS

% Private bath/shower: 20%
% Non-smoking: 100%
% Air conditioned: 0%
Car parking: Yes
Wheelchair access: No
Non-animal tested toiletries: No
Insecticides used? No
Pets welcome? No
Of animal origin: Feather pillows, wool rugs, down comforters
Nearby activities: Tennis, golf, bicycling, hiking, canoeing/kayaking, boating, water sports, cross-country skiing, downhill skiing, horseback riding, camping, yoga, fitness classes, exercise room, massage, juice fasting, educational lectures, antique shops, outdoor hot tub, art room, meditation classes, sun decks
Description: Our House Retreat is a beautiful five-bedroom contemporary home with large wraparound sun deck surrounded by woods, streams, organic

gardens, and wildlife in the heart of the Catskill mountains. Claudia and Lester (licensed massage and Reiki practitioners) provide a friendly, nurturing, peaceful environment with healthy home-cooked meals. Come as a guest and leave as a friend!

Forms of payment: *U.S. currency*—cash, travelers checks, personal checks

THE FARM SANCTUARY

P.O. Box 150
Watkins Glen, NY 14891 USA
Phone: 607-583-2225
Fax: 607-583-2041

Proprietor: Gene & Lori Bauston
Category: Bed & Breakfast
Location: Rural
Open all year? May to October only
Price: Inexpensive
Special packages: Yes
Reader discount: No
Child discount: No

MEALS

Included: B
Offered: B

Description: The Farm Sanctuary is a 175 acre working farm that is home to hundreds of rescued pigs, turkeys, cattle, goats, and other animals. During your stay, you'll tour the farm and meet and feed our farm animal friends. Give a pig a belly rub. Feed a sheep. Learn about farm animals. Tour our unique visitor center. Visit our country gift shop.

Forms of payment: *U.S. currency*—cash, travelers checks, personal checks; MC, VI

% Vegetarian: 100%
% Vegan: 100%
% Organic: 25%
Special diets: Yes
Nearby restaurants: Yes

ROOMS

% Private bath/shower: 0%
% Non-smoking: 100%
% Air conditioned: 0%
Car parking: Yes
Wheelchair access: Yes
Non-animal tested toiletries: yes
Insecticides used: No
Pets welcome: Yes
Of animal origin: Farm animals
Nearby activities: Outdoor pool, golf, bicycling, hiking, canoeing/ kayaking, boating, cross-country skiing, nutrition classes, horse-back riding, camping, yoga, fitness classes, exercise room, massage, educational lectures, sightseeing tours, nightclub, antique shops, museums, wineries

SIVANANDA ASHRAM YOGA RANCH

P.O. Box 195, Budd Rd.
Woodbourne, NY 12788 USA
Phone: 914-434-9242
Fax: 914-434-1032

Proprietor: Srinivasan
Category: Retreat
Location: Mountain
Open all year? Yes
Price: Inexpensive
Special packages: No
Reader discount: No
Child discount: Yes

MEALS

Included: L, D
Offered: L, D
% Vegetarian: 100%
% Vegan: 70%
% Organic: 60%
Special diets: Yes
Nearby restaurants: No

ROOMS

% Private bath/shower: 25%

% Non-smoking: 100%

% Air conditioned: 0%

Car parking: Yes

Wheelchair access: No

Non-animal tested toiletries: No

Insecticides used? No

Pets welcome? No

Of animal origin: Feather pillows, wool rugs, farm animals

Nearby activities: Hiking, cross-country skiing, horseback riding, camping, yoga, massage, juice fasting, educational lectures, sauna, swimming pond, meditation instruction

Description: Yoga vacations with 78 acres of secluded forests, panoramic view, swimming pond. Yoga program of twice-daily exercise, breathing, relaxation, vegetarian meals, positive thinking, and meditations. Yoga teachers-training course, sauna, guest lectures and workshops, cultural programs, family yoga.

Forms of payment: *U.S. currency*—cash, travelers checks, personal checks; MC, VI

SUNNY OAKS HOTEL

P.O. Box 297
Woodridge, NY 12789 USA
Phone: 800-679-4387 *(May-Oct);*
800-297-4488 *(Oct-May)*
Fax: 914-434-7580

Proprietor: Cynthia Arenson

Category: Hotel

Location: Lakefront, mountain

Open all year? Open Memorial Day to early October

Price: Inexpensive

Special packages: No

Reader discount: 10%

Child discount: Yes

MEALS

Included: B, L, D

Offered: B, L, D

% Vegetarian: 70%

% Vegan: 30%

% Organic: 10%

Special diets: Yes

Nearby restaurants: No

ROOMS

% Private bath/shower: 80%

% Non-smoking: 75%

% Air conditioned: 5%

Car parking: Yes

Wheelchair access: Yes

Non-animal tested toiletries: No

Insecticides used? No

Pets welcome? Yes

Of animal origin: Feather pillows

Nearby activities: Outdoor pool, tennis, bicycling, hiking, boating, yoga, fitness classes, massage, folk dancing, bridge, tai chi

Description: Sunny Oaks is an informal, inexpensive Catskill Mountain resort/B&B with pool, lake, yoga, tai chi, nature walks and delicious dining with vegetarian specialties. Hike, bike, visit nearby ashrams, or just relax. Suitable for groups, workshops and only 2 hours from New York City.

Forms of payment: *U.S. currency*—cash, travelers checks; MC, VI

WISE WOMAN CENTER

P.O. Box 64
Woodstock, NY 12498 USA
Phone: 914-246-8081
Fax: 914-246-8081

Proprietor: Susun S. Weed
Category: Retreat, workshop center
Location: Mountain, quaint village, resort town
Open all year? Apr. 15–Nov. 2 only
Price: Inexpensive
Special packages: Yes
Reader discount: No
Child discount: No

MEALS

Included: L
Offered: B, L, D
% Vegetarian: 100%
% Vegan: 100%
% Organic: 85%
Special diets: Yes
Nearby restaurants: Yes
Comments: Eggs and cheese served separately

ROOMS

% Private bath/shower: 0%
% Non-smoking: 100%
% Air conditioned: 0%
Car parking: No
Wheelchair access: No
Non-animal tested toiletries: No

Insecticides used? No
Pets welcome? No
Of animal origin: Farm animals
Nearby activities: Hiking, canoeing/ kayaking, nutrition classes, camping, yoga, massage, educational lectures, antique shops, museums
Description: The Wise Woman Center is a safe space for women—and men who love them—to empower themselves. Workshops with nationally

PEGGY MOTSCH

known teachers and work-exchange retreats focus on women's health and spirituality. Free information.

Forms of payment: *U.S. currency*—cash, travelers checks, personal checks

HIMALAYAN INSTITUTE

RR1, Box 400
Honesdale, PA 18431-9706 USA
Phone: 717-253-5551
Fax: 717-253-9078

Proprietor: N/A
Category: Retreat
Location: Mountain
Open all year? Yes
Price: Inexpensive
Special packages: No
Reader discount: No
Child discount: No

MEALS

Included: B, L, D
Offered: B, L, D
% Vegetarian: 100%
% Vegan: On request
% Organic: 50%
Special diets: Yes
Nearby restaurants: No

ROOMS

% Private bath/shower: 0%
% Non-smoking: 100%
% Air conditioned: 0%
Car parking: Yes
Wheelchair access: Yes
Non-animal tested toiletries: No
Insecticides used? No
Pets welcome? No
Of animal origin: Farm animals, wool rugs, live caged animals/birds
Nearby activities: Outdoor pool, tennis, hiking, water sports, cross-country skiing, downhill skiing, nutrition classes, camping, yoga, exercise room, massage, educational lectures, antique

shops, meditation, weekend seminars, residential programs

Description: Located in the rolling hills of the Pocono Mountains, the Himalayan Institute provides a wooded 400 acre

campus rich with wildlife, hiking trails, a pond, a nearby waterfall, clean air, and a quiet atmosphere—the perfect place to discover the best of yourself in a peaceful and healthy setting.

Forms of payment: *U.S. currency*—cash, travelers checks, personal checks; MC, VI

WHITE CLOUD INN

RR1, Box 215
Newfoundland, PA 18445 USA
Phone: 800-820-0320 or
717-676-3162

Proprietor: Dave Teel
Category: Bed & Breakfast
Location: Mountain
Open all year? Yes
Price: Moderate
Special packages: Yes
Reader discount: 10%
Child discount: Yes

MEALS

Included: B
Offered: B, L, D
% Vegetarian: 100%
% Vegan: 50%
% Organic: Varies
Special diets: Yes
Nearby restaurants: No

ROOMS

% Private bath/shower: 50%
% Non-smoking: 100%
% Air conditioned: 0%
Car parking: Yes
Wheelchair access: Yes
Non-animal tested toiletries: Yes
Insecticides used? No
Pets welcome? Yes
Of animal origin: None
Nearby activities: Tennis, golf, bicycling, hiking, canoeing/kayaking, boating, water sports, cross-country skiing, downhill skiing, horseback riding, camping, yoga, massage, antique shops, museums

Description: A simple and hospitable environment in the Pocono Mountains of northeastern Pennsylvania. Our vegetarian meals are served restaurant-style with guests able to choose from several different entrees each evening.

Forms of payment: *U.S. currency*—cash, travelers checks, personal checks; AX, MC, VI

VERMONT

WEST MOUNTAIN INN

**P.O. Box 481
Arlington, VT 05250 USA
Phone: 802-375-6516
Fax: 802-375-6553**

Proprietor: Wes and Maryann Carlson
Category: Full service country inn
Location: Mountain, rural
Open all year? Yes
Price: Moderate
Special packages: No
Reader discount: Yes; inquire directly
Child discount: Yes

MEALS

Included: B, D
Offered: B, D
% Vegetarian: 25%
% Vegan: On request
% Organic: 100%

Special diets: Yes

Nearby restaurants: Yes

ROOMS

% Private bath/shower: 100%

% Non-smoking: 100%

% Air conditioned: 100%

Car parking: Yes

Wheelchair access: Yes

Non-animal tested toiletries: Yes

Insecticides used? No

Pets welcome? No

Of animal origin: Farm animals, down comforters

Nearby activities: Tennis, golf, bicycling, hiking, canoeing/kayaking, boating, water sports, cross-country skiing, downhill skiing, horseback riding, camping, fitness classes, exercise room, massage, antique shops, museums

Description: West Mountain Inn is perched on 150 woodland acres overlooking the scenic Battenkill and the historic village of Arlington. We offer 15 individually decorated rooms, each with private bath. Outside is a world of natural beauty with trails for hiking, wonderful country roads along the Battenkill for walking or cycling, and in season a myriad of water sports. Special country shops and antique center in East Arlington, just minutes away. We are home to a busy bird feeding station, llamas in residence, and Willie the goat.

Forms of payment: *U.S. currency*—cash, travelers checks, personal checks; AX, MC, VI

THE INN OF THE SIX MOUNTAINS

Killington Road
Killington, VT 05751 USA
Phone: 800-228-4676 or
802-422-4302
Fax: 802-422-4321

Proprietor: James LeSage

Category: Resort, hotel

Location: Mountain, quaint village, resort town

Open all year? Yes

Price: Moderate

Special packages: Yes

Reader discount: Yes; inquire directly

Child discount: Yes

MEALS

Included: B

Offered: B, D

% Vegetarian: On request

% Vegan: On request

% Organic: Varies

Special diets: Inquire directly

Nearby restaurants: Yes

ROOMS

% Private bath/shower: 100%

% Non-smoking: 0%

% Air conditioned: 0%

Car parking: Yes

Wheelchair access: Yes

Non-animal tested toiletries: No

Insecticides used? No

Pets welcome? No

Of animal origin: Leather furniture

Nearby activities: Indoor pool, outdoor pool, tennis, golf, bicycling, hiking, canoeing/kayaking, boating, cross-country skiing, downhill skiing, horseback riding, nutrition classes, camping, fitness classes, exercise room, massage, sightseeing tours, nightclub, antique shops, museums

Description: With 103 luxurious rooms, we are located in the heart of Killington's night life and only one mile from the base lift. The Inn combines the charm and hospitality of a country inn with the convenient amenities of a four-season resort. Enjoy the simple pleasures of a roaring fire in a fieldstone fireplace, sunset over a mountain horizon, or a basket of fresh-picked apples awaiting your arrival. Add the pampered pleasure of a soothing sauna or hot tub (indoor or outdoor), therapeutic massage, or refreshing dip in either our indoor lap pool or outdoor swimming pool. Whether for a vacation or business gathering, romantic getaway or family reunion, this is your ideal destination for a memorable Vermont experience.

Forms of payment: *U.S. currency*—cash, travelers checks, personal checks; AX, MC, VI

ELIXIR RETREAT CENTER

RD 3, Box 71
St. Johnsbury, VT 05819 USA
Phone: 802-633-2225

Proprietor: Basira Mucha
Category: Retreat
Location: Mountain
Open all year? Open Apr. 30–Oct. 15
Price: Inexpensive
Special packages: No

Reader discount: 10%
Child discount: No

MEALS

Included: B, D
Offered: B, D
% Vegetarian: 10%
% Vegan: 90%
% Organic: 35%
Special diets: Yes
Nearby restaurants: No

ROOMS

% Private bath/shower: 0%
% Non-smoking: 100%
% Air conditioned: 0%
Car parking: Yes
Wheelchair access: No
Non-animal tested toiletries: No
Insecticides used? No
Pets welcome? No
Of animal origin: Wool rugs
Nearby activities: Indoor pool, outdoor pool, tennis, golf, bicycling, hiking, water sports, horseback riding, camping, fitness classes, exercise room, massage, antique shops, museums, Buddhist meditation center, art gallery, art classes

Description: This retreat center is for solo retreatants only. One is surrounded by the solitude of a lovely mountaintop. It is helpful if those visiting have already discovered some direction and have useful "practices" with which to continue on this path. Isolation is the key.

Forms of payment: *U.S. currency*—cash, travelers checks, personal checks

THE GREAT OUTDOORS INN

P.O. Box 2610
High Springs, FL 32643 USA
Phone: 904-454-1223
Fax: 904-454-1225

Proprietor: Tedd & Mary Greenwald
Category: Bed & Breakfast
Location: Countryside
Open all year? Yes
Price: Moderate
Special packages: Yes
Reader discount: No
Child discount: No

MEALS

Included: B
Offered: B, L, D
% Vegetarian: 95%
% Vegan: 50%
% Organic: 75%
Special diets: Yes
Nearby restaurants: Yes

ROOMS

% Private bath/shower: 100%
% Non-smoking: 100%
% Air conditioned: 100%
Car parking: Yes
Wheelchair access: Yes
Non-animal tested toiletries: Yes

Insecticides used? No
Pets welcome? See comments
Of animal origin: None
Nearby activities: Outdoor pool, golf, bicycling, hiking, canoeing/ kayaking, snorkeling, scuba diving, water sports, horseback riding, camping, massage, educational lectures, sightseeing tours, antique shops, museums

Description: Six spacious rooms on a 40 acre tree farm just minutes from quaint Gainesville, Florida, the #1 place to live in the USA. Gourmet vegetarian fare. Close to crystal clear rivers, springs, and virgin woods. See the real Florida far from the neon glow. On-site pool. Absolutely positively no smoking allowed.

Forms of payment: *U.S. currency* —cash, personal checks; AX, MC, VI, Discover
Comment: Some pets, not in rooms. Boarding on site.

SOUTHEASTERN U.S.

Florida
Georgia
North Carolina
Virginia
West Virginia

FIT FOR LIFE HEALTH RESORT AND SPA

**1460 S. Ocean Blvd.
Pompano Beach, FL 33062 USA
Phone: 305-941-6688
Fax: 305-943-1219**

Proprietor: Mort Pine
Category: Resort, spa
Location: Beachfront
Open all year? Yes
Price: Inexpensive
Special packages: Yes
Reader discount: No
Child discount: Yes

MEALS

Included: B, L, D
Offered: B, L, D
% Vegetarian: 100%
% Vegan: 100%
% Organic: 40%
Special diets: Yes
Nearby restaurants: Yes

ROOMS

% Private bath/shower: 100%
% Non-smoking: 100%
% Air conditioned: 100%
Car parking: Yes
Wheelchair access: No
Non-animal tested toiletries: No
Insecticides used? Yes
Pets welcome? No
Of animal origin: None
Nearby activities: Outdoor pool, tennis, golf, boating, snorkeling, scuba diving, water sports, nutrition classes, beach, yoga, fitness classes, exercise room, massage, juice fasting, weight loss classes, educational lectures, museums

Description: Fit For Life is a place of total health and fitness. A place to relax and renew your mind, body, and spirit. A place where you can lose weight safely, get in shape, and stay in shape. Our magnificent oceanfront location offers endless opportunities for sunbathing, swimming, sailing, and snorkeling.

Forms of payment: *U.S. currency*—cash, travelers checks, personal checks; AX, MC, VI

SAFETY HARBOR SPA AND FITNESS

**105 N. Bayshore Dr.
Safety Harbor, FL 34695 USA
Phone: 800-237-0155
Fax: 813-726-4268**

Proprietor: South Seas Resorts
Category: Spa
Location: Quaint village
Open all year? Inquire
Price: Moderate
Special packages: Yes
Reader discount: Inquire
Child discount: No

MEALS

Included: B, L, D
Offered: B, L, D
% Vegetarian: 25%
% Vegan: On request
% Organic: 5%
Special diets: Yes
Nearby restaurants: No

Description: One of Zagat Surveys top 10 spas in the US (1995). Tranquil waterfront location on 22 acres overlooking Tampa Bay. 172 guest rooms with double beds, 4 with king size. 2 suites. Features curative natural mineral waters, comprehensive skin and body treatments, 50,000 square foot fitness center with personal professional supervision, conference facilities for up to 300, ballroom, private meeting rooms, amphitheater. Call for brochure.

Forms of payment: *U.S. currency*— cash, travelers checks, personal checks; AX, MC, VI, Discover, Diners Club

ROOMS

% Private bath/shower: 100%
% Non-smoking: 80%
% Air conditioned: 100%
Car parking: Yes
Wheelchair access: Yes
Non-animal tested toiletries: No
Insecticides used? No
Pets welcome? Yes
Of animal origin: Leather furniture
Nearby activities: Indoor pool, outdoor pool, tennis, golf, bicycling, hiking, nutrition classes, yoga, 35 daily fitness classes, exercise room, massage, juice fasting, weight loss classes, educational lectures, museums, symphony, ballet, theater

WILDFLOWER INN
BED AND BREAKFAST

5218 Ocean Blvd.
Sarasota, FL 34242 USA
Phone: 941-346-1566
Fax: 941-346-7805

Proprietor: Ward Patton
Category: Small inn
Location: Quaint village, resort town
Open all year? Yes
Price: Moderate
Special packages: Yes
Reader discount: No
Child discount: Yes

MEALS

Included: None
Offered: B, L, D
% Vegetarian: 76%
% Vegan: 60%
% Organic: 30%
Special diets: Yes
Nearby restaurants: Yes
Comment: Lunch on weekends only. Self-catering units.

ROOMS

% Private bath/shower: 100%
% Non-smoking: 100%
% Air conditioned: 100%
Car parking: Yes
Wheelchair access: No
Non-animal tested toiletries: Yes
Insecticides used? No
Pets welcome? No
Of animal origin: None
Nearby activities: Tennis, golf, bicycling, hiking, canoeing/kayaking, boating, snorkeling, water sports, horseback riding, nutrition classes, camping, beach, yoga, fitness classes, exercise room, massage, juice fasting, educational lectures, sightseeing tours, nightclub, antique shops, museums

Description: Located a block from the Gulf of Mexico on beautiful Siesta Key, we have four 1BR apartments and a full-service restaurant that has been serving vegetarian, vegan, and macrobiotic meals since 1974. We are dedicated to serving wholesome foods for the health of the planet.

Forms of payment: *U.S. currency*—cash, travelers checks, personal checks; MC, VI

HIPPOCRATES HEALTH INSTITUTE

1443 Palmdale Court
West Palm Beach, FL 33411 USA
Phone: 407-471-8876
Fax: 407-471-9464

Proprietor: Brian R. Clemente
Category: Spa, retreat
Location: Suburban, lakefront, resort town
Open all year? Yes
Price: Moderate
Special packages: Yes
Reader discount: Yes; inquire directly
Child discount: No

MEALS

Included: B, L, D
Offered: B, L, D

% Vegetarian: 100%

% Vegan: 100%

% Organic: 100%

Special diets: Yes

Nearby restaurants: Yes

ROOMS

% Private bath/shower: 85%

% Non-smoking: 100%

% Air conditioned: 100%

Car parking: Yes

Wheelchair access: Yes

Non-animal tested toiletries: Yes

Insecticides used? No

Pets welcome? No

Of animal origin:
Leather
furniture

Nearby activities:
Outdoor pool,
tennis, golf,
hiking, boating,
snorkeling,
scuba diving,
water sports,
nutrition classes,
camping, beach,
yoga, fitness
classes, exercise
room, massage,
juice fasting, weight loss classes, educational lectures, sightseeing tours, nightclub, antique
shops, museums, cultural
center, shopping

Description: Hippocrates Health
Institute's 30 acre subtropical
forest estate provides a magnificent setting for the health-
conscious vacationer. Our
three-week program (shorter
stays also available) includes a
vegan vegetarian regimen, non-
stressful exercise, health analysis and counseling, massage
therapies, and daily lectures by
health experts. Palm Beach's
year-round mild climate and
superior air quality complete
the perfect scene for this
stress-free, healthy vacation!

Forms of payment: *U.S. currency*—cash,
travelers checks; AX, MC, VI,
Discover

WILDWOOD LIFESTYLE CENTER & HOSPITAL

U.S. Hwy. 11 and I-24
P.O. Box 129
Wildwood, GA 30757-0129 USA
Phone: 706-820-1493 or
800-634-WELL
Fax: 706-820-1474

Proprietor: Joyce Seay, Director
Category: Wellness center
Location: Mountain
Open all year? Yes
Price: Moderate
Special packages: Yes
Reader discount: No
Child discount: No

MEALS

Included: B, L, D
Offered: B, L, D
% Vegetarian: 100%
% Vegan: On request
% Organic: 50%
Special diets: Yes
Nearby restaurants: No

ROOMS

% Private bath/shower: 20%
% Non-smoking: 100%
% Air conditioned: 100%
Car parking: Yes
Wheelchair access: Yes
Non-animal tested toiletries: No
Insecticides used? Yes
Pets welcome? No
Of animal origin: Feather pillows
Nearby activities: Hiking, massage, weight loss classes, educational lectures

Description: A filigree of golden sunshine through southern pines on 25 miles of mountain trails. Nutritious deliciously satisfying meals. Under medical supervision enjoy natural methods—hydrotherapy, massage, lectures, and scheduled outings—in a Christian atmosphere for peace and restoration of mind and body.

Forms of payment: *U.S. currency*—cash, travelers checks, personal checks; AX, MC, VI, Discover

BEAUFORT HOUSE

**61 North Liberty St
Asheville, NC 28201 USA
Phone: 704-254-8334
Fax: 704-251-2082**

Proprietor: Robert &
    Jacqueline Glasgow
Category: Bed & Breakfast
Location: Mountain
Open all year? Yes
Price: Moderate
Special packages: Yes
Reader discount: Yes; inquire directly
Child discount: No

MEALS

Included: B
Offered: B
% Vegetarian: 100%
% Vegan: 100%
% Organic: 100%
Special diets: Yes
Nearby restaurants: Yes, 3 good vegetarian restaurants nearby

ROOMS

% Private bath/shower: 100%
% Non-smoking: 100%
% Air conditioned: 100%
Car parking: Yes
Wheelchair access: Yes
Non-animal tested toiletries: Yes
Insecticides used? No
Pets welcome? No
Of animal origin: Feather pillows, wool rugs, down comforters
Nearby activities: Outdoor pool, tennis, golf, bicycling, hiking, canoeing/kayaking, boating, cross-country skiing, downhill skiing, horseback riding, nutrition

classes, camping, yoga, fitness classes, exercise room, massage, juice fasting, educational lectures, sightseeing tours, nightclub, antique shops

Description: Relax in the casual elegance of our 100-year-old Victorian home. Enjoy movies in your own VCR in the privacy of your room or pull up a cozy rocker on our wraparound "gingerbread" porch and enjoy a glass of wine, lemonade, or tea. Choose among six exquisite guest suites, each individual in character. Our delicious home-cooked breakfast is made fresh from the purest ingredients and served with white linen and silver. Vegetarian, vegan, and macrobiotic diets are all easily catered for. The Asheville area has much to offer, including the Thomas Wolfe Memorial, Biltmore Estate, Smith McDowell House, Pack Place Arts & Science Center, and Chimney Rock Park.

Forms of payment: *U.S. currency*—cash, travelers checks, personal checks; MC, VI

DUCKETT HOUSE INN & FARM

P.O. Box 441
Hot Springs, NC 28743 USA
Phone: 704-622-7621

Proprietor: Brian Baker & Frank Matula
Category: Bed & Breakfast
Location: Mountain, quaint village, resort town
Open all year? Yes
Price: Moderate
Special packages: Yes
Reader discount: No
Child discount: No

MEALS

Included: B
Offered: B, D
% Vegetarian: 100%
% Vegan: 50%
% Organic: 100%
Special diets: Yes
Nearby restaurants: Yes

ROOMS

% Private bath/shower: 0%
% Non-smoking: 100%
% Air conditioned: 0%
Car parking: Yes
Wheelchair access: No
Non-animal tested toiletries: Yes
Insecticides used? No
Pets welcome? No
Of animal origin: Wool rugs, feather pillows, farm animals
Nearby activities: Outdoor pool, tennis, golf, bicycling, hiking, canoeing/kayaking, boating, cross-country skiing, downhill skiing, horseback riding, camping, exercise room, massage, antique shops, hot mineral springs, rafting

Description: Located on 5 beautiful acres bordering the Pisgah National Forest. Enjoy hiking on the Appalachian Trail, white water rafting, the Hot Springs Mineral Bath, the Biltmore House in Asheville, and the Great Smoky Mountains National Park.

Forms of payment: *U.S. currency*—cash, travelers checks, personal checks; MC, VI, Discover

ALPINE INN

P.O. Box 477
Little Switzerland, NC 28749 USA
Phone: 704-765-5380

Proprietor: Bill Cox & Sharon Smith
Category: Motel
Location: Mountain
Open all year? Open May–October
Price: Inexpensive/Moderate
Special packages: Yes
Reader discount: No
Child discount: No

MEALS

Included: B

Offered: B
% Vegetarian: 100%
% Vegan: On request
% Organic: 0%
Special diets: Yes
Nearby restaurants: No

ROOMS

% Private bath/shower: 100%
% Non-smoking: 0%
% Air conditioned: 0%
Car parking: Yes
Wheelchair access: No
Non-animal tested toiletries: No
Insecticides used? Yes
Pets welcome? No
Of animal origin: None
Nearby activities: Bicycling, hiking, boating, camping, antique shops, museums, gem stone mining, bookstores

Description: Located on secluded yet easily accessible Highway 226A, one mile west of the Blue Ridge Parkway in the hamlet of Little Switzerland. Our rooms are homey and cozy with a variety of accommodations available. Our breakfasts, which are optional, are served on the main balcony accompanied by a glorious sunrise. Little Switzerland offers a few restaurants, shopping, waterfalls, horseback riding, and gem mining in a relaxed atmosphere. A good setting for self-renewal, introspection, reflection, and establishing a greater affinity with nature.

Forms of payment: *U.S. currency*—cash, travelers checks, personal checks; MC, VI

MOUNTAIN MIST

142 Country Club Drive
Waynesville, NC 28786 USA
Phone: 704-452-1550

Proprietor: Joanna & Richard Swanson
Category: B&B, retreat
Location: Mountain, quaint village
Open all year? Varies, inquire directly
Price: Moderate
Special packages: Yes
Reader discount: Yes; inquire directly
Child discount: No

MEALS

Included: B, L, D
Offered: B, L, D
% Vegetarian: 100%
% Vegan: 100%
% Organic: 30%
Special diets: Yes
Nearby restaurants: Yes

ROOMS

% Private bath/shower: 100%
% Non-smoking: 100%
% Air conditioned: 20%
Car parking: Yes
Wheelchair access: No
Non-animal tested toiletries: Yes
Insecticides used? No
Pets welcome? No
Of animal origin: Feather pillows
Nearby activities: Indoor pool, outdoor pool, tennis, golf, bicycling, hiking, canoeing/kayaking, boating, downhill skiing, horseback riding, nutrition classes, yoga, fitness classes, exercise room, massage, juice fasting, educational lectures, weight loss classes, sightseeing

tours, antique shops, museums, white-water rafting, reiki, reflexology, psychic work, psychotherapy

Description: A warm, nurturing retreat in fresh, green, Smoky Mountains. Every room large, airy, luxurious, with private bathroom, TV, VCR, answer-

phone. Gourmet vegetarian and vegan food. Perfect for small groups. Meeting room available. Outdoor sports, shopping, only 27 miles from Asheville. You'll love us!

Forms of payment: *U.S. currency*—cash, travelers checks, personal checks; MC, VI

VIRGINIA

SATCHIDANANDA ASHRAM-YOGAVILLE

Rt. 1, Box 1720
Buckingham, VA 23921 USA
Phone: 804-969-3121
Fax: 804-969-1303

Proprietor: N/A
Category: Retreat
Location: Mountain
Open all year? Yes
Price: Moderate
Special packages: Yes
Reader discount: No
Child discount: Yes

MEALS

Included: B, L, D
Offered: B, L, D
% Vegetarian: 100%
% Vegan: 85%
% Organic: 50%
Special diets: Yes
Nearby restaurants: No

ROOMS

% Rooms bath/shower: 25%
% Non-smoking: 100%
% Air conditioned: 100%
Car parking: Yes
Wheelchair access: Yes
Non-animal tested toiletries: No

Insecticides used? No
Pets welcome? No
Of animal origin: Feather pillows
Nearby activities: Hiking, canoeing/

kayaking, boating, water sports, cross-country skiing, downhill skiing, nutrition classes, camping, yoga, fitness classes, exercise room, massage, juice fasting, weight loss classes, educational lectures, sightseeing tours, antique shops, museums, lake

Description: People of many faiths and backgrounds have come together to practice the principles of "Integral Yoga" under the guidance of the Reverend Sri Swami Satchidananda (Sri

Gurudev). Yogaville is situated on 750 acres of woodland along the James River, in the foothills of the Blue Ridge Mountains. This growing spiritual center strives to show how people can live together in harmony while still enjoying their individual differences. Join us for a day, overnight, a week, or longer. Programs include retreats, teacher training, meditation, hatha yoga workshops, and scriptural studies.

Forms of payment: *U.S. currency*—cash, travelers checks, personal checks; MC, VI

HARTLAND WELLNESS CENTER

P.O. Box 1
Rapidan, VA 22733 USA
Phone: 540-672-3100 X240
Fax: 540-672-2584

Proprietor: Will Evert, Director
Category: Christian health center
Location: Country
Open all year? Yes
Price: Moderate
Special packages: Yes
Reader discount: 10%
Child discount: No

MEALS
Included: B, L, D
Offered: B, L, D
% Vegetarian: 100%
% Vegan: 100%
% Organic: 80%
Special diets: Yes
Nearby restaurants: No

ROOMS
% Private bath/shower: 100%
% Non-smoking: 100%
% Air conditioned: 100%
Car parking: Yes
Wheelchair access: Yes
Non-animal tested toiletries: Yes
Insecticides used? No
Pets welcome? No
Of animal origin: Feather pillows
Nearby activities: Indoor pool, hiking, nutrition classes, exercise room, massage, juice fasting, educational lectures, sightseeing tours, hands-on cooking instruction

Description: Located away from the city in the Piedmont Valley of Virginia, we offer a health restoration program based on healthy lifestyle. Practical health lectures, stress management, individual counseling, massage, hydrotherapy, and lots of TLC are graciously offered in this elegant country estate. Visit our web site at http://www.hartland.edu/www/nuhealth.

Forms of payment: *U.S. currency*—cash, travelers checks, personal checks

STONEBRAKE COTTAGE

P.O. Box 1612
Shepherd Grade Road
Shepherdstown, WV 25443 USA
Phone: 304-876-6607

Proprietor: Anne Small

Category: Bed & Breakfast

Location: Rural, self-catering

Open all year? Yes

Price: Moderate

Special packages: Yes

Reader discount: Yes; inquire directly

Child discount: Yes

MEALS

Included: B

Offered: B

% Vegetarian: 100%

% Vegan: Guests' option

% Organic: 20%

Special diets: Yes

Nearby restaurants: Yes

Comments: Self-catering cottage stocked with breakfast food

ROOMS

% Private bath/shower: 100%

% Non-smoking: 100%

% Air conditioned: 100%

Car parking: Yes

Wheelchair access: No

Non-animal tested toiletries: No

Insecticides used? No

Pets welcome? No

Of animal origin: Farm animals, wool rugs

Nearby activities: Indoor pool, outdoor pool, tennis, golf, bicycling, hiking, canoeing/kayaking, boating, cross-country skiing, horseback riding, camping, yoga, fitness classes, massage, sightseeing tours, nightclub, antique shops, museums, theater, opera

Description: Stonebrake Cottage is located on a 140-acre farm. Rental of the cottage is private,

so guests are on their own for the weekend to walk or bike the C & O Canal, tour Harpers Ferry and the Antietam battle-fields, or browse through historic Shepherdstown's quaint shops and restaurants.

Forms of payment: *U.S. currency*—cash, travelers checks; MC, VI

Jamaica
Puerto Rico
St. John
St. Lucia
Mexico
Costa Rica
Peru

Caribbean, Mexico, Central & South America

JACKIE'S ON THE REEF

Negril, Jamaica, West Indies
Phone: 718-783-6763 or
809-957-4997
Fax: 718-783-6763

Proprietor: Jackie Lewis
Category: Spa
Location: Beachfront
Open all year? Yes
Price: Inexpensive
Special packages: Yes
Reader discount: Inquire directly
Child discount: No

MEALS

Included: B, L, D
Offered: B, L, D
% Vegetarian: 100%
% Vegan: 100%
% Organic: 75%
Special diets: Yes
Nearby restaurants: Yes
Comments: Chicken and fish served on request

ROOMS

% Private bath/shower: 100%
% Non-smoking: 100%
% Air conditioned: 0%
Car parking: Yes
Wheelchair access: Yes
Non-animal tested toiletries: Yes

CARIBBEAN

Jamaica
Puerto Rico
St. John
St. Lucia

Insecticides used? No
Pets welcome? No
Of animal origin: None
Nearby activities: Outdoor pool, bicycling, hiking, boating, snorkeling, scuba diving, water sports, nutrition classes, beach, yoga, fitness classes, exercise room, massage, juice fasting, weight loss classes, educational lectures, sightseeing tours, meditation, tai chi, past life work, herb farms, reflexology, facials
Description: Jackie's on the Reef is a casual island retreat that helps you to de-stress and retune your body and mind. We offer tranquillity, a total holistic spa to enjoy the essence of life.

We pamper you with natural foods to detoxify the body and treatments to enhance you spiritually. We grow our own vegetables and have the most beautiful scenery in the world. Send U.S. correspondence c/o Jackie Lewis, 364 Washington Avenue, Brooklyn, NY 11238.

Forms of payment: *U.S. currency*—cash, travelers checks; *Local currency* —cash

SWEPT AWAY RESORT

Negril, Jamaica, West Indies
U.S. Contact 4944 LeJeune Rd.
Coral Gables, FL 33146
Phone: 800-545-7937 or
305-666-2021
Fax: 305-666-8520

Proprietor: Lee Issa
Category: Resort
Location: Beachfront
Open all year? Yes
Price: Moderate
Special packages: Yes
Reader discount: No
Child discount: No

MEALS

Included: B, L, D
Offered: B, L, D
% Vegetarian: See comments
% Vegan: See comments
% Organic: Varies
Special diets: With advance request
Nearby restaurants: Yes
Comments: Each meal offers low
  calorie or vegetable dishes

ROOMS

% Private bath/shower: 100%
% Non-smoking: 0%
% Air conditioned: 100%
Car parking: Yes
Wheelchair access: Yes
Non-animal tested toiletries: No
Insecticides used? No
Pets welcome? No
Of animal origin: None
Nearby activities: Outdoor pools, ten-
  nis, golf, bicycling, canoeing/
  kayaking, boating, snorkeling,

scuba diving, water sports,
beach, yoga, fitness classes,
exercise room, massage, squash,
racquet ball, jogging track,
basketball

Description: The Caribbean's most
romantic 20-acre beachfront
resort for couples, featuring a
premier sports & fitness complex. Dining is a culinary
extravaganza with an array of
award-winning vegetarian
specialties. The fruit and veggie
bar also provides enticing
local delicacies. Swept Away
has a world of water sports,
unlimited golf, and much
more.

Forms of payment: *U.S. currency*—cash,
travelers checks; *Local currency*
—cash, travelers checks; AX,
MC, VI

GRATEFUL BED & BREAKFAST

**Box 568
Luquillo, Puerto Rico 00773
Phone: 809-889-4919**

Proprietor: Marty Soucie
Category: Bed & Breakfast
Location: Mountain, rainforest
Open all year? Yes
Price: Inexpensive
Special packages: No
Reader discount: No
Child discount: Yes

MEALS

Included: B
Offered: B, D
% Vegetarian: 100%
% Vegan: 50%
% Organic: 10%
Special diets: Yes
Nearby restaurants: Yes

ROOMS

% Private bath/shower: 15%
% Non-smoking: 100%

% Air conditioned: 0%
Car parking: Yes
Wheelchair access: No
Non-animal tested toiletries: No
Insecticides used? Yes
Pets welcome? No
Of animal origin: None
Nearby activities: Tennis, golf, hiking, canoeing/kayaking, snorkeling, scuba diving, horseback riding, beach, massage, sightseeing tours, nightclub, museums, rainforest trails, swimming holes, phosphorescent bay

Description: Imagine a fun and friendly tropical island B&B where staff and other guests treat you as one of the family. The personal attention is unmatched. You feel welcome and included—even before your arrival. That's why, in just 4 years, Grateful Bed & Breakfast has hosted guests from 44 states and several countries.

Forms of payment: *U.S. currency*—cash, personal checks

ANN WIGMORE INSTITUTE

P.O. Box 429
Rincon, Puerto Rico 00677
Phone: 787-868-6307
Fax: 787-868-2430

Proprietor: N/A

Category: Retreat, health education center

Location: Beachfront, rural

Open all year? Yes

Price: Moderate

Special packages: Yes

Reader discount: 5% Oct-May 30

Child discount: No

MEALS

Included: B, L, D

Offered: B, L, D

% Vegetarian: 100%

% Vegan: 100%

% Organic: 80%

Special diets: Yes

Nearby restaurants: Yes

ROOMS

% Private bath/shower: 30%

% Non-smoking: 100%

% Air conditioned: 0%

Car parking: Yes

Wheelchair access: Yes

Non-animal tested toiletries: Yes

Insecticides used? No

Pets welcome? No

Of animal origin: None

Nearby activities: Snorkeling, scuba diving, water sports, horseback riding, nutrition classes, beach, yoga, massage, weight loss classes, educational lectures, sightseeing tours, living raw foods

Description: The Ann Wigmore Institute, located near the sea in Aguada, Puerto Rico, is an oasis for reconnecting, rebuilding, and rejuvenating with nature through highly nutritious, easy to digest, raw living foods. We offer wheatgrass juice, hands-on experience, and a loving and supporting staff to create a self-healing, detoxifying, and revitalizing atmosphere.

Forms of payment: *U.S. currency*—cash, travelers checks, personal checks; AX, MC, VI

LA CASA DE VIDA NATURAL

P.O. Box 1916
Rio Grande, Puerto Rico 00745
Phone/Fax: 809-887-4359

Proprietor: Jane Goldberg
Category: Retreat
Location: Mountain
Open all year? Yes
Price: Inexpensive
Special packages: Yes
Reader discount: 10%
Child discount: No

MEALS

Included: B, L, D
Offered: B, L, D
% Vegetarian: 100%
% Vegan: 75%
% Organic: 40%
Special diets: Yes
Nearby restaurants: No

ROOMS

% Private bath/shower:
  30%
% Non-smoking: 100%
% Air conditioned: 0%
Car parking: Yes
Wheelchair access: No
Non-animal tested toiletries:
  Yes
Insecticides used? No
Pets welcome? No
Of animal origin: None
Nearby activities: Hiking, snorkeling,
  scuba diving, horseback riding,
  nutrition classes, yoga, beach,
  fitness classes, massage, educa-
  tional lectures, sightseeing
  tours, museums, meditation,

colonics, river body wraps,
Indian cleansing techniques

Description: La Casa provides an
opportunity for a back-to-basics
experience through a vision of
living harmoniously within the
natural world. Nestled in the
foothills of the famed Puerto
Rican rainforest, El Yunque,
with panoramic views of
mountain peaks and expansive
ocean.

Forms of payment: *U.S. currency*—cash,
travelers checks, personal
checks; MC, VI

The Specialness of St. John

Beautiful St. John surprises visitors in so many ways. It is almost no surprise how lovingly it caters to vegetarians. "Love City," in fact, is its Caribbean name. By contrast, St. Thomas is nicknamed "Rock City."

Love of animals is one of its most important features. The V.I. National Park comprises an astonishing two-thirds of the island boundaries and effectively protects numerous wild species. Unlike many preserves, hunting and trapping are totally illegal and these rules are not broken. Spearfishing is not allowed in the park waters and even the hand-harvesting of lobster, whelk, and conch is seasonally restricted.

However, the vegetarian liveliness here comes from more than just the rules of the park. Mindfulness of animal rights is so ingrained that a recent national park superintendent lost his job largely over the mistreatment of feral donkeys! Domestic animals have fund-raisers in their honor and are watched over by the St. John Animal Care Center and its proactive chief, Gina Burns.

The Omega Institute, long famous for its cutting-edge worldview and underlying spirituality, has held its winter programs here for years (with vegetarian

TRUNK BAY, ST. JOHN

CONSTANCE WALLACE

meals, of course). Stanley Selengut, the renowned environmental builder and eco-tourism expert has had both his first and his most recent project on little St. John.

Many health conscious people have made their homes here, as have many "new age" spiritually minded people. The New Agers have the support of some "old agers," naturalists, survivalists, and the vegetarian tenets of the Rastafarians. If there's a booth of fried fish in the ball park, there's also a Rasta with a giant cauldron of "ital" stew. While others are gorging at the Hyatt or Caneel Bay (the island's two hotels, which do not especially consider the vegetarian), you can be feasting at the Garden of Luscious Licks. "Licks," which was the Caribbean's first Ben & Jerry's franchise, has matured into a gourmet vegetarian and health food restaurant that would make any big city proud. Although they are not exclusively vegetarian, native chefs at The Gallery and The Inn at Tamarind Court know what you want: local favorites like johnny cakes, real mashed potatoes, sweet taro, plantains, and fungi (not mushrooms: just okra and corn meal). Even remote Coral Bay restaurants know what "no meat" really means. Rice can be found without chicken stock and refried beans without lard. The little roadside stand near the gas station makes an outstanding grain burger along with five kinds of fresh juices. Finally, the romantic Lucy's Restaurant, run by a charming down-island couple, has featured a beautiful vegetarian dinner for over a decade, accompanied by homemade banana cake, fried corn meal dumplings, and the best pumpkin soup you ever had.

—Jonathan Back, The Castle

THE CASTLE

Coral Bay
St. John, US Virgin Islands
Phone: 607-387-5877
Fax: 607-387-5566

Proprietor: Eve Abrams &
  Jonathan Back
Category: Rental home
Location: Mountain, panoramic
  ocean views
Open all year? Yes
Price: Moderate
Special packages:
  No
Reader discount:
  20%
Child discount: Yes

MEALS

Included: Self-
  catering
Offered: N/A
% Vegetarian: N/A
% Vegan: N/A
% Organic: N/A
Special diets: N/A
Nearby restaurants: Yes

ROOMS

% Private bath/shower: 100%
% Non-smoking: 100%
% Air conditioned: 0%
Car parking: Yes
Wheelchair access: No
Non-animal tested toiletries: Yes
Insecticides used? No
Pets welcome? No
Of animal origin: None
Nearby activities: Hiking, boating,
  snorkeling, scuba diving, water
  sports, beach, yoga, massage,

sightseeing tours, nightclub,
outdoor jacuzzi spa, astronomy

Description: The perfect getaway for
your adventurous spirit. A
secluded hideaway on a
windswept mountaintop,
bounded by the VI National
Park, and enjoying the most
extraordinary seascape. The
Castle is the only property on a
private, gated road. Lovingly

created over eight years by the
designers, the structure itself is
art, as well as a vehicle for art:
relics in the walls, fine mosaics,
a sculptured Japanese garden.
The structure is entirely of
stone, hand-hewn by master
masons from St. Lucia and
Nevis. Close by are the least
crowded of the Park's famous
beaches. Even on this quiet
side of St. John, there is a full
water sports center and several
shops, clubs, and restaurants
all within a ten minute drive.
You are invited for a magical
rendezvous! E-mail to Castle
STJ@aol.com or visit Website
http://pciweb.baka.com/web/
castle/

Forms of payment: *U.S. currency*—cash,
travelers checks, personal checks

CONCORDIA RESORT & ECO-TENTS

Estate Concordia
St. John, U.S. Virgin Islands
Phone: 800-392-9004 or
   212-472-9454
Fax: 212-861-6210

Proprietor: Stanley Selengut

Category: Studio apartments, self-catering

Location: Cliffs overlooking beach

Open all year? Yes

Price: Moderate

Special packages: No

Reader discount: No

Child discount: No

MEALS

Included: Self-catering

Offered: N/A

% Vegetarian: N/A

% Vegan: N/A

% Organic: N/A

Special diets: N/A

Nearby restaurants: Yes

ROOMS

% Private bath/shower: 100%

% Non-smoking: 0%

% Air conditioned: 0%

Car parking: Yes

Wheelchair access: No

Non-animal tested toiletries: No

Insecticides used? No

Pets welcome? No

Of animal origin: None

Nearby activities: Hiking, canoeing/ kayaking, boating, snorkeling, scuba diving, water sports,

camping, beach, outdoor pool

Description: These gorgeous, wind-swept units are on a cliff over-looking Salt Pond Bay and Ram Head Point. The well-equipped kitchen allows for self-catering and the seclusion is very sooth-ing. A rental vehicle is neces-sary for these units. Reminder: for the best selection, please stop in Cruz Bay to buy gro-ceries before your journey. Write c/o 17A East 73rd Street, New York, NY 10021.

Forms of payment: *U.S. currency*—cash, travelers checks, personal checks

HARMONY RESORT

Maho Bay
St. John, U.S. Virgin Islands
Phone: 800-392-9004
Fax: 212-861-6210

Proprietor: Stanley Selengut
Category: Resort
Location: Beachfront
Open all year? Yes
Price: Moderate
Special packages: No
Reader discount: No
Child discount: No

MEALS

Included: None
Offered: B, D
% Vegetarian: 15–25%
% Vegan: On request
% Organic: 0%
Special diets: Inquire directly
Nearby restaurants: Yes
Comments: Self-catering also

ROOMS

% Private bath/shower:
  100%
% Non-smoking: 0%
% Air conditioned: 0%
Car parking: Yes
Wheelchair access: Yes
Non-animal tested toiletries:
  No
Insecticides used? No
Pets welcome? No
Of animal origin: None
Nearby activities:
  Tennis, hiking, canoeing/kayak-
  ing, boating, snorkeling, scuba
  diving, water sports, camping,
  beach, yoga, massage

Description: Harmony Resort is a
  cluster of luxury studio apartments built on the principles
  of sustainable development.
  Harmony units have full
  kitchens. The facilities at Maho
  Bay Camps, including the
  restaurant, are also available
  to "Harmony" guests. Maho
  units feature a kitchenette,
  which also allows for the "self-
  catering" aspect often desired
  by vegetarians and vegans.
  These units are solar and wind
  powered and made with 70%
  recycled materials. Write c/o
  17A East 73rd Street, New York,
  NY 10021.

Forms of payment: *U.S. currency*—cash,
  travelers checks, personal
  checks

MAHO BAY CAMP

**Maho Bay
St. John, U.S. Virgin Islands
Phone: 800-392-9004
Fax: 212-861-6210**

Proprietor: Stanley Selengut
Category: Eco-resort camping
Location: Beachfront, hillside
Open all year? Yes
Price: Moderate
Special packages: No
Reader discount: No
Child discount: No

MEALS

Included: None
Offered: B, D
% Vegetarian: 15-25%
% Vegan: On request
% Organic: 0%
Special diets: Inquire
  directly
Nearby restaurants: Yes

ROOMS

% Private bath/shower: 0%
% Non-smoking: 0%
% Air conditioned: 0%
Car parking: Yes
Wheelchair access: No
Non-animal tested toiletries: No
Insecticides used? No
Pets welcome? No
Of animal origin: Wool rugs
Nearby activities: Hiking, canoeing/
  kayaking, boating, snorkeling,
  scuba diving, water sports,
  camping, beach, yoga, massage,
  educational lectures, sight-
  seeing tours

Description: Maho Bay is a resort camp designed to balance creature comforts and environmental sensitivity. Our tent cottages are hidden among the trees and connected by elevated walkways. Our white sandy beach offers privacy and a wide variety of quiet water sports including kayaking, windsurfing, snorkeling, and scuba. Write c/o 17A East 73rd Street, New York, NY 10021.

Forms of payment: *U.S. currency*—cash, travelers checks, personal checks

CHASE ESCAPES

Soufriere, St. Lucia, West Indies
Phone: 813-992-2684

Proprietor: Dian Chase

Category: B&B, resort, hotel, private home

Location: Beachfront, city center, mountain, quaint village, sea view

Open all year? Yes

Price: Inexpensive/Expensive

Special packages: Yes

Reader discount: Inquire directly

Child discount: Yes

MEALS

Included: Varies

Offered: B, L, D

% Vegetarian: On request

% Vegan: On request

% Organic: 80%

Special diets: Yes

Nearby restaurants: Yes

ROOMS

% Private bath/shower: 100%

% Non-smoking: 0%

% Air conditioned: 0%

Car parking: Yes

Wheelchair access: No

Non-animal tested toiletries: No

Insecticides used? No

Pets welcome? Yes

Of animal origin: Farm animals

Nearby activities: Outdoor pool, tennis, hiking, boating, snorkeling, scuba diving, water sports, horseback riding, beach, massage, sightseeing tours, nightclub, museums, arts & crafts

Description: Let Dian from Chase Escapes custom-design your St. Lucian holiday. Dian, a longtime resident of St. Lucia and a vegan herself, now offers individualized vacation packages for vegans. She'll create an itinerary which meets your exact desires. She'll even show you the most remote restaurants which offer vegans local cuisine. Everything from a car rental to the most luxurious all-inclusive resorts can be handled with a personal touch at discounted rates. Send U.S. correspondence c/o 27330 Matheson Ave., Bonita Springs FL 33923 USA.

Forms of payment: *U.S. currency*—cash, travelers checks

MEXICO

VILLA VEGETARIANA

Pino 114
Santa Maria Ahuacatitlan
Cuernavaca, Morelos, Mexico
Phone: 800-355-8667 or
 (52) 73 131044
Fax: 408-286-2066

Proprietor: Bill Mellentin
Category: Resort
Location: Suburban, mountain, quaint village, resort town
Open all year? Yes
Price: Inexpensive
Special packages: Yes
Reader discount: No
Child discount: Yes

MEALS

Included: B, L, D
Offered: B, L, D
% Vegetarian: 100%
% Vegan: 100%
% Organic: 0%
Special diets: Yes
Nearby restaurants: Yes

ROOMS

% Private bath/shower: 100%
% Non-smoking: 100%
% Air conditioned: 0%
Car parking: Yes
Wheelchair access: Yes
Non-animal tested toiletries: No
Insecticides used? No
Pets welcome? No
Of animal origin: Leather furniture
Nearby activities: Outdoor pool, tennis, golf, hiking, horseback riding, nutrition classes, yoga, fitness classes, exercise room, massage, juice fasting, weight loss classes, educational lectures, sightseeing tours, nightclub, antique shops, museums, tutoring in Spanish, ancient ruins

Description: Villa Vegetariana was founded in the 1960s to support the wholesome practices of natural hygiene—pure, live vegetarian foods, proper sleep, exercise, fasting, fresh air, water, and sunlight. Only one hour from Mexico City by luxury bus, we provide a comfortable resort setting, great vegetarian food, massage, health treatments, personalized and group exercise, interesting people, touring, Spanish lessons, and contact with the nature, culture, history, and art of Mexico. Visit our Website at http://www.livelyarts.com/villavege.html.

Forms of payment: *U.S. currency*—cash, travelers checks; *Local currency*—cash

RIO CALIENTE HOT SPRINGS SPA

La Primavera
Jalisco, Mexico
Phone: 415-615-9543
Fax: 415-615-0601

Proprietor: Caroline Durston
Category: Spa
Location: Mountain on volcanic hot river
Open all year? Yes
Price: Inexpensive
Special packages: Yes

Reader discount: No

Child discount: No

MEALS

Included: B, L, D

Offered: B, L, D

% Vegetarian: 100%

% Vegan: 85%

% Organic: Varies

Special diets: Yes

Nearby restaurants: No

ROOMS

% Private bath/shower: 100%

% Non-smoking: 100%

% Air conditioned: 0%

Car parking: Yes

Wheelchair access: No

Non-animal tested toiletries: No

Insecticides used? No

Pets welcome? No

Of animal origin: Feather pillows, farm animals

Nearby activities: Outdoor pool, hiking, horseback riding, yoga, fitness classes, exercise room, massage, sightseeing tours

Description: Beside a primeval volcanic hot springs, Rio Caliente provides a personal and relaxing retreat—quiet, unpretentious, friendly, and inexpensive. Choose privacy or companionship, exercise, yoga, and hiking or simply swim, sauna, sun, massage. Write c/o Spa Vacations, Ltd., P.O. Box 897, Millbrae, CA 94030.

Forms of payment: *U.S. currency*—cash, travelers checks, personal checks; *Local currency*—cash, travelers checks, personal checks

HOTEL SANTA FE

Calle Del Moro S/N
Puerto Escondido, Oaxaca, Mexico
Phone: (52) 958 20170
Fax: (52) 958 20260

Proprietor: Robin Cleaver
Category: Hotel
Location: Beachfront
Open all year? Yes
Price: Moderate
Special packages: Yes
Reader discount: Yes, inquire directly
Child discount: Yes

MEALS

Included: B
Offered: B, L, D
% Vegetarian: 70%
% Vegan: 25%
% Organic: 50%
Special diets: Yes
Nearby restaurants: Yes

ROOMS

% Private bath/shower: 100%
% Non-smoking: 50%
% Air conditioned: 100%
Car parking: Yes
Wheelchair access: Yes
Non-animal tested toiletries: Yes
Insecticides used? Yes
Pets welcome? No
Of animal origin: Feather pillows
Nearby activities: Outdoor pool, tennis, bicycling, water sports, horseback riding, massage, sightseeing tours, nightclub, scuba diving, snorkeling, boating, hiking, beach, yoga, fitness classes, exercise room, museums

Description: Splendidly situated on the beach in the unspoiled village of Puerto Escondido. Comfortable air-conditioned rooms furnished with colonial style furniture. Two famous beaches: Playa Zicatela for surfing, Playa Marinero for gentle picturesque relaxing. Pool, restaurant, bar, room service, baby-sitting, TV, laundry and medical services, private phone.

Forms of payment: *U.S. currency*—cash, travelers checks; *Local currency* —cash, travelers checks; MC, VI

MIRANDA'S VERANDA

**Umaran 122
San Miguel De Allende
Guanajuato 37700 Mexico
Phone: (52) 415 22659
Fax: (52) 415 21687**

Proprietor: Miranda & Eli Nadel

Category: Bed & Breakfast

Location: City center, mountain, quaint village, resort town

Open all year? Yes

Price: Moderate

Special packages: No

Reader discount: No

Child discount: No

MEALS

Included: B

Offered: B

% Vegetarian: On request

% Vegan: On request

% Organic: 20%

Special diets: Yes

Nearby restaurants: Yes

ROOMS

% Private bath/shower: 100%

% Non-smoking: 100%

% Air conditioned: 0%

Car parking: No

Wheelchair access: No

Non-animal tested toiletries: No

Insecticides used? No

Pets welcome? No

Of animal origin: Wool rugs, down comforters, feather pillows

Nearby activities: Outdoor pool, tennis, golf, bicycling, hiking, horseback riding, nutrition classes, camping, yoga, fitness classes, massage, sightseeing tours, nightclub, antique shops, museums, music festivals, painting, drawing, sculpture, weaving, pottery

Description: Located in a remodeled Mexican truck garage! Colorful historic charm and modern comfort in a town at an altitude of 6,200 feet that attracts many famous people. Perfect weather with many cultural

education and self-development opportunities. Local English newspaper supplied on request. Write c/o Box 16A, 907 Zaragaza St., Laredo, TX 78040-5927

Forms of payment: *U.S. currency*—cash, travelers checks, personal checks; *Local currency*—cash, travelers checks

RANCHO LA PUERTA

Tecate, Baja California, Mexico
Phone: 800-443-7565
Fax: 619-744-5007 (contact in CA)

Proprietor: Alex Szekely
Category: Spa
Location: Mountain, desert
Open all year? Yes
Price: Expensive
Special packages: Yes
Reader discount: No
Child discount: No

MEALS

Included: B, L, D
Offered: B, L, D
% Vegetarian: 95%
% Vegan: 85%
% Organic: 100%
Special diets: Yes
Nearby restaurants: No

ROOMS

% Private bath/shower: 100%
% Non-smoking: 100%
% Air conditioned: 0%
Car parking: Yes
Wheelchair access: No
Non-animal tested toiletries: Yes
Insecticides used? No
Pets welcome? No
Of animal origin: Leather furniture, farm animals, wool rugs
Nearby activities: Outdoor pool, tennis, hiking, water sports, nutrition classes, yoga, exercise room, fitness classes, massage, educational lectures, beauty treatments, organic garden tours, tai chi, weight loss, museums

Description: Spacious facilities at your command. Glorious gyms, 4 hot whirlpools, 3 swimming pools, miles and miles of hiking trails, 6 lighted tennis courts, and a caring and gifted staff encouraging you into fresh concepts of fitness and new insights into your own self. All nestled upon 1000 acres in Tecate, Baja California. Send correspondence c/o P.O. Box 463057, Escondido, CA 92046

Forms of payment: *U.S. currency*—cash, travelers checks; *Local currency*—cash, travelers checks, personal checks; AX, MC, VI

CENTRAL AMERICA

Costa Rica

HOTEL EL SAPO DORADO

**P.O. Box 9-5655
Monteverde, Costa Rica
Phone: (506) 645-5010
Fax: (506) 645-5180**

Proprietor: Hannah Lowther and Geovanny Arguedas
Category: Hotel
Location: Mountain, quaint village, cloud forest
Open all year? Yes
Price: Moderate
Special packages: Yes
Reader discount: No
Child discount: Yes

MEALS

Included: None
Offered: B, L, D
% Vegetarian: 50%
% Vegan: 30%
% Organic: 25%
Special diets: Yes
Nearby restaurants: No

ROOMS

% Private bath/shower: 100%
% Non-smoking: 0%
% Air conditioned: 0%
Car parking: Yes
Wheelchair access: Yes
Non-animal tested toiletries: No
Insecticides used? Once yearly
Pets welcome? No
Of animal origin: Farm animals
Nearby activities: Bicycling, hiking, horseback riding, camping, massage, juice fasting, educational lectures, sightseeing tours, nightclub, nature reserves, artist galleries, butterfly garden, serpentarium, canopy tour, hummingbird garden, cheese factory

Description: El Sapo Dorado offers ten Classic Mountain Suites and ten Sunset Terrace Suites set individually into the hillside above the restaurant. The lush grounds are spacious and quiet. We take health, comfort,

and happiness very seriously, emphasizing honest, efficient, informed service and clean, fresh, top quality ingredients. Come for tranquillity of mind, spirit, and body!

Forms of payment: *U.S. currency*—cash, travelers checks, personal checks; *Local currency*—cash

NOSARA RETREAT

**Nosara, Costa Rica
Phone: (506) 233-8057
Fax: (506) 680-0749**

Proprietor: Amba Stapleton
Category: Retreat
Location: Beachfront
Open all year? Open Nov.–July

Price: Moderate
Special packages: Yes
Reader discount: No
Child discount: Yes

MEALS

Included: B, L, D
Offered: B, L, D
% Vegetarian: 100%
% Vegan: 80%
% Organic: As available
Special diets: Yes
Nearby restaurants: No

ROOMS

% Private bath/shower: 100%
% Non-smoking: 100%
% Air conditioned: 0%
Car parking: Yes
Wheelchair access: No
Non-animal tested toiletries: Yes
Insecticides used? No
Pets welcome? No
Of animal origin: Feather pillows
Nearby activities: Outdoor pool, bicycling, hiking, canoeing/kayaking, boating, snorkeling, horseback riding, beach, yoga, fitness classes, exercise room, massage, juice fasting, educational lectures, sightseeing tours, boogie boarding, surfing
Description: We are a small, beautiful retreat center located on the Pacific coast of Costa Rica. We are set up best for private personal growth retreats or small intimate group programs. Our facility is elegant, yet designed so nature is at your fingertips. We believe that nature is the best teacher and healer, so we encourage lots of outdoor

activity. We also provide an environment for deep authentic relationship between guests and ourselves.
Forms of payment: *U.S. currency*—cash, travelers checks, personal checks; *Local currency*—cash

HOTEL ANTUMALAL

**Playa Junquillal, Aptdo 49
Santa Cruz, Guanacaste 5150
Costa Rica
Phone/Fax: (506) 680-0506**

Proprietor: Rosario Guarnieri / ask for Gunther or Renon
Category: Hotel
Location: Beachfront
Open all year? Yes
Price: Moderate
Special packages: Yes
Reader discount: 10%
Child discount: Yes

MEALS

Included: B, D
Offered: B, L, D
% Vegetarian: 25%
% Vegan: 10%
% Organic: 10%
Special diets: On request
Nearby restaurants: Yes

ROOMS

% Private bath/shower: 100%
% Non-smoking: 0%
% Air conditioned: 0%
Car parking: Yes
Wheelchair access: Yes
Non-animal tested toiletries: No

Insecticides used? Yes

Pets welcome? Yes

Of animal origin: Farm animals

Nearby activities: Outdoor pool, tennis, bicycling, hiking, canoeing/kayaking, snorkeling, scuba diving, water sports, horseback riding, camping, beach

Description: The Antumalal Hotel is located right on the beach of Playa Junquillal, one of the best beaches on the Pacific coast. Its 23 rooms and 9 villas are surrounded by a tropical garden in this natural habitat. In the ocean-view restaurant you can enjoy delicious food and an unforgettable sunset.

Forms of payment: *U.S. currency*—cash, travelers checks; *Local currency* —cash, travelers checks; AX, MC, VI, Diners Club

INSTITUTO DE ESPANOL CABO BLANCO

Cabuya
Puntarenas, Costa Rica
Phone: 800-684-0505

Proprietor: Tim and Valerie Pearson

Category: Seaside lodge

Location: Beachfront

Open all year? Open November-July

Price: Inexpensive

Special packages: Yes

Reader discount: 10%

Child discount: Yes

MEALS

Included: B, L, D

Offered: B, L, D

% Vegetarian: On request

% Vegan: On request

% Organic: Varies

Special diets: Yes

Nearby restaurants: Yes

ROOMS

% Private bath/shower: 0%

% Non-smoking: 100%

% Air conditioned: 0%

Car parking: Yes

Wheelchair access: No

Non-animal tested toiletries: No

Insecticides used? No

Pets welcome? No

Of animal origin: None

Nearby activities: Bicycling, hiking, canoeing/kayaking, boating, snorkeling, water sports, horseback riding, camping, beach, yoga, massage, juice fasting, educational lectures, sightseeing tours, bird-watching, medicinal tropical plants, women's agricultural project, Cabo Blanco ecological reserve, waterfall hikes

Description: Unique, family-owned Spanish Language Institute on remote Costa Rican coastline. Enjoy family hospitality, healthy meals, and professional instruction on a beautiful tropical beach. Portion of proceeds supports local school, ecological projects, and reforestation. E-mail to pearson@gate1.sbcc. cc.ca.us.

Forms of payment: *U.S. currency*—cash, travelers checks, personal checks

MACHU PICCHU PUEBLO HOTEL

**K W 110 Agvas Calientes
Machu Picchu WSW Peru
Phone: (51.1) 422-6574
Fax: (51.1) 422-4701**

Proprietor: Jose Koechlin Von Stein
Category: Hotel
Location: Mountain
Open all year? Yes
Price: Expensive
Special packages: No
Reader discount: No
Child discount: Yes

MEALS

Included: None
Offered: B, L, D
% Vegetarian: On
  request
% Vegan: On request
% Organic: Varies
Special diets: No
Nearby restaurants: No

ROOMS

% Private bath/shower: 100%
% Non-smoking: 0%
% Air conditioned: 0%
Car parking: No

Wheelchair access: No
Non-animal tested toiletries: No
Insecticides used? No
Pets welcome? No
Of animal origin: None
Nearby activities: Hiking, sightseeing
  tours.

Description: Elegant country hotel
  amidst a fabulous landscape
  surrounded by the high Andes
  mountains and fast mountain
  streams. Located near the
  famous ruins of Machu Picchu.
  50 double rooms, hot tub,
  sauna.

Forms of payment: *U.S. currency*—cash;
  AX, MC, VI

SOUTH AMERICA

Peru

United Kingdom and Ireland

MIDDLE RYLANDS

Redmoor
Near Bodmin, Cornwall PL30 5AR
England
Phone/Fax: (44) 01208 872316

Proprietor: Joan Dell
Category: Bed & Breakfast
Location: Quaint village, rural
Open all year? Yes
Price: Moderate
Special packages: No
Reader discount: 10%
Child discount: No

MEALS

Included: B
Offered: B
% Vegetarian: 100%
% Vegan: 100%
% Organic: As available
Special diets: None
Nearby restaurants: Yes

ROOMS

% Private bath/shower: 100%
% Non-smoking: 100%
% Air conditioned: 0%
Car parking: Yes
Wheelchair access: No
Non-animal tested toiletries: Yes
Insecticides used? No
Pets welcome? Yes

Of animal origin: None
Nearby activities: Hiking, beach, sight-seeing tours, antique shops, museums, nature reserves, neolithic settlements
Description: Middle Rylands is a charming traditional Cornish granite cottage with twin-bedded en-suite room. Both North and South Coasts are

within easy reach and Bodmin Moor is within a few minutes' drive. A 12th century inn serving vegan/vegetarian food is just a mile away. There are nature reserves nearby and the town of Plymouth is just a 30-mile drive.

Forms of payment: *Local currency*—cash

ENGLAND

London
South
Southwest

MONKTON WYLD COURT

Charmouth
Bridgeport, Dorset DT6 6DQ
England
Phone: (44) 01297 560342

Proprietor: N/A
Category: Holistic educational center
Location: Quaint village

Open all year? Yes
Price: Inexpensive
Special packages: No
Reader discount: No
Child discount: Yes

MEALS

Included: B, L, D
Offered: B, L, D
% Vegetarian: 100%
% Vegan: 50%
% Organic: 25%
Special diets: Yes
Nearby restaurants: Yes

ROOMS

% Private bath/shower: 0%
% Non-smoking: 100%
% Air conditioned: 0%
Car parking: Yes
Wheelchair access: No
Non-animal tested toiletries: Yes
Insecticides used? No
Pets welcome? No
Of animal origin: Wool rugs, feather pillows, farm animals, down comforters
Nearby activities: Indoor pool, tennis, golf, bicycling, hiking, boating, water sports, yoga, massage, educational lectures, sightseeing tours, antique shops, pottery, dance
Description: Monkton Wyld Court is a holistic education center run by a resident community, 3 miles from the sea at Lyme Regis. The house is set in 11 acres of organic farm and gardens which provide the vegetarian food for our visitors.
Forms of payment: *Local currency*—cash

POPLAR HERB FARM

Mark Road—Burtle
Bridgewater, Somerset TA7 8NB
England
Phone: (44) 01278 723170

Proprietor: Christine & Richard Fish
Category: Bed & Breakfast
Location: Quaint village

Open all year? Yes
Price: Inexpensive
Special packages: Yes
Reader discount: 5%
Child discount: Yes

MEALS

Included: B
Offered: B, D
% Vegetarian: 100%
% Vegan: 75%
% Organic: 90%
Special diets: Yes
Nearby restaurants: Yes

ROOMS

% Private bath/shower: 33%
% Non-smoking: 100%

UNITED KINGDOM & IRELAND

% Air conditioned: 0%

Car parking: Yes

Wheelchair access: No

Non-animal tested toiletries: Yes

Insecticides used? No

Pets welcome? Yes

Of animal origin: Farm animals

Nearby activities: Bicycling, hiking, antique shops, museums

Description: Peacefully situated organic herb nursery and small holding. Exclusively vegetarian and vegan. Seven miles west of Glastonbury with its sacred sites and Celtic mythology. Spacious gardens, including healing garden and astrological herb garden. Astrological counseling, meditation room, lots of friendly rescued animals. Ideal for walking, wildlife, and cycling.

Forms of payment: *U.S. currency*—cash; *Local currency*—cash

ARCHES HOTEL

132 Cotham Brow
Cotham
Bristol (Avon) BS6 6AE England
Phone/Fax: (44) 0117 924 7398

Proprietor: Mr. and Mrs. D. Lambert

Category: Hotel

Location: City center

Open all year? All except Christmas and New Year

Price: Moderate

Special packages: Yes

Reader discount: No

Child discount: No

MEALS

Included: B

Offered: B

% Vegetarian: 85%

% Vegan: 35%

% Organic: 5%

Special diets: With prior notice

Nearby restaurants: Yes

ROOMS

% Private bath/shower: 20%

% Non-smoking: 0%

% Air conditioned: 0%

Car parking: No

Wheelchair access: No

Non-animal tested toiletries: No

Insecticides used? No

Pets welcome? Yes

Of animal origin: Wool rugs

Nearby activities: Sightseeing tours, museums

Description: Set back off the road, this early Victorian house provides quiet, comfortable surroundings and a friendly welcome. All bedrooms are equipped with an ionizer which removes dust, smoke, and pollen. Continental breakfast is included and cooked breakfasts are an option with traditional, vegetarian, and vegan tastes catered for. Several restaurants within walking distance serve vege-

tarian and vegan dinners.

Forms of payment: *U.S. currency*—cash, travelers checks, personal checks; *Local currency*—cash, travelers checks; AX, MC, VI, Diners Club

FOXLOW GRANGE

**Harpur Hill
Buxton, Derbyshire SK17 9LU
England
Phone: (44) 01298 24507
Fax: (44) 01298 73011**

Proprietor: Mrs. Janet Smallbone
Category: Bed & Breakfast
Location: One mile from spa town
Open all year? Yes
Price: Moderate
Special packages: No
Reader discount: No
Child discount: No

MEALS

Included: B
Offered: B, D
% Vegetarian: 100%
% Vegan: On request
% Organic: 80%
Special diets: Yes
Nearby restaurants: Yes

ROOMS

% Private bath/shower: 100%
% Non-smoking: 100%
% Air conditioned: 0%
Car parking: Yes
Wheelchair access: No
Non-animal tested toiletries: Yes

Insecticides used? No
Pets welcome? No
Of animal origin: Wool rugs
Nearby activities: Indoor pool, tennis, golf, bicycling, hiking, horseback riding, antique shops, museums

Description: Foxlow Grange is an impressive stone-built Georgian-fronted farmhouse predating the 17th century. It is situated in Harpur Hill, a pleasant village less than a mile from the market cross of the

spa town of Buxton. The proprietress is a Cordon Vert chef who takes pride in offering the best in homemade vegetarian and vegan foods.

Forms of payment: *Local currency*—cash; MC, VI, Access, Eurocard

TEKELS PARK GUEST HOUSE

**Tekels Park
Camberley, Surrey GU15 2LF
England
Phone: (44) 01276 23159
Fax: (44) 01276 63723**

Proprietor: Mr. Whitehead
Category: Guesthouse, retreat
Location: Suburban, quaint village, resort town
Open all year? Yes
Price: Inexpensive/Moderate
Special packages: Yes
Reader discount: 5%
Child discount: Yes

MEALS

Included: B, L, D
Offered: B, L, D
% Vegetarian: 100%
% Vegan: 30%
% Organic: 20%
Special diets: Yes
Nearby restaurants: No

ROOMS

% Private bath/shower: 0%
% Non-smoking: 100%
% Air conditioned: 0%
Car parking: Yes
Wheelchair access: No
Non-animal tested toiletries: Yes
Insecticides used? No
Pets welcome? No
Of animal origin: None
Nearby activities: Camping, yoga, educational lectures, tai chi
Description: Fifty acres of private meadows and woodland. Owned by the Theosophical Society.

Forms of payment: *Local currency*—cash, travelers checks; MC, VI

LACOCK POTTERY

**The Tanyard
Church Street, Lacock
Chippenham, Wiltshire SN15 2LB
England
Phone: (44) 01249 730266**

Proprietor: David & Simone McDowell
Category: Bed & Breakfast

Location: Quaint village
Open all year? Yes
Price: Inexpensive/Moderate
Special packages: No
Reader discount: No
Child discount: Yes

MEALS

Included: B
Offered: B
% Vegetarian: On request
% Vegan: On request
% Organic: 90%
Special diets: Yes
Nearby restaurants: Yes

ROOMS

% Private bath/shower: 100%
% Non-smoking: 100%
% Air conditioned: 0%
Car parking: Yes
Wheelchair access: No
Non-animal tested toiletries: Yes
Insecticides used? No
Pets welcome? Yes
Of animal origin: Leather furniture, feather pillows, wool rugs, down comforters
Nearby activities: Golf, sightseeing tours, antique shops, museums, pottery, Stonehenge, Bath, Avebury

Description: Within this medieval village of Lacock lies the old workhouse, now Lacock Pottery and B&B. The workhouse has been tastefully converted to accommodate guests in comfortable and unique surroundings. Besides making and selling fine ceramics, we run residential pottery courses in the summer and at Easter. We take great pride in our organic vegetable gardens, which delight and surprise many of our guests.

Forms of payment: *Local currency*—cash, travelers checks

THE CROFT

Coverack, Cornwall TR12 6TF England
Phone: (44) 01326 280387

Proprietor: Peter Cheze-Brown
Category: Bed & Breakfast
Location: Seafront
Open all year? Yes
Price: Inexpensive
Special packages: Yes
Reader discount: No
Child discount: No

MEALS

Included: B
Offered: B, L, D
% Vegetarian: 100%
% Vegan: On request
% Organic: 10%
Special diets: Yes
Nearby restaurants: No

ROOMS

% Private bath/shower: 67%
% Non-smoking: 100%
% Air conditioned: 0%
Car parking: Yes
Wheelchair access: Yes
Non-animal tested toiletries: Yes
Insecticides used? No
Pets welcome? Dogs only
Of animal origin: Wool rugs, feather pillows
Nearby activities: Bicycling, hiking, canoeing/kayaking, scuba diving, water sports, camping, beach, wind surfing school
Description: Directly overlooking unspoiled bay, beach, and tiny harbor. Sea views from every room. Garden to cliff edge. On south West Cornish coastal footpath.

Forms of payment: *Local currency*—cash, travelers checks

MEREFIELD VEGETARIAN GUEST HOUSE

East Street
Crewkerne, Somerset TA18 7AB
England
Phone: (44) 01460 73112

Proprietor: Heather McQue
Category: Bed & Breakfast
Location: Country town
Open all year? Yes
Price: Inexpensive
Special packages: No
Reader discount: 10% for 3+ nights
Child discount: No

MEALS

Included: B, D
Offered: B, D
% Vegetarian: 100%
% Vegan: 90%
% Organic: 50%
Special diets: Yes
Nearby restaurants: Yes

ROOMS

% Private bath/shower: 33%
% Non-smoking: 0%
% Air conditioned: 0%
Car parking: Yes
Wheelchair access: No
Non-animal tested toiletries: Yes
Insecticides used? No
Pets welcome? No
Of animal origin: None
Nearby activities: Tennis, horseback riding, massage, nightclub, antique shops

Description: Exclusively vegetarian historic house dating back to 16th century. Walled gardens for guests' use. Imaginative vegetarian cuisine. Much seasonal home-grown produce. An ideal base for touring, visiting national trust gardens, walking, or just relaxing. Lyme Regis, Glastenbury, Bath, and Wells Cathedral all within easy reach.

Forms of payment: *Local currency*—cash, travelers checks

BEACONHILL EAST KENT FIELD CENTRE

Beaconhill
Great Mongeham
Deal, Kent CT14 0HW
England
Phone/Fax: (44) 01304 372809

Proprietor: Mr. H.A.R. Wiggins
Category: Bed & Breakfast
Location: Quaint village, nature reserve
Open all year? Yes
Price: Inexpensive
Special packages: Yes

Reader discount: No
Child discount: Yes

MEALS

Included: B, L, D
Offered: B, L, D
% Vegetarian: On request
% Vegan: On request
% Organic: 50%
Special diets: Yes
Nearby restaurants: No

ROOMS

% Private bath/shower: 0%
% Non-smoking: 100%
% Air conditioned: 0%
Car parking: Yes
Wheelchair access: No
Non-animal tested toiletries: Yes
Insecticides used? No
Pets welcome? No
Of animal origin: Wool rugs
Nearby activities: Golf, bicycling, hiking, fitness classes, sightseeing tours, gardens, music and art
Description: Beaconhill is a beautiful old country house set in a nature reserve near the sea and near Sandwich, Dover, and Canterbury. We offer walking, nature, English Heritage, art, and music. Fully inclusive holidays or bed and breakfast and dinner. Catering is to a very high standard using local produce imaginatively.
Forms of payment: *Local currency*—cash, travelers checks

EXMOOR LODGE

Chapel Street
Exmoor, Somerset TA24 7PY
England
Phone: (44) 01643 831694

Proprietor: Nigel Winter
Category: Guest house
Location: Quaint village
Open all year? Yes
Price: Moderate
Special packages: No
Reader discount: No
Child discount: No

MEALS

Included: B
Offered: B, D
% Vegetarian: 100%

% Vegan: 60%
% Organic: 40%
Special diets: Yes
Nearby restaurants: Yes

ROOMS

% Private bath/shower: 60%

% Non-smoking: 100%

% Air conditioned: 0%

Car parking: No

Wheelchair access: Yes

Non-animal tested toiletries: No

Insecticides used? No

Pets welcome? Yes

Of animal origin: Wool rugs

Nearby activities: Indoor pool, golf, hiking, horseback riding, wildlife tours, beach

Description: Located in the heart of Exmoor National Park, in the village of Exford overlooking the village green. Exclusively vegetarian and vegan. A set 3-course evening meal is offered, which is prepared fresh each day. A vegan option is always available. Heartbeat award for hygienic premises, encouraging healthy eating, and discouraging smoking.

Forms of payment: *Local currency*—cash, travelers checks

MCDONALD'S BARROW HOUSE

45 Barrow Road
London SW16 5PE
England
Phone: (44) 0181 6771925

Proprietor: Pauline McDonald

Category: Bed & Breakfast

Location: Suburban

Open all year? Yes, except Dec. 24–31

Price: Moderate

Special packages: No

Reader discount: No

Child discount: No

MEALS

Included: B

Offered: B

% Vegetarian: 100%

% Vegan: 75%

% Organic: 75%

Special diets: Yes

Nearby restaurants: Yes

ROOMS

% Private bath/shower: 0%

% Non-smoking: 100%

% Air conditioned: 0%

Car parking: Street parking only

Wheelchair access: No

Non-animal tested toiletries: Yes

Insecticides used? No

Pets welcome? No

Of animal origin: Wool rugs, down comforters, feather pillows

Nearby activities: Sightseeing tours, museums, central London within easy distance

Description: Barrow House is a comfortable, non-smoking family

home in a turn-of-the-century house. It is situated in a South London suburb, 15 minutes by overground train from Central London. We share our house and knowledge of London with our guests and make you feel at home.

Forms of payment: *Local currency*—cash, travelers checks

WAVERLEY HOUSE

130–134 Southampton Row
London WC1B 5AG
England
Phone: (44) 0171 833 3691
Fax: (44) 0171 837 3485

Proprietor: J. Chatwani
Category: Hotel
Location: City center
Open all year? Yes, except Dec. 25–26
Price: Moderate
Special packages: Yes
Reader discount: Yes, inquire directly
Child discount: Yes

MEALS

Included: B
Offered: B, L, D
% Vegetarian: 20%
% Vegan: 5%
% Organic: 0%
Special diets: Yes
Nearby restaurants: Yes
Comments: Kosher by prior arrangement

ROOMS

% Private bath/shower: 100%

% Non-smoking: 20%
% Air conditioned: 0%
Car parking: Yes
Wheelchair access: No
Non-animal tested toiletries: Yes
Insecticides used? No
Pets welcome? No
Of animal origin: None

Nearby activities: Indoor pool, tennis, golf, bicycling, boating, snorkeling, scuba diving, horseback riding, nutrition classes, fitness classes, exercise room, massage, juice fasting, weight loss classes, educational lectures, sightseeing tours, nightclub, antique shops, museums

Description: Located in historic Bloomsbury, the Waverley House Hotel is ideally placed for the West End and city and is close to such tourist attractions as the British Museum and Covent Garden. Each of our 109 bedrooms, including 2 suites and 9 executive rooms, offers luxurious accommodations with private bath, hair dryer, color TV linked to the latest satellite technology and movie channel, radio, direct-dial telephone, tea/coffee making facilities, and 24-hour room service. Our relaxed restaurant can easily cater to vegetarians (the owner is himself a vegetarian). Vegan meals are not normally served, but many local vegetarian restaurants cater to vegans.

Forms of payment: *U.S. currency*—cash, travelers checks; *Local currency*—cash, travelers checks; AX, MC, VI

MILK HOUSE

The Borough
Montacute, Somerset TA15 6XB
England
Phone: (44) 01935 823823

Proprietor: Lee & Bill Dufton
Category: Hotel
Location: Quaint village
Open all year? Yes, except Christmas
  and one month in summer
Price: Expensive
Special packages: Yes
Reader discount: 10% for 2+ days
Child discount: Yes

MEALS

Included: B, D
Offered: B, D
% Vegetarian: 33%
% Vegan: 16%
% Organic: 90%
Special diets: Yes
Nearby restaurants: No

ROOMS

% Private bath/shower: 100%

% Non-smoking: 100%
% Air conditioned: 0%
Car parking: Yes
Wheelchair access: Yes
Non-animal tested toiletries: Yes
Insecticides used? No
Pets welcome? No
Of animal origin: Wool rugs, feather
  pillows
Nearby activities: Outdoor pool, golf,
  bicycling, hiking, horseback
  riding, nutrition classes, educational lectures, sightseeing
  tours, antique shops, museums,
  mansion houses, exquisite
  gardens
Description: Milk House is a golden-
  stone 15th century rambling
  old house with a beautiful garden and creeper-covered terrace. It is furnished with
  antiques and offers a friendly,
  personal, and relaxed atmosphere.
Forms of payment: *Local currency*—cash;
  VI

LANDS END YOUTH HOSTEL

**Letcha Vean—St. Just
Penzance, Cornwall TR19 7NT
England
Phone: (44) 01736 788437
Fax: (44) 01736 787337**

Proprietor: Tracy Wright

Category: Hostel

Location: Rural coast

Open all year? Mid-February to end of October only

Price: Inexpensive

Special packages: Yes

Reader discount: No

Child discount: Yes

MEALS

Included: None

Offered: B, L, D

% Vegetarian: 70%

% Vegan: 15%

% Organic: 10%/
See comment

Special diets: Yes

Nearby restaurants: No

Comments: Can have 100% organic with one week's advance notice

ROOMS

% Private bath/shower: 0%

% Non-smoking: 99%

% Air conditioned: 0%

Car parking: Yes

Wheelchair access: No

Non-animal tested toiletries: No

Insecticides used? No

Pets welcome? No

Of animal origin: Wool rugs, feather pillows

Nearby activities: Golf, bicycling, hiking, water sports, camping, beach, sightseeing tours, museums, guided walks of ancient sites

Description: This friendly hostel has open log fires, good food, and wonderful sea views. Spectacular coastline (seals and dolphins can often be seen), clear sandy beaches and wildflowers, as well as desolate moorland studded with stone circles, neolithic burial mounds, and standing stones.

Forms of payment: *Local currency*—cash, travelers checks; MC, VI

HALF HOUSE

**Military Road
Rye, East Sussex TN31 7NY
England
Phone: (44) 01797 223404**

Proprietor: N.J. & A.N. Bennett

Category: Bed & Breakfast

Location: Small medieval town

Open all year? Yes

Price: Moderate

Special packages: No
Reader discount: No
Child discount: Yes

MEALS

Included: B
Offered: B
% Vegetarian: 20%
% Vegan: 1%
% Organic: 50%
Special diets: Yes
Nearby restaurants: Yes

ROOMS

% Private bath/shower: 33%
% Non-smoking: 100%
% Air conditioned: 0%
Car parking: Yes
Wheelchair access: No
Non-animal tested toiletries: No
Insecticides used? No
Pets welcome? No
Of animal origin: Wool rugs
Nearby activities: Indoor pool, tennis, golf, bicycling, hiking, horse-

HALF HOUSE

back riding, camping, beach, sightseeing tours, nightclub, antique shops, museums

Description: A delightful Edwardian period home decorated in Laura Ashley style. Lovely bedrooms have color TVs and complimentary beverage tray. Parking is easy and we are 5 minutes walk to town center.

Forms of payment: *Local currency*—cash, travelers checks; MC, VI, Delta, Access

JEAKE'S HOUSE

**Mermaid St.
Rye, E. Sussex TN31 7ET
England
Phone: (44) 01797 222828
Fax: (44) 01797 222623**

Proprietor: Mrs. Jenny Hadfield
Category: Bed & Breakfast
Location: Quaint village
Open all year? Yes
Price: Inexpensive

Special packages: Yes
Reader discount: No
Child discount: Yes

MEALS

Included: B
Offered: B
% Vegetarian: 75%
% Vegan: 25%
% Organic: 75%
Special diets: Yes
Nearby restaurants: Yes

ROOMS

% Private bath/shower: 90%

% Non-smoking: 0%

% Air conditioned: 0%

Car parking: No

Wheelchair access: No

Non-animal tested toiletries: Yes

Insecticides used? No

Pets welcome? Yes

Of animal origin: Feather pillows, down comforters

Nearby activities: Bicycling, hiking, horseback riding, beach, fitness classes, sightseeing tours, nightclub, antique shops, museums, historic interest

Description: Enjoy traditional luxury in the beautiful setting of 17th century Jeake's House in the medieval cobbled streets of Rye. Each individually restored room carefully combines the elegance of the past with all modern amenities. High standards of comfort and attentive service. Situated in the heart of the Sussex countryside, ancient Rye is the perfect touring base.

Forms of payment: *Local currency*—cash, travelers checks; MC, VI

WOODCOTE HOTEL

The Saltings, Lelant
St. Ives, Cornwall TR26 3DL
England
Phone: (44) 01736 753147

Proprietor: John & Pamela Barrett

Category: Hotel

Location: Estuary and bird sanctuary

Open all year? Mar.–Oct. only

Price: Moderate

Special packages: No

Reader discount: No

Child discount: Yes

MEALS

Included: B, D

Offered: B, D

% Vegetarian: 100%

% Vegan: 50%

% Organic: 50%

Special diets: Yes

Nearby restaurants: No

ROOMS

% Private bath/shower: 50%

% Non-smoking: 100%

% Air conditioned: 0%

Car parking: Yes

Wheelchair access: No

Non-animal tested toiletries: No

Insecticides used? No

Pets welcome? No

Of animal origin: None

Nearby activities: Indoor pool, outdoor pool, golf, hiking, boating, snorkeling, scuba diving, water sports, horseback riding, beach, sightseeing tours, antique shops, museums

Description: Established in the early 1920s to cater exclusively for vegetarians, Woodcote is the UK's oldest vegetarian hotel! Situated on its own grounds with a small secluded wood to the rear, our small family-run hotel overlooks the beautiful tidal estuary and bird sanctuary of Hayle. Convenient to St. Ives and Penzance, the hotel is also within easy reach of sea and coastal walks, quiet bays, and sandy beaches. An ideal center for touring, yet able to provide a restful retreat.

Forms of payment: *Local currency*—cash, travelers checks

THE EDGECLIFFE HOTEL

**7 Clarence Gardens
Shanklin, Isle of Wight PO37 6HA
England
Phone/Fax: (44) 01983 866199**

Proprietor: Gary Bateson

Category: Hotel

Location: Beachfront, quaint village, resort town

Open all year? Yes

Price: Moderate

Special packages: Yes

Reader discount: 5%

Child discount: Yes

MEALS

Included: B, D

Offered: B, D

% Vegetarian: 50%

% Vegan: 0%

% Organic: 20%

Special diets: Yes

Nearby restaurants: No

ROOMS

% Private bath/shower: 60%

% Non-smoking: 100%

% Air conditioned: 0%

Car parking: No

Wheelchair access: No

Non-animal tested toiletries: No

Insecticides used? No

Pets welcome? No

Of animal origin: None

Nearby activities: Indoor pool, outdoor pool, tennis, golf, bicycling, hiking, canoeing/kayaking, boating, water sports, horseback riding, camping, beach, yoga, fitness classes, exercise room, massage, sightseeing tours, antique shops, museums

Description: Charming, friendly, completely non-smoking hotel with a relaxed atmosphere. Tastefully decorated and furnished with a delightful garden. Food is of the highest standard from a full and varied menu. Large portions are our byword. Many rooms have beautiful views. Close to the cliff top and the famous cliff top walk.

Forms of payment: *Local currency*—cash, travelers checks; AX, MC, VI

ROSEGLEN HOTEL

**12 Palmerston Road
Shanklin, Isle of Wight PO37 6AS
England
Phone/Fax: (44) 01983 863164**

Proprietor: F.R. & J.E. Barrass

Category: Hotel

Location: Beachfront, quaint village, resort town

Open all year? Yes, except Christmas

Price: Moderate

Special packages: No

Reader discount: 5%

Child discount: Yes

MEALS

Included: B, D

Offered: B, D

% Vegetarian: 10%

% Vegan: 1%

% Organic: 10%

Special diets: Yes

Nearby restaurants: Yes

ROOMS

% Private bath/shower: 75%

% Non-smoking: 0%

% Air conditioned: 0%

Car parking: Street parking only

Wheelchair access: Yes

Non-animal tested toiletries: Yes

Insecticides used? No

Pets welcome? Yes

Of animal origin: Feather pillows

Nearby activities: Indoor pool, golf, bicycling, hiking, water sports, horseback riding, beach, fitness classes, exercise room, massage, sightseeing tours, nightclub, museums

Description: Friendly family-run hotel only yards from town center and very close to beach, lift, cliff walks, and Shanklin Old Village. All bedrooms offer color TV/radio, hospitality tray, hair dryer, and direct dial telephone. Well-stocked lounge bar with separate darts/pool room. Vegetarian cuisine prepared by vegetarians. Full central heating.

Forms of payment: *Local currency*—cash, travelers checks; AX, MC, VI, Access

SEASHELLS HOTEL

**7 Burlington Road
Swanage, Dorset BH19 1LR
England
Phone: (44) 01929 422794**

Proprietor: Brian Slater

Category: Hotel

Location: Beachfront, resort town, hills

Open all year? Inquire directly

Price: Inexpensive/ Moderate

Special packages: Yes

Reader discount: No

Child discount: Yes

MEALS

Included: B, D

Offered: B, D

% Vegetarian: 100%

% Vegan: 75%

% Organic: Varies

Special diets: Yes

Nearby restaurants: Yes

ROOMS

% Private bath/shower: 100%

% Non-smoking: 100%

% Air conditioned: 0%

Car parking: Yes

Wheelchair access: Yes

Non-animal tested toiletries: Yes

Insecticides used? No

Pets welcome? No

Of animal origin: Wool rugs, feather pillows

Nearby activities: Indoor pool, tennis, golf, bicycling, hiking, canoeing/kayaking, boating, snorkeling, scuba diving, water sports, horseback riding, camping, beach, yoga, fitness classes, exercise room, massage, weight loss classes, sightseeing tours, nightclub, antique shops, museums

Description: We are an exclusively vegetarian and non-smoking family hotel situated opposite a safe sandy beach in a little resort town surrounded by the beautiful Purbeck Hills. The Dorset coastal path is wonderful and passes the end of our

road: spectacular walking! Our food is bountiful and lovingly prepared by Brian. We cater for diets happily and offer a selection of vegetarian wines and beers also.

Forms of payment: *Local currency*—cash, travelers checks, personal checks

THE STANNARY

Mary Tavy
Tavistock, Devon PL19 9QB
England
Phone: (44) 01822 810897
Fax: (44) 01822 810898

Proprietor: Michael Cook and
  Alison Fife
Category: Restaurant with guest rooms
Location: Quaint village, national
  park
Open all year? See comment
Price: Expensive
Special packages: Yes
Reader discount: No
Child discount: No

MEALS

Included: B, D
Offered: B, D
% Vegetarian: 100%
% Vegan: 50%
% Organic: 30%
Special diets: With advance notice
Nearby restaurants: No

ROOMS

% Private bath/shower: 33%
% Non-smoking: 100%
% Air conditioned: 0%
Car parking: Yes
Wheelchair access: No
Non-animal tested toiletries: Yes
Insecticides used? No
Pets welcome? No
Of animal origin: Wool rugs, feather
  pillows
Nearby activities: Horseback riding,
  camping, antique shops,
  museums, hiking

Description: An elegant house with a
  beautiful restaurant in
  Victorian style with many
  antiques, plus three guest bed-
  rooms. Highly creative food.
  Stannary country wines.
  Everything here is unique.
  Situated on the edge of
  Dartmoor.

Forms of payment: *Local currency*—cash,
  travelers checks; AX, MC, VI

Comment: Restaurant open and
  guest rooms available on
  Friday, Saturday, and Sunday
  evenings, Valentine's Day,
  and New Year's Eve. Closed
  December 25–26. B&B (no
  dinner) available other times:
  Call to request.

BROOKESBY HALL HOTEL

Hesketh Road
Torquay, Devon TQ1 2LN
England
Phone: (44) 01803 292194

Proprietor: Edward & Hilda Baker
Category: Hotel
Location: Resort town
Open all year? Open March-October
Price: Moderate
Special packages: Yes
Reader discount: No
Child discount: Yes

MEALS

Included: B, D
Offered: B, D
% Vegetarian: 100%
% Vegan: 30%
% Organic: 60%

Special diets: Yes

Nearby restaurants: Yes

ROOMS

% Private bath/shower: 80%

% Non-smoking: 80%

% Air conditioned: 0%

Car parking: Yes

Wheelchair access: No

Non-animal tested toiletries: Yes

Insecticides used? No

Pets welcome? Yes

Of animal origin: Leather furniture, wool rugs, feather pillows

Nearby activities: Indoor pool, outdoor pool, tennis, golf, bicycling, hiking, boating, water sports, horseback riding, camping, beach, yoga, fitness classes, exercise room, massage, juice fasting, weight loss classes, educational lectures, sightseeing tours, nightclub, antique shops, museums

Description: Brookesby Hall, catering solely for vegetarians and vegans, is an elegant Victorian villa which, while modernized, retains many original features. It is quietly situated in an exclusive conservation area of Torquay, a resort town known as the "Queen of the English Riviera," and enjoys glorious sea views across Torbay.

Forms of payment: *U.S. currency*—cash, travelers checks; *Local currency* —cash, travelers checks

NUT TREE FARM

Stoughton Cross
Wedmore, Somerset BS28 4QP
England
Phone/Fax: (44) 01934 712404

Proprietor: Ann & Melvin Firmager

Category: Bed & Breakfast

Location: Rural

Open all year? Yes, except December 25–26

Price: Inexpensive

Special packages: No

Reader discount: No

Child discount: Yes

MEALS

Included: B

Offered: B

% Vegetarian: Varies

% Vegan: Varies

BROOKESBY HALL

% Organic: As available

Special diets: Yes

Nearby restaurants: Yes

Comment: Extensive vegetarian/ vegan menu

ROOMS

% Private bath/shower: 100%

% Non-smoking: 100%

% Air conditioned: 0%

Car parking: Yes

Wheelchair access: One room

Non-animal tested toiletries: Where available

Insecticides used? No

Pets welcome? No

Of animal origin: Wool rugs

Nearby activities: Indoor pool, outdoor pool, golf, bicycling, hiking, horseback riding, beach, yoga, fitness classes, exercise room, massage, educational lectures, sightseeing tours, antique shops, museums, art gallery, wood turning school

Description: Sixteenth-century former farmhouse in peaceful 2 acres of semi-wild garden and orchard, 1-1/2 miles from the historic village of Wedmore. Elm beams, log fires. Probably the most extensive breakfast menu in the UK. All diets catered for. Our children vegetarian/vegan. Internationally recognized sculptural wood turner.

Forms of payment: *Local currency*—cash, travelers checks; MC, VI

ENGLAND

East Anglia
Midlands
Northeast
Northwest

SHADES OF GREEN VEGETARIAN RESTAURANT

**Upper Arley
Bewdley, Worcestershire DY12 1X4
England
Phone/Fax: (44) 01299 861311**

Proprietor: Brian Maynard-Rolling
Category: Bed & Breakfast
Location: Quaint village
Open all year? Yes
Price: Inexpensive
Special packages: No
Reader discount: No
Child discount: Yes

MEALS

Included: B
Offered: B, L, D
% Vegetarian: 100%
% Vegan: On request
% Organic: 30%
Special diets: Yes
Nearby restaurants: No

ROOMS

% Private bath/shower: 0%
% Non-smoking: 100%
% Air conditioned: 0%
Car parking: Yes
Wheelchair access: No
Non-animal tested toiletries: No
Insecticides used? No
Pets welcome? Yes
Of animal origin: Feather pillows, wool rugs
Nearby activities: Indoor pool, golf, bicycling, hiking, canoeing/ kayaking, boating, camping, fitness classes, exercise room, antique shops, museums, steam railway

Description: Shades of Green is set in one of the prettiest villages in the UK. Formerly a 17th century vicarage, it is 40 meters from River Severn and offers views of the Severn Valley and steam railway. Half an hour from the famous iron bridge and museums near Telford.

Forms of payment: *Local currency*—cash, travelers checks; MC, VI, JCB

RICHARD'S BACKPACKERS HOSTEL

**157 Wanlip Lane
Birstall, Leicester LE4 4GL
England
Phone: (44) 0116 2673107**

SUMMER HOUSE, RICHARD'S BACKPACKERS HOSTEL

Proprietor: Richard Allen
Category: Hostel
Location: Suburban
Open all year? Yes
Price: Inexpensive
Special packages: Yes
Reader discount: See comment
Child discount: No

MEALS

Included: None

Offered: B, D

% Vegetarian: See comment

% Vegan: See comment

% Organic: See comment

Special diets: Yes

Nearby restaurants: Yes

Comments: All meals made to order. Many items organically grown. 10% discount on bed fee, 3 nights maximum (larger discount on 4 nights or more) for mentioning this book.

ROOMS

% Private bath/shower: 0%

% Non-smoking: 100%

% Air conditioned: 0%

Car parking: No

Wheelchair access: No

Non-animal tested toiletries: No

Insecticides used? No

Pets welcome? No

Of animal origin: None

Nearby activities: Indoor pool, bicycling, hiking, sightseeing tours, nightclub, antique shops, museums, wildlife parks

Description: A small, cozy, non-smoking backpacker's hostel catering for cyclists, backpackers, and other young tourists. Good healthy food, homemade bread and cakes. Easy access (3 miles) from city center, frequent bus service 7 days a week. Money exchange in village.

Forms of payment: *Local currency*—cash, travelers checks

ROSE COTTAGE VEGETARIAN BED & BREAKFAST

**6 Hart Lane
Bodham, Norfolk NR25 6NT
England
Phone: (44) 01263 588589**

Proprietor: Megan Joyce

Category: Bed & Breakfast

Location: Beachfront, resort town, countryside

Open all year? Yes, except Christmas

Price: Inexpensive

Special packages: No

Reader discount: No

Child discount: Yes

MEALS

Included: B

Offered: B, D

% Vegetarian: 100%

% Vegan: On request

% Organic: 90%

Special diets: Yes

Nearby restaurants: No

ROOMS

% Private bath/shower: 0%

% Non-smoking: 100%

% Air conditioned: 0%

Car parking: Yes

Wheelchair access: No

Non-animal tested toiletries: Yes

Insecticides used? No

Pets welcome? No

Of animal origin: Wool rugs

Nearby activities: Indoor pool, tennis, golf, bicycling, hiking, horseback riding, beach, yoga, sightseeing tours, antique shops, museums, stately homes, birdwatching

Description: Rose Cottage is in a small village close to beach and sea, open fields and wood, salt marshes and heathland. Share the peace of this comfortable home. Log fires in the winter and alfresco eating in the summer in a lovely garden. Exclusively vegetarian/vegan.

Forms of payment: *Local currency*—cash

BRADFORD OLD WINDMILL

**4 Masons Lane
Bradford-on-Avon, Wiltshire
BA15 1QN
England
Phone: (44) 01225 866842
Fax: (44) 01225 866648**

Proprietor: Priscilla & Peter Roberts

Category: Bed & Breakfast

Location: Quaint village

Open all year? Yes

Price: Moderate

Special packages: Yes

Reader discount: No

Child discount: Yes

MEALS

Included: B

Offered: B, D

% Vegetarian: 60%

% Vegan: 20%

% Organic: 30%

Special diets: Yes

Nearby restaurants: Yes

ROOMS

% Private bath/shower: 100%

% Non-smoking: 100%

% Air conditioned: 0%

Car parking: Yes

Wheelchair access: No

Non-animal tested toiletries: Yes

Insecticides used? No

Pets welcome? No

Of animal origin: Wool rugs, down comforters, feather pillows

Nearby activities: Indoor pool, bicycling, hiking, canoeing/kayaking, boating, sightseeing tours, antique shops, museums

Description: Step back to a more caring, sharing world at this Cotswold stone tower former windmill with its dreamy views, cottage garden, and mellow old pine furniture. Patchwork quilts and masses of books and maps complete the relaxed atmosphere. The vegetarian/vegan meals use recipes collected from far flung parts of the world by the well-traveled owners.

Forms of payment: *U.S. currency*—cash, travelers checks; *Local currency*—cash, travelers checks; AX, MC, VI, Access

NEW PALLYARDS

Hethersgill
Carlisle, Cumbria CA6 6HZ
England
Phone/Fax: (44) 01228 577308

Proprietor: Mrs. G.A. Elwen
Category: Bed & Breakfast
Location: Countryside
Open all year? Yes
Price: Inexpensive
Special packages: No
Reader discount: 10%
Child discount: Yes

MEALS

Included: B
Offered: B, L, D

% Vegetarian: 25%
% Vegan: On request
% Organic: 50%
Special diets: None
Nearby restaurants: No
Comments: Packed lunch offered. Always vegetarian options.

ROOMS

% Private bath/shower: 100%
% Non-smoking: 50%
% Air conditioned: 0%
Car parking: Yes
Wheelchair access: Yes
Non-animal tested toiletries: No
Insecticides used? No
Pets welcome? See comments
Of animal origin: Leather furniture, wool rugs
Nearby activities: Water sports, cross-country skiing, downhill skiing, horseback riding, camping, beach, educational lectures, yoga, sightseeing tours, antique shops, museums

Description: New Pallyards is a small mixed farm of 65 acres set in historic northeast Cumbria close to the border with Scotland. Offering both self-catering and serviced accommodation, it is central for visiting Hadrian's Wall, Carlisle, Kielder Forest, Mill shops, Gretna Green, and the lake district. Awarded "Best Breakfast in Britain" from Salon Culinaire Award.

Forms of payment: *Local currency*—cash, travelers checks; MC, VI

Comments: Pets welcome by arrangement (some rooms)

UNITED KINGDOM & IRELAND

CASTLE COTTAGE

Castle Square
Castle Acre, Norfolk PE32 2AT
England
Phone/Fax: (44) 1760 755888

Proprietor: Nigel & Jacky Walker
Category: Bed & Breakfast
Location: Quaint village
Open all year? Yes
Price: Moderate
Special packages: No
Reader discount: 5%
Child discount: Yes

MEALS

Included: B
Offered: B
% Vegetarian: 100%
% Vegan: 100%
% Organic: 75%
Special diets: Yes
Nearby restaurants: No

ROOMS

% Private bath/shower: 0%
% Non-smoking: 100%
% Air conditioned: 0%
Car parking: Yes
Wheelchair access: No
Non-animal tested toiletries: No
Insecticides used? No
Pets welcome? No
Of animal origin: Feather pillows, wool rugs
Nearby activities: Hiking, bicycling, yoga, nutrition classes, massage, antique shops

Description: Castle Cottage is comfortably modernized with original oak beams and Inglenook fireplace. There is one single room for short or long stays, which converts to a small twin-bedded room. The garden backs directly on the great moat of a ruined Norman castle, built circa 1070.

Forms of payment: *U.S. currency*—cash, travelers checks; *Local currency* —cash, travelers checks

VEGI VENTURES HOLIDAYS

Castle Cottage, Castle Square
Castle Acre, Norfolk PE32 2AJ
England
Phone/Fax: (44) 01760 755888

Proprietor: Nigel Walker
Category: Holidays and house parties
Location: Varied
Open all year? Inquire directly
Price: Inexpensive/Moderate
Special packages: Yes
Reader discount: 5%

VEGI VENTURES HOLIDAYS, PORTUGAL, 1990

Child discount: Inquire directly

MEALS

Included: B, D
Offered: B, L, D
% Vegetarian: 100%
% Vegan: 90%
% Organic: 75%
Special diets: Yes
Nearby restaurants: No

ROOMS

% Private bath/shower: Varies
% Non-smoking: 100%
% Air conditioned: Varies
Car parking: N/A
Wheelchair access: Varies
Non-animal tested toiletries: Varies
Insecticides used? Varies
Pets welcome? Inquire directly
Of animal origin: Feather pillows, wool rugs
Nearby activities: Bicycling, snorkeling, water sports nutrition classes, massage, educational lectures, beach, yoga, sight-seeing tours
Description: We provide holidays and house parties with great vegetarian and vegan food, often with a macrobiotic option. Holidays are for friendly groups of 10-30 people. Destinations include: Crete, Peru, Bali, the English lake district, and Christmas and New Year on the west coast of Wales.

Forms of payment: *U.S. currency*—cash, travelers checks; *Local currency* —cash, travelers checks
Comments: We use a variety of establishments.

THE OLD RED LION

**Bailey St.
Castle Acre, Norfolk PE32 2AG
England
Phone: (44) 01760 755557**

Proprietor: Alison Loughlin
Category: B&B, retreat
Location: Quaint village
Open all year? Yes
Price: Inexpensive
Special packages: No
Reader discount: No
Child discount: No

MEALS

Included: B
Offered: B

% Vegetarian: 100%

% Vegan: 100%

% Organic: 70%

Special diets: Yes

Nearby restaurants: No

ROOMS

% Private bath/shower: 0%

% Non-smoking: 100%

% Air conditioned: 0%

Car parking: Yes

Wheelchair access: No

Non-animal tested toiletries: Yes

Insecticides used? No

Pets welcome? Yes

Of animal origin: None

Nearby activities: Bicycling, hiking, boating, water sports, horse-back riding, nutrition classes, camping, beach, yoga, exercise room, educational lectures, sightseeing tours

Description: The Old Red Lion is centrally situated and carries on the tradition of serving travelers who seek restoration and repose. Private rooms, dormitories, and fully equipped self-catering units are available. Communally served meals are exclusively wholefood/vegetarian. Main attractions are the ruins of Cluniac Priory, gracing the wooded slopes of the River Nar and the castle earthworks—an irresistible natural playground for walking or scaling to enjoy a spectacular view over the valley.

Forms of payment: *Local currency*—cash, travelers checks; AX, MC, VI

WESTERN HOUSE

High St.

Cavendish, Suffolk CO10 8AR

England

Phone: (44) 01787 280550

Proprietor: Peter Marshall

Category: Bed & Breakfast

Location: Quaint village

Open all year? Yes

Price: Inexpensive

Special packages: No

Reader discount: No

Child discount: Yes

MEALS

Included: B

Offered: B

% Vegetarian: 100%

% Vegan: On request

% Organic: 90%

Special diets: Yes

Nearby restaurants: No

ROOMS

% Private bath/shower: 0%

% Non-smoking: 70%

% Air conditioned: 0%

Car parking: Yes

Wheelchair access: No

Non-animal tested toiletries: Yes

Insecticides used? No

Pets welcome? No

Of animal origin: Wool rugs, feather pillows

Nearby activities: Inquire directly

Description: Lovely Tudor house in beautiful village of Cavendish within easy reach of other quaint villages.

Forms of payment: *Local currency*—cash

COTSWOLD CYCLING COMPANY

**48 Shurdington Rd.
Cheltenham, Gloucestershire
GL53 0JE
England
Phone: (44) 0144 250642
Fax: (44) 0144 529730**

Proprietor: Steve Short & Don Muir
Category: Outdoor adventure
Location: Cotswolds
Open all year? Yes
Price: Moderate
Special packages: Yes
Reader discount: 10%
Child discount: Yes

MEALS

Included: B
Offered: B
% Vegetarian: 15%
% Vegan: 5%
% Organic: 5%
Special diets: Yes
Nearby restaurants: No
Comments: All establishments offer vegetarian and vegan meals

ROOMS

% Private bath/shower: 50%
% Non-smoking: 20%
% Air conditioned: 0%
Car parking: Yes
Wheelchair access: No
Non-animal tested toiletries: No
Insecticides used? No
Pets welcome? Yes
Of animal origin: Accommodations vary
Nearby activities: Bicycling

Description: Set in the heart of England, the Cotswolds are Britain's largest area of outstanding natural beauty and can truly claim to offer the ideal country for all cyclists, novice to enthusiast. Your cycling holiday will guide you away from the crowds and along some of the many hundreds of miles of peaceful country lanes and tracks which

cover the area. Should you find that none of our itineraries quite matches your ideal, we will custom-build your own personal holiday. Accommodations are at family run hotels and guest houses and include traditional English breakfast as well as vegetarian and vegan.

Forms of payment: *Local currency*—cash, travelers checks; AX, MC, VI, JCB

HALLERY HOUSE HOTEL

**48 Shurdington Rd.
Cheltenham, Gloucestershire
GL53 0JE
England
Phone: (44) 01242 578450
Fax: (44) 01242 529730**

Proprietor: Steve & Angie
Category: Hotel
Location: City center
Open all year? Yes
Price: Moderate
Special packages: Yes
Reader discount: 5%
Child discount: Yes

MEALS

Included: B
Offered: B, D
% Vegetarian: 20%
% Vegan: 5%
% Organic: 50%
Special diets: Yes
Nearby restaurants: Yes

ROOMS

% Private bath/shower: 65%
% Non-smoking: 25%
% Air conditioned: 0%
Car parking: Yes
Wheelchair access: No
Non-animal tested toiletries: Yes
Insecticides used? No
Pets welcome? Yes
Of animal origin: Feather pillows, down comforters
Nearby activities: Bicycling, hiking, horseback riding, fitness classes, massage, sightseeing tours, nightclub, antique shops, museums

Description: This Victorian house dating from 1837 has 16 bedrooms, most with en-suite facilities and all with satellite TV and hospitality tray. Children are welcome and special diets can be easily accommodated with notice. The hotel is within walking distance of the elegant Montpellier district of Cheltenham with its antique shops, fashion houses, wine bars, and restaurants. We can also offer cycling holidays and hot air ballooning.

Forms of payment: *Local currency*—cash, travelers checks; AX, MC, VI, JCB, Diners Club

Comments: 2 dogs, 2 cats, tropical fish, and a daughter

GLYN & SALLY TUDOR

**Lost Leet Mill
Hopton Heath
Craven Arms, Shropshire SY7 0QB
England
Phone: (44) 01547 530384**

Proprietor: Glyn & Sally Tudor
Category: Bed & Breakfast
Location: Country hamlet
Open all year? Yes
Price: Inexpensive
Special packages: No
Reader discount: 10%
Child discount: Yes

MEALS

Included: B
Offered: B, L
% Vegetarian: 90%
% Vegan: 10%
% Organic: 90%
Special diets: None
Nearby restaurants: No

ROOMS

% Private bath/shower: 0%
% Non-smoking: 100%
% Air conditioned: 0%
Car parking: Yes
Wheelchair access: No
Non-animal tested toiletries: No
Insecticides used? No
Pets welcome? No
Of animal origin: None
Nearby activities: Indoor pool, golf, bicycling, hiking, horseback riding, yoga, fitness classes, exercise room, massage, sightseeing tours, antique shops, museums

Description: Situated in the glorious Clun Valley on the Welsh/Shropshire Border, this is the place for peace, walking, magnificent scenery and abundant wildlife. Historic Ludlow, famous for its summer arts festival, is 10 miles away. Shrewsbury 30 miles, Hereford 30 miles. Welcome to A.E. Houseman country.

Forms of payment: *Local currency*—cash

HOLMHEAD

Hadrian's Wall
Greenhead via Carlisle,
Northumberland CA6 7HY
England
Phone/Fax: (44) 016977 47402

Proprietor: Brian & Pauline Staff
Category: Guest house
Location: Countryside
Open all year? Yes
Price: Inexpensive
Special packages: Yes
Reader discount: 5%
Child discount: Yes

MEALS

Included: B
Offered: B, L, D
% Vegetarian: 4%
% Vegan: 1%
% Organic: 5%
Special diets: Yes
Nearby restaurants: No
Comments: Packed
   lunches available

ROOMS

% Private bath/shower: 100%
% Non-smoking: 100%
% Air conditioned: 0%
Car parking: Yes
Wheelchair access: Yes
Non-animal tested toiletries: Yes
Insecticides used? No
Pets welcome? No
Of animal origin: Feather pillows, farm
   animals, wool rugs
Nearby activities: Indoor pool, outdoor
   pool, tennis, golf, bicycling,
   hiking, canoeing/kayaking,

boating, water sports, horseback riding, camping, educational lectures, sightseeing
tours, antique shops, museums,
Hadrian's Wall, castles, excavat-
ed Roman remains

Description: Enjoy fine food and hospitality with a personal touch
   in a non-smoking atmosphere.
   This lovely old farmhouse is
   built with Hadrian's Wall stone
   near spectacular remains. Cozy
   bedrooms with shower/wc.

Quality home cooking, guests
dine together at candlelight
table. BTA excellence award for
breakfasts. Self-catering annex,
French windows onto patio,
private garden. All diets catered
for with prior notice and assis-
tance.

Forms of payment: *Local currency*—cash,
   travelers checks; MC, VI

AMADEUS

**115 Franklin Road
Harrogate, N. Yorkshire HG1 5EN
England
Phone: (44) 01423 505151**

Proprietor: Sylvia Barnes
Category: B&B, hotel
Location: Resort town
Open all year? Yes, except
    December 24–26.
Price: Moderate
Special packages: No
Reader discount: No
Child discount: Yes

MEALS

Included: B
Offered: B, D
% Vegetarian: 50%
% Vegan: 50%
% Organic: 10%
Special diets: Yes
Nearby restaurants: Yes

ROOMS

% Private bath/shower: 80%
% Non-smoking: 100%
% Air conditioned: 0%
Car parking: Yes
Wheelchair access: No
Non-animal tested toiletries: Yes
Insecticides used? No
Pets welcome? Yes
Of animal origin: Wool rugs, down
    comforters, feather pillows
Nearby activities: Indoor pool, tennis,
    golf, bicycling, hiking, horse-
    back riding, fitness classes,
    exercise room, massage, sight-
    seeing tours, nightclub, antique

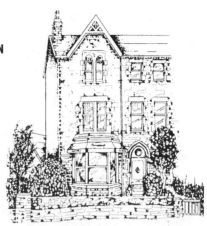

shops, museums, Turkish bath
& sauna, aromatherapy

Description: An elegant Victorian
    home near the center of the
    spa town of Harrogate. Enjoy
    superb vegetarian/vegan cui-
    sine freshly prepared by us or
    dine out at the local vegetarian
    bistro. Only 20 miles from York
    and the Yorkshire Dales
    National Park.

Forms of payment: *Local currency*—cash,
    travelers checks

WHARFEDALE HOUSE HOTEL

**28 Harlow Moor Drive
Harrogate, N. Yorkshire HG2 0JY
England
Phone: (44) 01423 522233**

Proprietor: H. & P. Quinn
Category: B&B, hotel
Location: Resort town, gardens and
    woodlands
Open all year? Yes
Price: Moderate
Special packages: Yes

WHARFEDALE HOUSE HOTEL

exercise room, massage, weight loss classes, sightseeing tours, nightclub, antique shops, museums, private guided tours

Description: Wharfedale House is spacious, welcoming, and comfortable, with visitors from all over the world. It's our delight to open the treasure chest of Yorkshire so that all our visitors experience "the real thing," from the beautiful dales to the Farne Islands, to the moors and the dramatic east coastline and towns and villages. Don't forget your camera and that special sense of adventure for magical tours only we provide.

Forms of payment: *Local currency*—cash, travelers checks

Reader discount: No

Child discount: Yes

MEALS

Included: B

Offered: B, L, D

% Vegetarian: 30%

% Vegan: 5%

% Organic: 10%

Special diets: Yes

Nearby restaurants: Yes

ROOMS

% Private bath/shower: 100%

% Non-smoking: 0%

% Air conditioned: 0%

Car parking: Yes

Wheelchair access: No

Non-animal tested toiletries: Yes

Insecticides used? No

Pets welcome? Yes

Of animal origin: Wool rugs

Nearby activities: Indoor pool, tennis, golf, hiking, boating, horseback riding, yoga, fitness classes,

PROSPECT COTTAGE

Bank End
Ingleton via Carnforth
N. Yorkshire LA6 3HE
England
Phone: (44) 015242 41328

Proprietor: Lauraine Palmeri

Category: Bed & Breakfast

Location: Mountain, quaint village

Open all year? Yes

Price: Inexpensive

Special packages: Yes

Reader discount: Yes, for 2+ nights

Child discount: Yes

MEALS

Included: B

Offered: B

% Vegetarian: 100%

% Vegan: On request

% Organic: Varies

Special diets: Yes

Nearby restaurants: Yes

ROOMS

% Private bath/shower: 100%

% Non-smoking: 100%

% Air conditioned: 0%

Car parking: On street

Wheelchair access: No

Non-animal tested toiletries: Yes

Insecticides used? No

Pets welcome? Yes

Of animal origin: Feather pillows, down comforters

Nearby activities: Outdoor pool, hiking, camping, sightseeing tours, caving

Description: Inexpensive vegetarian/ vegan B&B at picturesque Prospect Cottage, conveniently based in quaint village of Ingelton, home of the famous Waterfalls Walk, center for the Yorkshire dales, and close to lake district. Fells, caves, wooded glens, and mountainous limestone scenery of breathtaking beauty are nearby.

Forms of payment: *Local currency*—cash

PONDEN HALL

**Stanbury
Keighley, W. Yorkshire BD22 0HR
England
Phone: (44) 01535 644154**

Proprietor: Brenda Taylor

Category: Bed & Breakfast

Location: Moorland

Open all year? Yes, except Christmas

Price: Moderate

Special packages: No

Reader discount: Yes; inquire directly

Child discount: Yes

MEALS

Included: B

Offered: B, L, D

% Vegetarian: 30%

% Vegan: 5%

% Organic: 10%

Special diets: Yes

Nearby restaurants: Yes

Comments: Packed lunch offered

ROOMS

% Private bath/shower: 1%

% Non-smoking: 100%

% Air conditioned: 0%

Car parking: Yes

Wheelchair access: Yes

Non-animal tested toiletries: No

Insecticides used? No

Pets welcome? Yes

Of animal origin: Feather pillows, wool rugs, down comforters

Nearby activities: Hiking, horseback riding, camping, massage, antique shops, museums

Description: Ponden Hall is a listed Elizabethan farmhouse with a Georgian extension, situated on the Pennine Way amid glorious moors and farm land. Good food, informal hospitality, peace and quiet. Come find the peace and relaxing way of life of another era.

Forms of payment: *Local currency*—cash, travelers checks

PENRHOS COURT HOTEL

**Penrhos Court
Kington, Herefordshire HR5 3LH
England
Phone: (44) 01544 230720
Fax: (44) 01544 230754**

Proprietor: Daphne Lambert
Category: Hotel
Location: Countryside
Open all year? Yes
Price: Expensive
Special packages: Yes
Reader discount: No
Child discount: Free under age 5

MEALS

Included: B
Offered: B, D
% Vegetarian: 75%
% Vegan: 20%
% Organic: 75%
Special diets: Yes
Nearby restaurants: Yes

ROOMS

% Private bath/shower: 100%
% Non-smoking: 100%

% Air conditioned: 0%
Car parking: Yes
Wheelchair access: Yes
Non-animal tested toiletries: Yes
Insecticides used? No
Pets welcome? No
Of animal origin: Wool rugs
Nearby activities: Tennis, golf, bicycling, hiking, horseback riding, nutrition classes, antique shops, museums, canoeing/kayaking, boating

Description: Thirteenth-century timber frame manor house building with many unique features. The house and outbuildings form a courtyard around a lovely pond an d grassed area. Superb bedrooms. Delicious food and wine.

Forms of payment: *Local currency*—cash, travelers checks; AX, VI

LUPTON TOWER COUNTRY HOUSE VEGETARIAN HOTEL

**Lupton near Kirkby, Lonsdale
Cumbria LA6 2PR
England
Phone: (44) 015395 67400**

Proprietor: Mrs. A. Paget
Category: Hotel
Location: Countryside
Open all year? Yes
Price: Moderate
Special packages: No
Reader discount: 10%
Child discount: Yes

MEALS

Included: B
Offered: B, D
% Vegetarian: 100%
% Vegan: 5%
% Organic: 50%
Special diets: Yes
Nearby restaurants: No

ROOMS

% Private bath/shower: 100%
% Non-smoking: 100%
% Air conditioned: 0%
Car parking: Yes
Wheelchair access: Yes
Non-animal tested toiletries: Yes
Insecticides used? No
Pets welcome? No
Of animal origin: Wool rugs
Nearby activities: Hiking, boating, water sports
Description: Lupton Tower is a peaceful country hotel on 7 acres between the lake district and the Yorkshire dales with easy access to the motorway network. We are well-known for our excellent vegetarian cuisine.

Forms of payment: *Local currency*—cash, travelers checks; MC, VI

CHESTNUT HOUSE

**Crosby Garrett
Kirby Stephen, Cumbria CA17 4PR
England
Phone: (44) 017683 71230**

Proprietor: Stephanie & John Dewhurst
Category: Guest house
Location: Quaint village
Open all year? Yes
Price: Inexpensive
Special packages: Yes
Reader discount: No
Child discount: Yes

MEALS

Included: B, D
Offered: B, L, D
% Vegetarian: 100%
% Vegan: 20%
% Organic: 20%
Special diets: Yes

Nearby restaurants: No

ROOMS

% Private bath/shower: 0%

% Non-smoking: 100%

% Air conditioned: 0%

Car parking: Yes

Wheelchair access: No

Non-animal tested toiletries: Yes

Insecticides used? No

Pets welcome? Yes

Of animal origin: None

Nearby activities: Bicycling, hiking, antique shops

Description: Tucked away in beautiful countryside between the lake district and the Yorkshire dales, our traditional cottage provides cozy and relaxing accommodation and mouth-watering meals. We use our own organic vegetables when available. Good walking/cycling. Perfect for exploring Northern England with chance to unwind in a real English village.

Forms of payment: *Local currency*—cash, travelers checks

THE LION INN

**Blaney Ridge
Kirnbymoorside, N. Yorkshire YO6 6LQ
England
Phone: (44) 01751 417320
Fax: (44) 01751 417717**

Proprietor: Barry Crossland

Category: Hotel

Location: Countryside

Open all year? Yes

Price: Moderate

Special packages: Yes

Reader discount: No

Child discount: Yes

MEALS

Included: None

Offered: B, L, D

% Vegetarian: 15%

% Vegan: 5%

% Organic: Varies

Special diets: Yes

Nearby restaurants: No

ROOMS

% Private bath/shower: 70%

% Non-smoking: 0%

% Air conditioned: 0%

Car parking: Yes

Wheelchair access: Yes

Non-animal tested toiletries: No

Insecticides used? No

Pets welcome? Yes

Of animal origin: None

Nearby activities: Indoor pool, outdoor pool, tennis, golf, bicycling, hiking, canoeing/kayaking, boating, cross-country skiing, horseback riding, camping, museums

Description: Sixteenth-century house, set amidst the beautiful North Yorkshire moors. Breathtaking views over Rosedale and Farndale. Superb candelight a la carte restaurant, open log fires, beamed ceilings.

Forms of payment: *U.S. currency*—cash, travelers checks; *Local currency* —cash, travelers checks; MC, VI

REGENCY GUEST HOUSE

**The Street
Neatishead, Norfolk NR12 8AD
England
Phone: (44) 01692 630233**

Proprietor: Alan and Sue Wrigley

Category: Bed & Breakfast

Location: Quaint village

Open all year? Yes

Price: Moderate

Special packages: Yes

Reader discount: Inquire directly

Child discount: Yes

MEALS

Included: B

Offered: B, L, D

% Vegetarian: See comments

% Vegan: See comments

% Organic: See comments

Special diets: Yes

Nearby restaurants: Yes

Comments: Vegetarian/vegan meals on request. Packed lunches and light suppers also served. Very small restaurant. Special terms for 3–day breaks.

ROOMS

% Private bath/shower: 50%

% Non-smoking: 0%

% Air conditioned: 0%

Car parking: Yes

Wheelchair access: No

Non-animal tested toiletries: Yes

Insecticides used? No

Pets welcome? Yes

Of animal origin: None

Nearby activities: Indoor pool, outdoor pool, bicycling, boating, horseback riding, beach, sightseeing tours, antique shops, museums, wildlife and bird-watching

Description: Seventeenth-century house of character in picturesque, unspoiled village in the heart of the Norfolk Broads. Five minutes' walk from the public mooring. Ideal holiday center for all boating activities, walking, and cycling. Easy access to bird-watching and wildlife facilities. All rooms are individually Laura Ashley decorated and tastefully furnished with color TV, radio, tea-making facilities. Very generous breakfasts.

Forms of payment: *Local currency*—cash

CHANDLERS

Honing
North Walsham, Norfolk NR28 9QW
England
Phone: (44) 01692 536504

Proprietor: Mrs. J.S. White

Category: Bed & Breakfast

Location: Quaint village

Open all year? Yes, except Christmas
and New Year

Price: Inexpensive

Special packages: No

Reader discount: No

Child discount: Yes

MEALS

Included: B

Offered: B, D

% Vegetarian: 75%

% Vegan: 25%

% Organic: 90%

Special diets: Yes

Nearby restaurants: No

ROOMS

% Private bath/shower: 0%

% Non-smoking: 100%

% Air conditioned: 0%

Car parking: Yes

Wheelchair access: No

Non-animal tested toiletries: Yes

Insecticides used? No

Pets welcome? Yes

Of animal origin: Farm animals, wool
rugs

Nearby activities: Golf, bicycling,
hiking, boating, horseback
riding, beach, antique shops,
museums, bird watching

Description: A small bed and breakfast establishment able to
accommodate individual
requirements. Our large
Victorian house is in a rural
setting with a spacious garden
surrounded by countryside.
Quiet roads make travel by
bike/car to Norwich, Norfolk
Broads, and many other attractions a pleasure. The sea is 10
minutes away.

Forms of payment: *Local currency*—cash

PINE TREES

Holly Lane—Blofield
Norwich, Norfolk NR13 4BY
England
Phone: (44) 01603 713778

Proprietor: Jean Eldred

Category: Bed & Breakfast

Location: Countryside

Open all year? Yes, except Dec. 23–25

Price: Inexpensive

Special packages: Yes

Reader discount: Yes, for 2+ nights

Child discount: Yes

MEALS

Included: B
Offered: B
% Vegetarian: 10%
% Vegan: 1%
% Organic: 0%
Special diets: Yes
Nearby restaurants: Yes

ROOMS

% Private bath/shower: 100%
% Non-smoking: 100%
% Air conditioned: 0%
Car parking: Yes
Wheelchair access: No
Non-animal tested toiletries: No
Insecticides used? No

Pets welcome? No
Of animal origin: None
Nearby activities: Boating, horseback riding, beach, sightseeing tours, nightclub, antique shops, museums
Description: Bed and breakfast accommodation in self-contained ground floor suite of large modern country house set in 1-1/2 acre garden. Quiet rural situation one mile from A-47, close to Norwich, the Broads, and Norfolk coast. Private bathroom and entrance. Color TV, tea/coffee facilities. Non-smokers only. All diets catered for.
Forms of payment: *Local currency*—cash

COTSWOLD HOUSE

363 Banbury Rd.
Oxford, Oxfordshire OX2 7PL
England
Phone/Fax: (44) 01865 310558

Proprietor: Jim & Anne O'Kane
Category: Bed & Breakfast
Location: City center
Open all year? Yes
Price: Inexpensive
Special packages: No
Reader Discount: No
Child discount: Yes

MEALS

Included: B
Offered: B
% Vegetarian: 100%
% Vegan: On request

% Organic: 0%
Special diets: Yes
Nearby restaurants: Yes

ROOMS

% Private bath/shower: 100%
% Non-smoking: 100%
% Air conditioned: 0%
Car parking: Yes

Wheelchair access: No

Non-animal tested toiletries: No

Insecticides used? No

Pets welcome? No

Of animal origin: Leather furniture, feather pillows

Nearby activities: Sightseeing tours, museums, hiking, botanical gardens, biking, castles

Description: Cotswold House is situated in the leafy suburb of North Oxford, almost two miles from City Centre. All rooms have en-suite facilities and the premises are totally nonsmoking. Special breakfasts include a wholesome vegetarian breakfast with fresh fruit and Anne's home-made muesli.

Forms of payment: *Local currency*—cash, travelers checks

YEW TREE COTTAGE

**Grove Lane—Redlynch
Salisbury, Wiltshire SP5 2NR
England
Phone: (44) 01725 511730**

Proprietor: Angela Churchill

Category: Bed & Breakfast

Location: Quaint village

Open all year? Yes, except Christmas and New Year

Price: Moderate

Special packages: No

Reader discount: 10% for 3+ nights

Child discount: Yes

MEALS

Included: B

Offered: B

% Vegetarian: 10%

% Vegan: 5%

% Organic: 0%

Special diets: Yes

Nearby restaurants: No

ROOMS

% Private bath/shower: 0%

% Non-smoking: 100%

% Air conditioned: 0%

Car parking: Yes

Wheelchair access: No

Non-animal tested toiletries: No

Insecticides used? No

Pets welcome? No

Of animal origin: Feather pillows, down comforters, wool rugs

Nearby activities: Golf, bicycling, hiking, horseback riding, camping, massage

Description: Situated in the "new Forest" Heritage village of Redlynch, near Salisbury, Yew Tree Cottage stands in a large garden overlooking a grazing paddock and an ideal base from which to explore the southern

counties. The area is superb for walking and riding, and golfing facilities are close by. Salisbury is 20 minutes' drive away, Stonehenge not much farther.

Forms of payment: *Local currency*—cash

THE GYPSY VEGETARIAN GUEST HOUSE

Ranworth—Church Rd. Ravenscar Scarborough, N. Yorkshire UO13 OLZ England
Phone: (44) 01723 870366

Proprietor: Karen Dickinson
Category: Guest house
Location: Quaint coastal village
Open all year? Yes
Price: Inexpensive
Special packages: No
Reader discount: No
Child discount: Yes

MEALS

Included: B, L, D
Offered: B, L, D
% Vegetarian: 100%
% Vegan: 100%
% Organic: 40%
Special diets: Yes
Nearby restaurants: Yes

ROOMS

% Private bath/shower: 0%
% Non-smoking: 100%
% Air conditioned: 0%
Car parking: Yes
Wheelchair access: No
Non-animal tested toiletries: Yes
Insecticides used? No

Pets welcome? Yes
Of animal origin: Wool rugs
Nearby activities: Indoor pool, outdoor pool, tennis, golf, bicycling, hiking, boating, scuba diving, water sports, horseback riding, camping, beach, yoga, massage, sightseeing tours, nightclub,

antique shops, museums, full body aromatherapy massage

Description: Ranworth is the former village vicarage. Built in 1894, it is a Victorian villa construct-ed of locally quarried stone. We opened as a whole food vege-tarian guest house in 1985 and offer very friendly comfortable accommodations. We have an English cottage garden with summer house and beautiful cats, and we serve delicious cruelty-free food.

Forms of payment: *Local currency*—cash, travelers checks

SANSBURY PLACE VEGETARIAN GUEST HOUSE

Duke Street
Settle, N. Yorkshire
England
Phone: (44) 01729 823840

Proprietor: Sue & Dave Stark

Category: Guest house

Location: Market town

Open all year? Yes, except last three weeks in January

Price: Moderate

Special packages: No

Reader discount: No

Child discount: No

MEALS

Included: B

Offered: B, L, D

% Vegetarian: 100%

% Vegan: 75%

% Organic: 60%

Special diets: Yes

Nearby restaurants: Yes

Comments: Packed lunches available

ROOMS

% Private bath/shower: 0%

% Non-smoking: 100%

% Air conditioned: 0%

Car parking: Yes

Wheelchair access: No

Non-animal tested toiletries: Yes

Insecticides used? No

Pets welcome? No

Of animal origin: Wool rugs, feather pillows

Nearby activities: Indoor pool, bi-
cycling, hiking, horseback riding, antique shops, museums, caving, potholing

Description: Sansbury Place is a spacious Victorian House with splendid views of the surrounding hills, a secluded garden, off-road parking, and accommodations for five guests. Sample imaginative vegetarian cooking, relax in front of open fires, and explore our famous Settle-Carlisle railway line and beautiful limestone scenery.

Forms of payment: *Local currency*—cash, travelers checks

PARKFIELD GUEST HOUSE

3 Broad Walk
Stratford-upon-Avon, Warwickshire
CV37 6HS
England
Phone: (44) 01789 293313

Proprietor: Jo & Roger Pettitt
Category: Bed & Breakfast
Location: Small cultural town
Open all year? Yes
Price: Inexpensive
Special packages: No
Reader discount: 10%
Child discount: Yes

MEALS

Included: B
Offered: B
% Vegetarian: 90%
% Vegan: 25%
% Organic: 10%
Special diets: Yes
Nearby restaurants: Yes

ROOMS

% Private bath/shower: 72%
% Non-smoking: 100%
% Air conditioned: 0%
Car parking: Yes
Wheelchair access: No
Non-animal tested toiletries: Yes
Insecticides used? No
Pets welcome? No
Of animal origin: Feather pillows,
  wool rugs
Nearby activities: Indoor pool, tennis,
  golf, bicycling, hiking, boating,
  yoga, fitness classes, massage,
  sightseeing tours, nightclub,
antique shops, museums, Royal
Shakespeare Theatre

Description: Elegant Victorian house,
  quietly situated in the old town
  port of Stratford only a few
  minutes from town center,
  river, and theater. Delicious
  breakfasts with wide choice
  and all ingredients homemade,
  free range, and organic where
  possible.

Forms of payment: *Local currency*—cash,
  travelers checks; MC, VI, JCB,
  Diners Club

WINTON HOUSE

**The Green, Upper Quinton
Stratford-upon-Avon, Warwickshire
CV37 8SX
England
Phone: (44) 01789 720500**

Proprietor: Mrs. G. Lyon

Category: Bed & Breakfast

Location: Quaint village, resort town

Open all year? Yes

Price: Moderate

Special packages: Yes

Reader discount: No

Child discount: Yes

MEALS

Included: B

Offered: B

% Vegetarian: 75%

% Vegan: 25%

% Organic: Varies

Special diets: Yes

Nearby restaurants:
  Yes

ROOMS

% Private bath/shower:
  100%

% Non-smoking:
  100%

% Air conditioned: 0%

Car parking: Yes

Wheelchair access: No

Non-animal tested toiletries: Yes

Insecticides used? No

Pets welcome? No

Of animal origin: Feather pillows,
  down comforters

Nearby activities: Bicycling, hiking

Description: Historic Victorian farmhouse in area of outstanding
  natural beauty 6 miles from
  Stratford-upon-Avon. Ideally
  situated for touring and
  cycling, cycles available. En-
  suite bedrooms with antique
  4-poster beds and handmade
  quilts enjoy country views.
  Heartbeat Award–winning
  breakfasts include a special
  which changes daily. Homemade jam and fruit fresh from
  our own orchard. Two village
  pubs.

Forms of payment: *U.S. currency*—cash;
  Local currency—cash; Eurocheck

DAIRY GUEST HOUSE

3 Scarcroft Road
York, N. Yorkshire YO2 1ND
England
Phone: (44) 01904 639367

Proprietor: Keith Jackman
Category: Bed & Breakfast
Location: City center
Open all year? Closed some of
  December and all of January
Price: Inexpensive
Special packages: No
Reader discount: No
Child discount: Yes

MEALS

Included: B
Offered: B
% Vegetarian: On
  request
% Vegan: On request
% Organic: Varies
Special diets: Yes
Nearby restaurants: No

ROOMS

% Private bath/shower:
  50%
% Non-smoking: 100%
% Air conditioned: 0%
Car parking: Yes
Wheelchair access: No
Non-animal tested toiletries: No
Insecticides used? No
Pets welcome? No
Of animal origin: Wool rugs, down
  comforters, feather pillows
Nearby activities: Indoor pool, tennis,
  bicycling, hiking, boating,
  museums

Description: Situated in central York,
  the Dairy is just 200 yards
  south of the medieval city walls
  and an easy stroll to York's
  many attractions and museums. Well-equipped cottage-
  style rooms surround a
  flower-filled courtyard. Some
  en-suite. One four-poster.
  Informal atmosphere. Offers
  traditional or vegetarian B&B.

Forms of payment: *Local currency*—cash,
  travelers checks

SCOTLAND

AVINGORMACK GUEST HOUSE

**Boat of Garten
Inverness-shire PH24 3BT Scotland
Phone: (44) 01479 831614**

Proprietor: Jan & Matthew Ferguson
Category: Bed & Breakfast
Location: Mountain
Open all year? Closed November
Price: Moderate

Special packages: Yes
Reader discount: 10% on room
Child discount: Yes

MEALS

Included: B, D
Offered: B, D
% Vegetarian: 100%
% Vegan: 70%
% Organic: 75%
Special diets: Yes
Nearby restaurants: No

ROOMS

% Private bath/shower: 50%
% Non-smoking: 100%
% Air conditioned: 0%
Car parking: Yes
Wheelchair access: No
Non-animal tested toiletries: Yes
Insecticides used? No

Pets welcome? No
Of animal origin: None
Nearby activities: Golf, bicycling, hiking, canoeing/kayaking, water sports, cross-country skiing, downhill skiing, horseback riding, camping, sightseeing tours, antique shops, museums, castles, whiskey distilleries, Findhorn Foundation

Description: The spectacular mountain scenery from our guest house has to be seen to be believed. Just as our award-winning food has to be tasted. Excellent location to explore the Highlands. Near to the Findhorn Foundation. S.T.B. 3 crowns highly commended.

Forms of payment: *Local currency*—cash, travelers checks; MC, VI

WILD EXPLORER HOLIDAYS

**Skye Environmental Centre
Broadford
Isle of Skye IV49 9AQ Scotland
Phone/Fax: (44) 01471 822487**

Proprietor: Paul Yoxon
Category: Wildlife center
Location: Beachfront, mountain, quaint village

Open all year? Yes
Price: Inexpensive/Moderate
Special packages: Yes
Reader discount: 10%
Child discount: Yes

MEALS

Included: B, L, D
Offered: B, L, D
% Vegetarian: 60%
% Vegan: 15%
% Organic: 15%
Special diets: Yes
Nearby restaurants: Yes

ROOMS

% Private bath/shower: 50%
% Non-smoking: 100%
% Air conditioned: 0%
Car parking: Yes
Wheelchair access: No
Non-animal tested toiletries: Yes
Insecticides used? No
Pets welcome? No
Of animal origin: Wool rugs
Nearby activities: Educational lectures, sightseeing tours, museums, wildlife trips
Description: Wild Explorer Holidays specializes in wildlife holidays in Scotland. All profits go into our charity which works in the fields of wildlife conservation and environmental education.
Forms of payment: Local currency—cash, travelers checks; MC, VI

DENARD VEGETARIAN BED & BREAKFAST

**Glen Cloy Rd.
Brodick, Isle of Arran
Strathclyde KA27 8VA Scotland
Phone: (44) 01770 302475**

Proprietor: Jill & Ramesh Lele
Category: Bed & Breakfast
Location: Island, quiet rural
Open all year? Re-opening in 1998
Price: Inexpensive/Moderate
Special packages: No
Reader discount: 10%
Child discount: Yes

MEALS

Included: B
Offered: B, L, D
% Vegetarian: 100%
% Vegan: 30%
% Organic: As available
Special diets: Yes
Nearby restaurants: No

ROOMS

% Private bath/shower: 0%
% Non-smoking: 100%
% Air conditioned: 0%
Car parking: Yes
Wheelchair access: No
Non-animal tested toiletries: No
Insecticides used? No
Pets welcome? By arrangement only
Of animal origin: Wool rugs
Nearby activities: Indoor pool, tennis, golf, bicycling, hiking, boating, water sports, horseback riding, camping, beach, exercise room, museums

Description: Cheerful family-run house close to sea and mountains. Stunning scenery and local wildlife are nearby. Owners are active craftspeople. We cater for individuals and provide an interesting environment in which to relax and enjoy Arran. Packed lunches and dinner by arrangement.

Forms of payment: *U.S. currency*—cash, travelers checks, personal checks; *Local currency*—cash, travelers checks

THE ROSSAN

Auchencairn
Castle Douglas
Dumfries and Galloway DG7 1QR
Scotland
Phone: (44) 01556 640269

Proprietor: Mrs. Bardsley
Category: Bed & Breakfast
Location: Beachfront, quaint village
Open all year? Yes
Price: Inexpensive
Special packages: Yes
Reader discount: No
Child discount: Yes

MEALS

Included: B, D
Offered: B, D
% Vegetarian: 85%
% Vegan: See description
% Organic: 95% in summer, as available in winter.
Special diets: Yes
Nearby restaurants: Yes

ROOMS

% Private bath/shower: 0%
% Non-smoking: 100%
% Air conditioned: 0%
Car parking: Yes
Wheelchair access: No
Non-animal tested toiletries: No
Insecticides used? No
Pets welcome? Dogs on leash may sleep in room.
Of animal origin: None
Nearby activities: Golf, bicycling, hiking, boating, horseback riding, beach
Description: An early Victorian ex-manse set on an acre of grounds between the Screel Hills and the sea. The house overlooks the bay and is a convenient center for touring Galloway, bird-watching, painting, golfing, pony trekking, and yachting. The nearby Ewart Library in Dunfries is excellent for tracing ancestry. Vegetarian and gluten-free diets are always available. Vegan and other special diets can be catered for with advance notice.
Forms of payment: *U.S. currency*—travelers checks; *Local currency*—cash; AX

JULIE & BRIAN NEATH

**Culag
Carr Brae
Dornie
Kyle, Ross-shire IV40 8HA Scotland
Phone: (44) 01599 555341**

Proprietor: Brian Neath
Category: Bed & Breakfast
Location: Woodland
Open all year? Closed over Christmas/ New Year only
Price: Inexpensive
Special packages: No
Reader discount: No
Child discount: Yes

MEALS

Included: B
Offered: B, D
% Vegetarian: 100%
% Vegan: 100%
% Organic: 10%
Special diets: Yes
Nearby restaurants: Yes

ROOMS

% Private bath/shower: 0%
% Non-smoking: 100%
% Air conditioned: 0%
Car parking: Yes
Wheelchair access: No
Non-animal tested toiletries: Yes
Insecticides used? No
Pets welcome? No
Of animal origin: Wool rugs
Nearby activities: Indoor pool, bicycling, hiking, boating, mountaineering
Description: Exclusively vegan bed & breakfast in modern bungalow

set amongst some of the finest scenery in the Scottish Highlands. Surrounded by native broad-leaved woodland with spectacular views of mountains and sea lochs from all rooms. Very quiet and relaxing. Warm, friendly welcome. Dairy milk is available for non-vegans, but soy milk is used for all cooking purposes.

Forms of payment: *Local currency*—cash, travelers checks

THE GREEN DOOR

**10 Greenhill Terrace
Edinburgh EH10 4BS Scotland
Phone: (44) 01314 470245**

Proprietor: Mr. & Mrs. Newall-Watson
Category: Bed & Breakfast
Location: City center
Open all year? Yes
Price: Inexpensive/Moderate
Special packages: Yes
Reader discount: 5%
Child discount: Yes

MEALS

Included: B
Offered: B, L, D
% Vegetarian: 100%
% Vegan: 30%
% Organic: 20%
Special diets: Yes
Nearby restaurants: Yes

ROOMS

% Private bath/shower: 0%
% Non-smoking: 100%
% Air conditioned: 0%
Car parking: Yes
Wheelchair access: No
Non-animal tested toiletries: No
Insecticides used? No
Pets welcome? No
Of animal origin: Wool rugs, down comforters, feather pillows
Nearby activities: Indoor pool, tennis, golf, bicycling, hiking, canoeing/kayaking, boating, water sports, downhill skiing, horseback riding, nutrition classes, camping, beach, yoga, fitness classes, exercise room, massage, juice fasting, weight loss classes, educational lectures, sightseeing tours, nightclub, antique shops, museums
Description: Situated in a central yet quiet, leafy, residential part of Edinburgh. We offer flexible accommodation with a family atmosphere in a large, traditional Victorian townhouse. Ideally located (buses, trains, etc.), it makes a perfect base from which to explore and enjoy the delights of this historic, enchanting city.
Forms of payment: *Local currency*—cash

MINTON HOUSE

Findhorn
Forres
Moray IV36 0YY Scotland
Phone: (44) 01309 690819
Fax: (44) 01309 691583

Proprietor: Judith Meynell
Category: Retreat, conference center
Location: Beachfront, quaint village
Open all year? Open April-December
Price: Moderate
Special packages: Yes
Reader discount: No
Child discount: Yes

MEALS

Included: B
Offered: B, D
% Vegetarian: 100%
% Vegan: 70%
% Organic: 60%
Special diets: Yes
Nearby restaurants: Yes

ROOMS

% Private bath/shower: 60%
% Non-smoking: 100%
% Air conditioned: 0%
Car parking: Yes
Wheelchair access: Yes
Non-animal tested toiletries: No
Insecticides used? No
Pets welcome? No
Of animal origin: Leather furniture, wool rugs, down comforters, feather pillows, farm animals
Nearby activities: Indoor pool, hiking, canoeing/kayaking, boating, water sports, horseback riding, camping, beach, yoga, massage,

educational lectures, sightseeing tours, Findhorn Foundation

Description: Minton House has been developed as a residential center and a retreat center honoring all the main spiritual traditions. It has become a haven particularly for stressed professional people who appreciate the opportunity to be still, nourish and renew the spirit, and rediscover their source of peace and inspiration.

Forms of payment: *Local currency*—cash, travelers checks

NEVIS VIEW

**14 Farrow Drive
Corpach
Fort William
Inverness-shire PH33 7JW Scotland
Phone: (44) 01397 772447
Fax: (44) 01397 772800**

Proprietor: Mrs. Barbara Grieve

Category: Bed & Breakfast

Location: Mountain, lakefront, quaint village

Open all year? Inquire directly

Price: Inexpensive

Special packages: No

Reader discount: 5% for 5+ days

Child discount: Yes

MEALS

Included: B

Offered: B, L, D

% Vegetarian: On request

% Vegan: On request

% Organic: Varies

Special diets: Inquire directly

Nearby restaurants: No

Comments: Packed lunches available

ROOMS

% Private bath/shower: 0%

% Non-smoking: 100%

% Air conditioned: 0%

Car parking: Yes

Wheelchair access: No

Non-animal tested toiletries: No

Insecticides used? No

Pets welcome? Yes

Of animal origin: None

Nearby activities: Indoor pool, golf, bicycling, hiking, cross-country skiing, downhill skiing, horseback riding, camping, fitness classes, museums

Description: A warm welcome awaits you. Quiet, located near Fort William. Well-equipped and comfortably furnished bedrooms. Superb views of the surrounding hills and lochs. An excellent base for exploring the local area.

Forms of payment: *Local currency*—cash, travelers checks; MC, VI

RHU MHOR GUEST HOUSE

Alma Road
Fort William
Inverness-shire PH33 6BP Scotland
Phone: (44) 01397 702213

Proprietor: Ian M. Macpherson
Category: Guest house
Location: Suburban

Open all year? Open Easter–October
Price: Inexpensive
Special packages: No
Reader discount: No
Child discount: Yes

MEALS

Included: B
Offered: B, D
% Vegetarian: On request
% Vegan: On request
% Organic: 5%
Special diets: Yes
Nearby restaurants: No

ROOMS

% Private bath/shower: 0%
% Non-smoking: 0%
% Air conditioned: 0%
Car parking: Yes

Wheelchair access: No
Non-animal tested toiletries: No
Insecticides used? No
Pets welcome? Yes
Of animal origin: Wool rugs, down comforters, feather pillows
Nearby activities: Indoor pool, tennis, golf, bicycling, hiking, boating, downhill skiing, horseback riding, camping, exercise room, sightseeing tours, museums
Description: Rhu Mhor, built in 1925, is situated within a steep acre of wild garden overlooking Loch Linnhe and the hills of Loch Fil. The house, which has been in our family since 1972, is just ten minutes' walk from the town center, railway station, and bus services.
Forms of payment: *Local currency*—cash, travelers checks

BALKISSOCK LODGE

Balkissock by Ballantrae
Ballantrae
Girvan
Ayrshire KA26 0LP Scotland
Phone/Fax: (44) 01645 831537

Proprietor: Janet & Adrian Beale
Category: Bed & Breakfast
Location: Countryside
Open all year? Yes
Price: Moderate
Special packages: Yes
Reader discount: 10%
Child discount: No

MEALS

Included: B, D

Offered: B, L, D
% Vegetarian: 33%
% Vegan: On request
% Organic: Varies
Special diets: Yes
Nearby restaurants: No

ROOMS

% Private bath/shower: 100%
% Non-smoking: 100%
% Air conditioned: 0%
Car parking: Yes
Wheelchair access: Yes
Non-animal tested toiletries: No
Insecticides used? No
Pets welcome? No
Of animal origin: None
Nearby activities: Indoor pool, tennis, golf, hiking, beach
Description: At least 200 years old, this charming lodge is delightfully situated in the hills above

the coastal village of Ballantrae. This peaceful "off the beaten track" location is much sought by nature and country lovers and convenient for numerous golf courses and the Irish ferry. Taste of Scotland recommended.

Forms of payment: *U.S. currency*—cash; *Local currency*—cash, travelers checks; MC, VI

BAILLEBOIDEACH

4 Lephin
Glendale
Isle of Skye IV55 8WJ Scotland
Phone: (44) 01470 511376

Proprietor: Janet Kernachan
Category: Bed & Breakfast
Location: Quaint village
Open all year? Open March–Sept.
Price: Inexpensive
Special packages: No
Reader discount: 10% for 2+ nights
Child discount: Yes

MEALS

Included: B

Offered: B, D
% Vegetarian: On request
% Vegan: 0%
% Organic: 0%
Special diets: Yes
Nearby restaurants: Yes

ROOMS

% Private bath/shower: 0%
% Non-smoking: 100%
% Air conditioned: 0%
Car parking: Yes
Wheelchair access: No
Non-animal tested toiletries: No
Insecticides used? No
Pets welcome? Yes

Of animal origin: Feather pillows, farm animals

Nearby activities: Indoor pool, golf, bicycling, hiking, canoeing/ kayaking, boating, snorkeling, scuba diving, water sports, horseback riding, camping, beach, fitness classes, exercise room, massage, antique shops, museums, castles, distillery, birdwatching

BAILLEBQIDEACH

Description: Warm, friendly welcome at our modern crofthouse situated in scattered township in lovely glen with view to Outer Hebrides. Ample scope for walking, bird-watching, museums. Seven miles from Dunnegan Castle, home of clan Macleod. French/German spoken.

Forms of payment: *Local currency*—cash, travelers checks

GLENDALE VEGETARIAN GUEST HOUSE

Mandally
Invergarry
Inverness-shire PH35 4HP Scotland
Phone: (44) 01809 501282

Proprietor: Michelle Riers

Category: Guest house

Location: Mountain, quaint village

Open all year? Yes

Price: Inexpensive

Special packages: Yes

Reader discount: No

Child discount: Yes

MEALS

Included: B

Offered: B, L, D

% Vegetarian: 100%

% Vegan: 50%

% Organic: 25%

Special diets: Yes

Nearby restaurants: No

ROOMS

% Private bath/shower: 20%

% Non-smoking: 0%

% Air conditioned: 0%

Car parking: Yes

Wheelchair access: Yes

Non-animal tested toiletries: Yes

Insecticides used? No

Pets welcome? Yes

Of animal origin: None

Nearby activities: Indoor pool, tennis, golf, bicycling, hiking, canoeing/kayaking, boating, snorkeling, scuba diving, water sports, cross-country skiing, downhill skiing, horseback riding, camping, sightseeing tours, antique shops, museums, guided walks, castles, climbing

Description: Excellent vegan/vegetarian Scottish and international cuisine prepared by our trained vegetarian chef in our spacious and comfortable guest house, set amidst glorious Highland scenery. Great walking and sightseeing country with castles, hills, lochs, waterfalls, and diverse wildlife in abundance. Warm welcome.

Forms of payment: *Local currency*—cash, travelers checks

RAASAY OUTDOOR CENTRE

**Raasay House
Isle of Raasay by Kyle
Ross-shire IV40 8PB Scotland
Phone: (44) 0147 8660 266
Fax: (44) 0147 8660 200**

Proprietor: Lyn Rowe
Category: Outdoor adventure
Location: Beachfront, mountain, island
Open all year? Open April–October
Price: Moderate
Special packages: No
Reader discount: No
Child discount: Yes

MEALS

Included: B, L, D
Offered: B, L, D
% Vegetarian: On request
% Vegan: On request
% Organic: 10%
Special diets: Yes
Nearby restaurants: No

ROOMS

% Private bath/shower: 0%
% Non-smoking: 90%
% Air conditioned: 0%

Car parking: Yes
Wheelchair access: No
Non-animal tested toiletries: No
Insecticides used? No
Pets welcome? Yes
Of animal origin: Feather pillows
Nearby activities: Hiking, canoeing/kayaking, boating, water sports, camping
Description: Raasay is a small, close-knit crofting community which extends a warm welcome to visitors. Raasay abounds with wildlife and plants and features of archeological interest. Discover this island through the many walking tours, from 20 minutes to 2-1/2 hours.

Forms of payment: *Local currency*—cash

CHORAIDH CROFT FARM PARK

**94 Laid
Loch Eriboll Side, via Altnaharra
Lairg, Sutherland IV27 4UN Scotland
Phone: (44) 01971 511235**

Proprietor: Lesley Smith
Category: Bed & Breakfast
Location: Sea loch
Open all year? Open Easter–Nov.; or by advance booking only
Price: Moderate
Special packages: Yes
Reader discount: Inquire directly
Child discount: Yes

MEALS

Included: B
Offered: B, L, D
% Vegetarian: 20%
% Vegan: On request

% Organic: 2%

Special diets: Yes

Nearby restaurants: Yes

ROOMS

% Private bath/shower: 33%

% Non-smoking: 100%

% Air conditioned: 0%

Car parking: Yes

Wheelchair access: No

Non-animal tested toiletries: No

Insecticides used? No

Pets welcome? No

Of animal origin: Farm animals, feather pillows, wool rugs, live caged animals/birds

Nearby activities: Golf, bicycling, hiking, snorkeling, camping, beach, sightseeing tours, museums, craft shops

Description: Modern bungalow on Scotland's most northerly farm park. See over 40 breeds of animals, the crofting museum, and the cuddle corner—for close encounters of the furry kind. Delicious home baking and tempting meals available in the tea room. Perfect venue for artists, photographers, bird and animal enthusiasts of all ages.

Forms of payment: *Local currency*—cash, travelers checks

....

LINNE MHUIRICH

**Unapool, Croft Road
Kylesku Via Lairg
Sutherland IV27 4HW Scotland
Phone: (44) 01971 502227**

Proprietor: Fiona MacAulay

Category: Bed & Breakfast

Location: Quaint village, lochside

Open all year? Open Easter–November; other times by arrangement only

Price: Moderate

Special packages: Yes

Reader discount: For one week+; inquire

Child discount: Yes

MEALS

Included: B

Offered: B, L, D

% Vegetarian: See description

% Vegan: 0%

% Organic: As available

Special diets: None

Nearby restaurants: No

ROOMS

% Private bath/shower: 33%

% Non-smoking: 100%

% Air conditioned: 0%

Car parking: Yes

Wheelchair access: No

Non-animal tested toiletries: Yes

Insecticides used? No

Pets welcome? Yes

Of animal origin: Feather pillows, farm animals, wool rugs

Nearby activities: Hiking, beach

Description: Fiona and Diarmid MacAulay welcome non-smokers to their modern crofthouse, superbly situated on a hillside overlooking Loch Glencoul. Guests return annually for the comfort, attention, peace, and delicious "Taste of Scotland" food. Fiona has attended the Vegetarian Cookery School. Beverage trays in bedrooms. We provide 100% vegetarian meals if we have resident vegetarians. We also provide meat and fish for other guests. We do not feel able to cater for vegans, but are highly regarded by vegetarians.

Forms of payment: *Local currency*—cash, travelers checks

GORDON ARMS HOTEL

**Kincardine O'Neil
Royal Deeside
Aberdeenshire AB34 5AA Scotland
Phone: (44) 013398 84236
Fax: (44) 013398 84401**

Proprietor: Bryn Wayte
Category: Hotel
Location: Quaint village
Open all year? Yes
Price: Moderate
Special packages: Yes
Reader discount: 10%
Child discount: Yes

MEALS

Included: B
Offered: B, L, D

% Vegetarian: 20%
% Vegan: 15%
% Organic: 15%
Special diets: Yes
Nearby restaurants: No

ROOMS

% Private bath/shower: 90%
% Non-smoking: 0%
% Air conditioned: 0%
Car parking: Yes
Wheelchair access: No
Non-animal tested toiletries: No
Insecticides used? No
Pets welcome? Yes
Of animal origin: None

Nearby activities: Tennis, golf, bicycling, hiking, horseback riding, antique shops

Description: Small family-run hotel in the oldest village on Royal Deeside, set amidst beautiful scenery and numerous castles. Former Victorian coach inn with many period antiques.

Extensive menus include vegetarian and vegan, organic wines, and real ales. Comfortable en-suite rooms. Scottish Tourist Board 3 crowns.

Forms of payment: *Local currency*—cash, travelers checks; AX, MC, VI

QUIRAING LODGE

Staffin
Isle of Skye IV51 9JS Scotland
Phone: (44) 01470 562330

Proprietor: Kate Money
Category: B&B, retreat
Location: Beachfront, mountain
Open all year? Yes
Price: Moderate
Special packages: No
Reader discount: No
Child discount: Yes

MEALS

Included: B
Offered: B, L, D
% Vegetarian: 100%
% Vegan: 50%
% Organic: 10%
Special diets: Yes
Nearby restaurants: Yes

ROOMS

% Private bath/shower: 0%
% Non-smoking: 100%
% Air conditioned: 0%
Car parking: Yes
Wheelchair access: No
Non-animal tested toiletries: No
Insecticides used? No
Pets welcome? Outdoors only

Of animal origin: Wool rugs
Nearby activities: Bicycling, hiking, meditation and retreat facilities
Description: Warm and welcoming family atmosphere. Spectacular scenic location offering a tranquil base from which to explore the beauty and magic of Skye. Built in 1850 and surrounded by an acre of garden, the house is situated on the shore with river and mountain close by.
Forms of payment: *Local currency*—cash, travelers checks

JENNY'S BOTHY

Dellachuper
Corgarff
Strathdon
Aberdeenshire AB36 8YP Scotland
Phone: (44) 019756 51446 or (44) 019756 51449

Proprietor: Jenny Smith
Category: Retreat
Location: Mountain
Open all year? Yes

Price: Inquire
Special packages: No
Reader discount: 10%
Child discount: Yes

MEALS

Included: Self-catering
Offered: N/A
% Vegetarian: N/A
% Vegan: N/A
% Organic: N/A
Special diets: N/A
Nearby restaurants: Yes

ROOMS

% Private bath/shower: 50%
% Non-smoking: 0%
% Air conditioned: 0%
Car parking: Yes
Wheelchair access: No
Non-animal tested toiletries: No
Insecticides used? No
Pets welcome? Yes
Of animal origin: Wool rugs
Nearby activities: Bicycling, hiking, canoeing/kayaking, cross-country skiing, downhill skiing, horseback riding, camping, massage, museums

Description: Situated in an area of outstanding natural beauty, Jenny's Bothy is a rustic camp, comprising one large and one smaller room. Wood-burning stove, kitchen facilities, shower and WC. Ideal for individuals, families, and small groups. Paradise for children. Downhill and cross-country skiing in winter. Suitable as a quiet retreat.

Forms of payment: *Local currency*—cash

THE CENTRE OF LIGHT

**Tigh Na Bruaich
Struy, By Beauly
Inverness-shire IV4 7JU Scotland
Phone: (44) 01463 761254
Fax: (44) 01463 761247**

Proprietor: Linda Christie
Category: Retreat
Location: Mountain
Open all year? Yes
Price: Moderate
Special packages: No
Reader discount: No
Child discount: No

MEALS

Included: B, L, D
Offered: B, L, D
% Vegetarian: 100%
% Vegan: 50%
% Organic: 60%
Special diets: Yes
Nearby restaurants: Yes

ROOMS

% Private bath/shower: 0%

% Non-smoking: 100%

% Air conditioned: 0%

Car parking: Yes

Wheelchair access: No

Non-animal tested toiletries: Yes

Insecticides used? No

Pets welcome? No

Of animal origin: Wool rugs, down comforters, feather pillows

Nearby activities: Meditation, therapy, healing

Description: Be nourished by nature and get clear guidance on how to create a more positive and happy life. Workshops and retreats in meditation, color healing, and therapy are held in the peaceful, natural surroundings of the Highlands.

Forms of payment: *U.S. currency*—cash; *Local currency*—cash

BED AND BREAKFAST

**3 Castle Terrace
Ullapool
Ross-shire IV26 2XD Scotland
Phone: (44) 01854 612409**

Proprietor: Penny Ross Browne

Category: Bed & Breakfast

Location: Beachfront, mountain, quaint village

Open all year? Open May–Oct.

Price: Moderate

Special packages: No

Reader discount: 5% except August

Child discount: Yes

MEALS

Included: B

Offered: B

% Vegetarian: 100%

% Vegan: On request

% Organic: 20%

Special diets: Yes

Nearby restaurants: Yes

ROOMS

% Private bath/shower: 0%

% Non-smoking: 100%

% Air conditioned: 0%

Car parking: Yes

Wheelchair access: No

Non-animal tested toiletries: Yes

Insecticides used? No

Pets welcome? Yes

Of animal origin: Wool rugs

Nearby activities: Indoor pool, golf, bicycling, hiking, boating, camping, beach, sightseeing tours, antique shops, museums, mountaineering, exercise room, geological interest

Description: Bungalow set in a quiet part of fishing village has magnificent views of a mountain, the Summer Isles, and sunset. Clean pretty rooms, centrally heated with family atmosphere. Garden available. Informative, hospitable hostess serves delicious vegetarian-only breakfasts with homemade jams, fruit, etc.

Forms of payment: *Local currency*—cash, travelers checks

THE CEILIDH PLACE

**West Argyle St.
Ullapool
Ross-shire IV26 2TY Scotland
Phone: (44) 01854 612103
Fax: (44) 01854 612886**

Proprietor: Jean Urquhart

Category: Hotel

Location: Quaint village

Open all year? Yes

Price: Inexpensive/Expensive

Special packages: Yes

Reader discount: No

Child discount: Yes

MEALS

Included: B

Offered: B, L, D

% Vegetarian: 50%

% Vegan: 10%

% Organic: 20%

Special diets: Yes

Nearby restaurants: No

ROOMS

% Private bath/shower: 40%

% Non-smoking: 5%

% Air conditioned: 0%

Car parking: Yes

Wheelchair access: No

Non-animal tested toiletries: Yes

Insecticides used? No

Pets welcome? Yes

Of animal origin: Feather pillows, wool rugs

Nearby activities: Indoor pool, tennis, bicycling, hiking, canoeing/kayaking, boating, snorkeling, camping, beach, fitness classes, exercise room, massage, theater

Description: We aim to be environmentally friendly. I am vegetarian as are many of the staff. We are a small, lovely complex with food, sitting room, bookshop, cultural activities, art exhibitions, hotel, bunkhouse, bakery, and drapers shop!

Forms of payment: *U.S. currency*—cash, travelers checks; *Local currency*—cash, travelers checks; AX, MC, VI, Diners Club, Switch

TAIGH NA MARA

**The Shore
Ardindrean
Loch Broom
Ullapool IV23 2SE Scotland
Phone/Fax: (44) 01854 655282**

Proprietor: Jackie & Tony Weston

Category: Retreat, hotel

Location: Beachfront, mountain, lakefront

Open all year? Yes

Price: Moderate

Special packages: No

Reader discount: 10% off season

Child discount: Yes

MEALS

Included: B, D

Offered: B, L, D

% Vegetarian: 100%

% Vegan: 100%

% Organic: 50%

Special diets: Yes

Nearby restaurants: Yes

ROOMS

% Private bath/shower: 33%

% Non-smoking: 100%

% Air conditioned: 0%

Car parking: Yes

Wheelchair access: No

Non-animal tested toiletries: Yes

Insecticides used? No

Pets welcome? Yes

Of animal origin: None

Nearby activities: Indoor pool, tennis, golf, bicycling, hiking, canoeing/kayaking, boating, snorkeling, scuba diving, water sports, camping, beach, sightseeing tours, antique shops, museums

Description: Voted Vegetarian Hotel of the Year for location, service, and creative cooking, this secluded and idyllic lochside home is also the Vegetarian Information Centre for the Highlands. Tony and Jackie have recently published a book which captures the enchantment of Highland life called *Rainbows & Wellies—The Taigh Na Mara Cookbook.*

Forms of payment: *Local currency*—cash, travelers checks; MC, VI, Switch, Delta

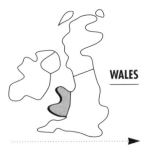

WALES

DINMOR GUEST HOUSE

**Penmon, Beaumaris
Anglesey
Gwynedd LL58 8SN Wales
Phone: (44) 01248 490395**

Proprietor: Mary Korn
Category: Bed & Breakfast
Location: Beachfront, mountain
Open all year? Yes
Price: Inexpensive
Special packages: Yes
Reader discount: No
Child discount: Yes

MEALS

Included: B
Offered: B
% Vegetarian: 100%
% Vegan: 50%
% Organic: 20%
Special diets: Yes
Nearby restaurants: Yes

ROOMS

% Private bath/shower: 60%

% Non-smoking: 60%
% Air conditioned: 0%
Car parking: Yes
Wheelchair access: No
Non-animal tested toiletries: No
Insecticides used? No
Pets welcome? Yes
Of animal origin: Feather pillows, wool rugs
Nearby activities: Indoor pool, golf, bicycling, hiking, canoeing/kayaking, boating, horseback riding, beach, museums
Description: None provided.
Forms of payment: *Local currency*—cash, travelers checks

HEAD FOR THE HILLS

**Garth
Builth
Powys Wales
Phone: (44) 01591 620388**

Proprietor: Laurence Golding
Category: Outdoor adventure
Location: Mountain, quaint village, lakefront
Open all year? Open Easter–Oct.
Price: Inexpensive
Special packages: Yes
Reader discount: 10%
Child discount: Yes

MEALS

Included: B, L, D
Offered: B, L, D
% Vegetarian: 100%
% Vegan: On request
% Organic: 15%
Special diets: Yes

Nearby restaurants: No

ROOMS

% Private bath/shower: N/A

% Non-smoking: N/A

% Air conditioned: N/A

Car parking: No

Wheelchair access: No

Non-animal tested toiletries: Yes

Insecticides used? No

Pets welcome? No

Of animal origin: Wool rugs

Nearby activities: Hiking, camping

Description: Disappear into the landscape for several days with a small guided group of walkers. Using ancient, often forgotten trails we penetrate the past and have adventures with nature in Wales and England. Staff travel ahead with luggage and a superb camp (with personal tents) and prepare our famous vegetarian cuisine.

Forms of payment: *U.S. currency*—personal checks; *Local currency*—cash, travelers checks

BICYCLE BEANO

Erwood
Builth Wells
Powys LD2 3PQ Wales
Phone: (44) 01982 560471

Proprietor: Jane Barnes & Rob Green

Category: Outdoor adventure

Location: ·Various venues

Open all year? Open Easter–Sept.

Price: Moderate

Special packages: Yes

Reader discount: No

Child discount: Yes

MEALS

Included: B, D

Offered: B, D

% Vegetarian: 100%

% Vegan: 5%

% Organic: 20%

Special diets: Yes

Nearby restaurants: No

ROOMS

% Private bath/shower: 50%

% Non-smoking: 100%

% Air conditioned: 0%

Car parking: Yes

Wheelchair access: Yes

Non-animal tested toiletries: No

Insecticides used? No

Pets welcome? No

Of animal origin: Varies

Nearby activities: Indoor pool, bicycling, hiking, canoeing/kayaking, boating, horseback riding, camping, beach, sightseeing tours, antique shops, museums, volleyball, juggling, unicycling

Description: Really special cycling holidays in mid-Wales, Pembrokeshire coast, and the unspoiled Welsh border country. Exclusively whole food vegetarian cuisine and spectacular non-macho rides. Stay in such fantastic venues as an Elizabethan castle, a traditional Welsh tavern, or a stately home, etc. Guided groups, detailed route sheets, bike mechanic. All on peaceful, beautiful lanes.

Forms of payment: *Local currency*—cash, travelers checks

PENTRE BACH

**Llwyngwril
Near Dolgellau
Gwynedd LL37 2JU Wales
Phone: (44) 01341 250294
Fax: (44) 01341 250885**

Proprietor: Nick and Margaret Smyth
Category: Bed & Breakfast
Location: Mountain,
quaint village
Open all year? Yes
Price: Moderate
Special packages: No
Reader discount: No
Child discount: No

MEALS

Included: B
Offered: B, L, D
% Vegetarian: 66%
% Vegan: 33%
% Organic: 80%
Special diets: Yes
Nearby restaurants: No

ROOMS

% Private bath/shower: 100%
% Non-smoking: 100%
% Air conditioned: 0%
Car parking: Yes
Wheelchair access: No
Non-animal tested toiletries: Yes
Insecticides used? No
Pets welcome? No
Of animal origin: Wool rugs, farm
animals
Nearby activities: Indoor pool, tennis,
golf, bicycling, hiking, canoeing/
kayaking, boating, horseback
riding, camping, beach, sight-

seeing tours, antique shops,
table tennis, croquet

Description: Relax in our large, warm,
peaceful farmhouse, breakfast
whenever you choose, enjoy
fresh air and spectacular
scenery of mountains and sea
on the doorstep. Return to can-
dlelit dinner prepared by mid-
Wales Cook of the Year 1994.

We have our own free-range
eggs and organic produce.
Castles, steam railways nearby.
Local train station and bus
service.

Forms of payment: *Local currency*—cash,
travelers checks; MC, VI

BUCK FARM

**Hanmer
Clwyd SY14 7LX Wales
Phone: (44) 01948 830339**

Proprietor: Cedric E. Sumner
Category: Bed & Breakfast
Location: Quaint village
Open all year? Yes
Price: Moderate
Special packages: No
Reader discount: No
Child discount: Yes

MEALS

Included: B
Offered: B, L, D
% Vegetarian: 30%
% Vegan: 3%
% Organic: 50%
Special diets: By prior arrangement only
Nearby restaurants: No

ROOMS

% Private bath/shower: 33%
% Non-smoking: 100%
% Air conditioned: 0%
Car parking: Yes
Wheelchair access: Yes
Non-animal tested toiletries: No
Insecticides used? No
Pets welcome? See comments
Of animal origin: Feather pillows, farm animals, wool rugs, down comforters
Nearby activities: Indoor pool, golf, hiking, sightseeing tours, antique shops, museums, walking on country lanes and public footpaths
Description: Our simple yet sophisticated Tudor farmhouse is well known for its excellent vegetarian and non-vegetarian country cooking. Vegans and others on special diets also eat well here. Gardens, woodland, books, music. Within easy reach of Chester. An outstanding touring base for North Wales and the Welsh border country. No smoking.
Forms of payment: *Local currency*—cash, travelers checks

Comments: Picnic lunches available. Pets allowed by arrangement but never in the house.

CYFEILIOG GUEST HOUSE

**Bont Dolgadfan
Llanbrynmair
Powys SY19 7BB Wales
Phone: (44) 01650-521231**

Proprietor: A. and E. Fox
Category: Guest house
Location: Quaint village, riverside
Open all year? Yes
Price: Inexpensive
Special packages: No
Reader discount: No
Child discount: Yes

MEALS

Included: B, D
Offered: B, D
% Vegetarian: On request
% Vegan: On request
% Organic: 50%
Special diets: On request

Nearby restaurants: No

ROOMS

% Private bath/shower: 33%

% Non-smoking: 100%

% Air conditioned: 0%

Car parking: Yes

Wheelchair access: No

Non-animal tested toiletries: No

Insecticides used? No

Pets welcome? No

Of animal origin: Feather pillows, wool rugs

Nearby activities: Indoor pool, tennis, golf, bicycling, hiking, canoeing/kayaking, water sports, horseback riding, beach, sightseeing tours, antique shops, museums, Centre for Alternative Technology

Description: Liz & Andrew Fox invite you to share their 18th century beamed home in the unspoiled countryside of mid Wales. Ideal for touring or just relaxing. Vegetarian and vegan cuisine our specialty. Home-grown vegetables, wine list. Ideal area for walkers, bird-watchers, naturalists, artists, and those who love the countryside. The villages and towns are welcoming with craft shops and interesting features recording their history.

Forms of payment: *Local currency*—cash, travelers checks

GWALIA

Cemmaes
Machynlleth
Powys SY20 9PU Wales
Phone: (44) 01650-511377

Proprietor: Olivia & Harry Chandler

Category: Bed & Breakfast

Location: Mountain, countryside

Open all year? Yes

Price: Inexpensive

Special packages: No

Reader discount: No

Child discount: Yes

MEALS

Included: B

Offered: B, D

% Vegetarian: 100%

% Vegan: 50%

% Organic: 90%

Special diets: Yes

Nearby restaurants: Yes

ROOMS

% Private bath/shower: 0%

% Non-smoking: 100%

% Air conditioned: 0%

Car parking: Yes

Wheelchair access: No

Non-animal tested toiletries: Yes

Insecticides used? No

Pets welcome? Yes

Of animal origin: Feather pillows, farm animals

Nearby activities: Bicycling, hiking, canoeing/kayaking, massage

Description: Gwalia is a small family farm, 700 feet up in the Welsh hills overlooking the mountains of Southern Snowdonia. We produce our own organic vegetables, fruit, eggs, milk, yoghurt, home-baked bread, jam, and marmalade, and we cook wholesome whole food meals. Guests enjoy their own sitting room with a log fire and spring water. We have a small lake in a conservation area for swimming and canoeing. The unspoiled area is excellent for bird and badger watching and walking. The Centre for Alternative Technology is nine miles away.

Forms of payment: *Local currency*—cash

THE OLD RECTORY HOTEL

Maentwrog
Gwynedd LL41 4HN Wales
Phone: (44) 01766 590305

Proprietor: Sue Herbert

Category: B&B, hotel

Location: Mountain

Open all year? Yes; restaurant seasonal

Price: Inexpensive

Special packages: Yes

Reader discount: No

Child discount: Yes

MEALS

Included: B

Offered: B, L, D

% Vegetarian: 50%

% Vegan: 10%

% Organic: 10%

Special diets: Yes

Nearby restaurants: No

ROOMS

% Private bath/shower: 100%

% Non-smoking: 100%

% Air conditioned: 0%

Car parking: Yes

Wheelchair access: No

Non-animal tested toiletries: Yes

Insecticides used? No

Pets welcome? Yes

Of animal origin: Leather furniture, feather pillows, wool rugs

Nearby activities: Hiking, canoeing/kayaking, water sports, horseback riding, camping, beach

Description: The Old Rectory Hotel stands on its own grounds in the delightful Vale of Ffestiniog in the village of Maentwrog. The whole atmosphere is one of peaceful existence. The Old Rectory is over 400 years old. Main house or budget annex rooms are all en-suite with tea facilities. Home-cooked vegetarian food is available by advance order (restaurant seasonal). Weekly discounts.

Forms of payment: *Local currency*—cash, travelers checks; VI

WARPOOL COURT HOTEL

St. Davids
Pembrokeshire SA62 6BN Wales
Phone: (44) 01437-720300
Fax: (44) 01437-720676

Proprietor: Peter Trier
Category: Hotel
Location: Quaint village
Open all year? Open February to December
Price: Moderate
Special packages: Yes
Reader discount: No
Child discount: Yes

MEALS

Included: B, D
Offered: B, L, D
% Vegetarian: 25%

% Vegan: 2%
% Organic: 5%
Special diets: Yes
Nearby restaurants: Yes

ROOMS

% Private bath/shower: 100%
% Non-smoking: 0%
% Air conditioned: 0%
Car parking: Yes
Wheelchair access: No
Non-animal tested toiletries: No
Insecticides used? No
Pets welcome? Yes
Of animal origin: Feather pillows

Nearby activities: Indoor pool, tennis, golf, bicycling, hiking, canoeing/kayaking, boating, water sports, horseback riding, beach, exercise room

Description: Privately owned 25-bedroom hotel overlooking St. Brides bay and islands beyond. Set in 7 acres with easy access to the coastal path, St. Davids Cathedral, and the Bishops Palace. Sandy beaches and castles abound in the area which is also well-known for its wide variety of wildlife. The hotel has an award-winning restaurant.

Forms of payment: *Local currency*—cash, travelers checks; AX, MC, VI, Diners Club

DAFS GUESTHOUSE

116 Bryn Rd.
Brynmill
Swansea
West Glamorgan SA2 0AT Wales
Phone/Fax: (44) 01792 475731

Proprietor: Denice Feben-Smith

Category: Bed & Breakfast

Location: Beachfront, near city center

Open all year? Yes

Price: Inexpensive

Special packages: Yes

Reader discount: 10%

Child discount: Yes

MEALS

Included: B

Offered: B, D

% Vegetarian: 75%

% Vegan: 5%

% Organic: 0%

Special diets: Yes

Nearby restaurants: No

ROOMS

% Private bath/shower: 0%

% Non-smoking: 100%

% Air conditioned: 0%

Car parking: On street

Wheelchair access: No

Non-animal tested toiletries: No

Insecticides used? No

Pets welcome? No

Of animal origin: 3 cats

Nearby activities: Indoor pool, tennis, golf, bicycling, hiking, water sports, horseback riding, camping, beach, yoga, fitness classes, exercise room, massage, weight loss classes, educational lectures, sightseeing tours, nightclub, antique shops, museums, historic castles, cave complex

Description: Experience the culture and history of Wales and the outstanding natural beauty of the Gower, Swansea, birthplace of Dylan Thomas. Historic castles, unspoiled golden

beaches, colorful parks, spectacular coastal cliffs, and wild moorland pony herds. Great walking, riding, and cycling country. E-mail to afswales @cix.compulink.co.uk.

Forms of payment: *Local currency*—cash

TREMEIFION VEGETARIAN HOTEL

**Soar Road
Talsarnau
Gwynedd LL47 6UH Wales
Phone: (44) 01766 770491**

Proprietor: Maureen Jackson

Category: Hotel

Location: Beachfront, mountain, estuary

Open all year? Yes, except early January.

Price: Moderate

Special packages: Yes

Reader discount: 5%

Child discount: Yes

MEALS

Included: B, D

Offered: B, D

% Vegetarian: 100%

% Vegan: 50%

% Organic: 10%

Special diets: Yes

Nearby restaurants: No

ROOMS

% Private bath/shower: 100%

% Non-smoking: 100%

% Air conditioned: 0%

Car parking: Yes

Wheelchair access: No

Non-animal tested toiletries: Yes

Insecticides used? No

Pets welcome? Yes

Of animal origin: Wool rugs

Nearby activities: Golf, hiking, horseback riding, camping, beach, castles, slate mines

Description: Tremeifion has spectacular views over the river estuary and the Snowdonia mountain range. Excellent home-cooked vegetarian cuisine, organic wines available. Relaxing and peaceful environment within three acres of private land. Non-smoking throughout. Ideal access to beaches and mountain walks.

Forms of payment: *Local currency*—cash, travelers checks

Comments: Winter weekends special price. Inquire.

WOLFSCASTLE POTTERY

Wolfcastle
Pembrokeshire SA62 5LZ Wales
Phone/Fax: (44) 01437 741609

Proprietor: Philip Cunningham
Category: Retreat
Location: Quaint village
Open all year? Open Easter-October.
Price: Moderate
Special packages: Yes
Reader discount: 5%
Child discount: No

MEALS

Included: B, L, D
Offered: B, L, D
% Vegetarian: 75%
% Vegan: 10%
% Organic: 90%
Special diets: Yes
Nearby restaurants: Yes

ROOMS

% Private bath/shower: 0%
% Non-smoking: 100%
% Air conditioned: 0%
Car parking: Yes
Wheelchair access: No
Non-animal tested toiletries: Yes
Insecticides used? No
Pets welcome? No
Of animal origin: None
Nearby activities: Indoor pool, tennis, golf, bicycling, hiking, canoeing/kayaking, boating, snorkeling, scuba diving, water sports, beach, yoga, fitness classes, massage, sightseeing tours, pottery classes
Description: An idyllic setting. The

Pottery is in a sheltered tranquil valley, the home of Maddy and Phillip Cunningham. A warm atmosphere to make new friends, have fun, develop new interests and skills. Courses in pottery-making, Swedish massage, aromatherapy, and yoga are offered. Surfing, snorkeling, rock climbing, tennis, or just relaxing are other options.

Guests stay in a Welsh stone cottage adjoining the main house. The food is delicious, healthy, and professionally prepared using organic vegetables and fruit from our garden.

Forms of payment: *Local currency*—cash, travelers checks; MC, VI

IRELAND

BOG VIEW HOSTEL

**Lougher
Inch
Annascaul
Co. Kerry, Ireland
Phone/Fax: (353) 066 58125**

Proprietor: Susan Barrett and
  John Coakley
Category: Self-catering hotel
Location: Mountain, quaint village
Open all year? Open May–October
Price: Inexpensive
Special packages: Yes
Reader discount: 10%
Child discount: Yes

MEALS

Included: None
Offered: B
% Vegetarian: 90%
% Vegan: 40%
% Organic: 70%
Special diets: Yes
Nearby restaurants: Yes
Comments: Will also cook
  meals with advance notice

ROOMS

% Private bath/shower: 0%
% Non-smoking: 100%
% Air conditioned: 0%
Car parking: Yes
Wheelchair access: Yes
Non-animal tested toiletries: No
Insecticides used? No
Pets welcome? No
Of animal origin: Farm animals, feath-
  er pillows
Nearby activities: Indoor pool, golf,
  bicycling, hiking, canoeing/
kayaking, boating, water sports,
horseback riding, nutrition
classes, beach, yoga, fitness
classes, massage, sightseeing
tours, museums
Description: Bog View Hostel is
  small, friendly and cozy.
  Accommodation is provided
  in dorms or private rooms and
  our large garden offers opportunities for outdoor games. John
  and Susan offer good, friendly
  Irish hospitality.
Forms of payment: *Local currency*—cash

BAVARIA HOUSE

**Garrymore
Ballinagh
Co. Cavan, Ireland
Phone: (353) 049 37452**

Proprietor: Ilse Kiebler
Category: Bed & Breakfast
Location: Quaint village
Open all year? Open Apr.–Oct.
Price: Moderate
Special packages: No
Reader discount: No

Child discount: No

MEALS

Included: B
Offered: B, L, D
% Vegetarian: 95%
% Vegan: 5%
% Organic: 98%
Special diets: Yes
Nearby restaurants: No

ROOMS

% Private bath/shower: 33%
% Non-smoking: 100%
% Air conditioned: 0%
Car parking: Yes
Wheelchair access: No
Non-animal tested toiletries: No
Insecticides used? No
Pets welcome? No
Of animal origin: None
Nearby activities: Outdoor pool, tennis, golf, bicycling, boating, horseback riding, fitness classes, exercise room, massage, sightseeing tours, nightclub, antique shops, museums
Description: Bavaria House is a 19th century home with a unique atmosphere, ideal for relaxation. It is also a central point to discover the historical places of Ireland. We love cooking and serve superb and healthy food with our own organically grown vegetables, fruits, and herbs. We are environmentally friendly, cater for vegetarians, vegans, fruitarians, and gluten-free. English and German spoken.
Forms of payment: *Local currency*—cash

MURRAY'S FARMHOUSE

**Knockmoyleen
Ballycroy
Co. Mayo, Ireland
Phone: (353) 098 49120**

Proprietor: Sheila & John Murray
Category: Bed & Breakfast
Location: Mountain, quaint village
Open all year? Yes, except Christmas
Price: Inexpensive
Special packages: No
Reader discount: No
Child discount: Yes

MEALS

Included: B, D
Offered: B, D
% Vegetarian: 75%
% Vegan: 10%
% Organic: 75%
Special diets: Yes
Nearby restaurants: No

ROOMS

% Private bath/shower: 0%
% Non-smoking: 100%
% Air conditioned: 0%
Car parking: Yes
Wheelchair access: No
Non-animal tested toiletries: Yes
Insecticides used? No
Pets welcome? Yes
Of animal origin: Farm animals
Nearby activities: Golf, bicycling, hiking, horseback riding, bio-dynamic clinic
Description: Between the Wephin Mountains and the sea lies our cozy farmhouse—famous for its organically grown fruit and

MURRAY'S FARMHOUSE

vegetables, whole meal bread, preserves, and country wines. Explore spectacular Achill Island and Mulranny with its riding stables and sandy beaches, Westport, Ceide Fields, Bellacorick Bog train, Killala and Bio-Dynamic Clinic.

Forms of payment: *Local currency*—cash

GREEN LODGE

Trawnamadree
Ballylickey
Bantry
Co. Cork, Ireland
Phone: (353) 027 66146

Proprietor: Chris Domegan
Category: Self-catering
Location: Quaint village
Open all year? Yes
Price: Inexpensive
Special packages: No
Reader discount: No

Child discount: Yes

MEALS

Included: None
Offered: None
% Vegetarian: N/A
% Vegan: N/A
% Organic: N/A
Special diets: N/A
Nearby restaurants: Yes
Comments: Vegan wholefoods and organic home-grown vegetables are available on site

ROOMS

% Private bath/shower: 100%
% Non-smoking: 0%
% Air conditioned: 0%
Car parking: Yes
Wheelchair access: Yes
Non-animal tested toiletries: Yes
Insecticides used? No
Pets welcome? No
Of animal origin: None
Nearby activities: Golf, bicycling, hiking, canoeing/kayaking, boating,

horseback riding, camping, beach, paragliding, ancient mystical and sacred sites

Description: Situated in a beautiful part of West Cork, peaceful yet convenient, 8km from Bantry Town and 3km from the coast. Accommodation is in a single-story terrace in an enclosed courtyard next to a lovely mature garden amidst 10 acres of semi-wooded grounds. Organic orchard and garden.

Forms of payment: *Local currency*—cash, travelers checks

CHRYSALIS

**Donard
Co. Wicklow, Ireland
Phone: (353) 045 404713**

Proprietor: Ann Maria Dunne
Category: Retreat, holistic center
Location: Mountain
Open all year? Yes, except Christmas
Price: Moderate
Special packages: Yes
Reader discount: No
Child discount: No

MEALS

Included: B, L, D
Offered: B, L, D
% Vegetarian: 100%
% Vegan: 30%
% Organic: 10%
Special diets: Yes
Nearby restaurants: No

ROOMS

% Private bath/shower: None
% Non-smoking: 100%
% Air conditioned: None
Car parking: Yes
Wheelchair access: No
Non-animal tested toiletries: No
Insecticides used? No
Pets welcome? No
Of animal origin: Wool rugs, feather pillows
Nearby activities: Golf, bicycling, hiking, canoeing/kayaking, boating, horseback riding, camping, massage, sauna, craft shop
Description: A holistic center specializing in residential courses on many aspects of personal growth and spirituality, with facilities for private group bookings. Peaceful setting in mature garden. Rectory dates from 1711.

Forms of payment: *Local currency*—cash; MC, VI

BAILE AN TSLEIBHE

**Upper Ardbane
Downings
Co. Donegal, Ireland
Phone: (353) 074 55661**

Proprietor: Moira O'Neill

Category: Bed & Breakfast

Location: Mountain, quaint village, seaside

Open all year? Yes

Price: Inexpensive

Special packages: Yes

Reader discount: No

Child discount: Yes

MEALS

Included: B

Offered: B, D

% Vegetarian: 80%

% Vegan: 20%

% Organic: 60%

Special diets: Yes

Nearby restaurants: No

ROOMS

% Private bath/shower: 0%

% Non-smoking: 0%

% Air conditioned: 0%

Car parking: Yes

Wheelchair access: No

Non-animal tested toiletries: No

Insecticides used? No

Pets welcome? Yes

Of animal origin: Farm animals, down comforters, feather pillows

Nearby activities: Indoor pool, tennis, golf, bicycling, hiking, canoeing/kayaking, boating, snorkeling, water sports, horseback riding, beach, massage

Description: Wild and romantic, peaceful and timeless, Baile-an-Tsleibhe is a homey and secluded B&B situated in the hills of the scenic Rosguill Peninsula overlooking the Atlantic Ocean. Accommodations in the beautifully restored old cottage are comfortable and charming. Traditional antique furniture, 4-poster bed. Open turf fires. Real Ireland.

Forms of payment: *Local currency*—cash, travelers checks

THE EWE, ART & CRAFT RETREAT

**Goleen
West Cork, Ireland
Phone/Fax: (353) 028 35492**

Proprietor: Sheena Wood

Category: Retreat

Location: Mountain, quaint village

Open all year? Yes

Price: Moderate

Special packages: Yes

Reader discount: No

Child discount: No

MEALS

Included: B

Offered: B

% Vegetarian: 100%

% Vegan: On request

% Organic: 50%

Special diets: Yes

Nearby restaurants: Yes

Comments: Essentially self-catering

ROOMS

% Private bath/shower: 100%

% Non-smoking: 100%

% Air conditioned: 0%

Car parking: Yes

Wheelchair access: No

Non-animal tested toiletries: No

Insecticides used? No

Pets welcome? No

Of animal origin: Feather pillows

Nearby activities: Golf, bicycling, hiking, boating, snorkeling, scuba diving, water sports, horseback riding, camping, beach, art, classes in pottery, weaving, papier mache, painting, drawing

Description: In a spectacular setting overlooking the Atlantic, The Ewe, Art and Craft Retreat is a unique creative center offering courses in arts and craft to all ages from the beginner to the inspiration-seeking professional. Bright spacious studios, galleries, a shop and self-catering lodges are set around a tranquil courtyard garden. A wonderful creative escape! Courses in pottery and all aspects of ceramics,

weaving, textile technique, papier mache, painting, drawing, and much more.

Forms of payment: *Local currency*—cash, travelers checks

INSE BUI HOUSE

Lough Cutra Drive
Inchaboy
Gort
Co. Galway, Ireland
Phone: (353) 091 32509
Fax: (353) 091 32748

Proprietor: Norma Slattery
Category: Bed & Breakfast
Location: Mountain, lakefront
Open all year? Open Mar.–Oct.
Price: Moderate
Special packages: No
Reader discount: Yes, inquire directly
Child discount: Yes

MEALS

Included: B
Offered: B
% Vegetarian: 20%
% Vegan: 5%
% Organic: Varies
Special diets: None
Nearby restaurants: Yes

ROOMS

% Private bath/shower: 100%
% Non-smoking: 0%
% Air conditioned: 0%
Car parking: Yes
Wheelchair access: No

Non-animal tested toiletries: Yes
Insecticides used? No
Pets welcome? Yes
Of animal origin: Wool rugs, farm
    animals
Nearby activities: Tennis, golf, bicy-
    cling, hiking, boating, water
    sports, horseback riding, camp-
    ing, beach, exercise room,
    massage
Description: Situated in the foothills
    of Slieve Aughty Mountains
    overlooking woods, lakes, castle,
    and famous Burren Region.
    Organic garden, sheep, and
    horses. Family Homes of
    Ireland member. Nature lovers
    paradise.
Forms of payment: *Local currency*—cash,
    travelers checks

KARUNA FLAME

c/o Celtic Farm
Grange
Co. Sligo, Ireland
Phone: (353) 071 63337

Proprietor: Epona O'Donovan
Category: B&B, retreat
Location: Mountain, quaint village
Open all year? Yes, by reservation
    only
Price: Moderate
Special packages: No
Reader discount: 10%, must show book
Child discount: Yes

MEALS

Included: B, D
Offered: B, D
% Vegetarian: 100%

% Vegan: On request
% Organic: 100%
Special diets: Yes
Nearby restaurants: No

ROOMS

% Private bath/shower: 50%
% Non-smoking: 100%
% Air conditioned: None
Car parking: Yes
Wheelchair access: Yes
Non-animal tested toiletries: Yes
Insecticides used? No
Pets welcome? Yes
Of animal origin: Farm animals
Nearby activities: Indoor pool, outdoor pool, tennis, golf, bicycling, hiking, canoeing/kayaking, boating, snorkeling, scuba diving, water sports, horseback riding, nutrition classes, camping, beach, yoga, fitness classes, exercise room, massage, educational lectures, sightseeing tours, antique shops, museums
Description: Traditional cottage on 3-1/2 acres of wild mountain land looking out across 100 miles of sea/forest/mountains.

Garden of organic vegetables and fruit. Library of Celtic art, history, stories of the area and landscape. Warm and friendly atmosphere.

Forms of payment: *Local currency*—cash, travelers checks

CUSSENS COTTAGE

Bulgaden
Ballygrennan
Kilmallock
Co. Limerick, Ireland
Phone: (353) 063 98926

Proprietor: Ita West
Category: Guest house
Location: Rural
Open all year? Yes
Price: Inexpensive
Special packages: Yes
Reader discount: No
Child discount: Yes

MEALS

Included: B
Offered: B, L, D
% Vegetarian: 100%

% Vegan: On request
% Organic: 60%
Special diets: Yes
Nearby restaurants: No

ROOMS

% Private bath/shower: 100%
% Non-smoking: 100%
% Air conditioned: 0%
Car parking: Yes
Wheelchair access: No
Non-animal tested toiletries: No
Insecticides used? No
Pets welcome? Yes
Of animal origin: None
Nearby activities: Tennis, golf, bicycling, hiking, canoeing/kayak-
ing, boating, horseback riding,
nightclub, museums, castles,
ruins
Description: B&B prices with hotel
services. Your own front door
so that you can come and go as
you please. A trav-
elogue provided
free, with places of
interest for you to
visit. Three-course
evening meals
vegan/ vegetarian
every night—if
required—for under
10.00 punt. Stay
here and see the
real Ireland.
Forms of payment: *Local
currency*—cash,
travelers checks;
Eurocheck
Comments: We accept deposits in
advance in any currency

BURREN HAVEN

St. Brendan's Rd.
Lisdoonvarna
Co. Clare, Ireland
Phone: (353) 065 74366

Proprietor: Kathleen Purcell
Category: Bed & Breakfast
Location: Small town near sea
Open all year? Open April–October
Price: Inexpensive
Special packages: Yes
Reader discount: Yes, inquire directly
Child discount: Yes

MEALS

Included: B, D
Offered: B, D
% Vegetarian: 12%
% Vegan: 12%
% Organic: 50%
Special diets: Yes
Nearby restaurants: No

ROOMS

% Private bath/shower: 3%
% Non-smoking: 0%
% Air conditioned: 0%

Car parking: Yes

Wheelchair access: Yes

Non-animal tested toiletries: Yes

Insecticides used? No

Pets welcome? Yes

Of animal origin: Leather furniture, wool rugs, feather pillows

Nearby activities: Tennis, bicycling, hiking, water sports, massage, pubs, dancing, magnesia/sulphur waters

Description: A friendly family home, approved by the Family Homes of Ireland. Vegetarians and vegans welcomed. The town is small but friendly, full of lively pubs and bars with traditional music and dancing. Cliffs of Mohes, and the famous Burren coastline is a unique experience to those who have never seen its lunar-like landscape.

Forms of payment: *Local currency*—cash; MC, VI

SLIEVE AUGHTY RIDING CENTRE

**Kylebrack West
Loughrea
Co. Galway, Ireland
Phone: (353) 0509 45246**

Proprietor: Esther Zyderlaan

Category: Guest house

Location: Mountain, forest

Open all year? Yes

Price: Moderate

Special packages: Yes

Reader discount: No

Child discount: No

MEALS

Included: B, L, D

Offered: B, L, D

% Vegetarian: 50%

% Vegan: 25%

% Organic: 80%

Special diets: Yes

Nearby restaurants: No

ROOMS

% Private bath/shower: 100%

% Non-smoking: 100%

% Air conditioned: 100%

Car parking: Yes

Wheelchair access: No

Non-animal tested toiletries: Yes

Insecticides used? No

Pets welcome? No

Of animal origin: Farm animals, wool rugs, down comforters

Nearby activities: Outdoor pool, tennis, golf, bicycling, boating, horseback riding, sightseeing tours

Description: Small friendly guest house with organic vegetable garden and cheese dairy. Special equestrian holidays organized, trail riding, and lessons can be arranged. Small groups only.

Forms of payment: *Local currency*—cash

MR. & MRS. PETER UPSON

**Shielbaggan
Ramsgrange
Co. Wexford, Ireland
Phone: (353) 051 562465
Fax: (353) 051 28646**

Proprietor: Mr. & Mrs. Peter Upson

Category: Guest house

Location: Farm

Open all year? Yes

Price: Inexpensive/ Moderate

Special packages: No

Reader discount: Yes, inquire directly

Child discount: Yes

MEALS

Included: B, L, D

Offered: B, L, D

% Vegetarian: 50%

% Vegan: 10%

% Organic: 50%

Special diets: Yes

Nearby restaurants: Yes

ROOMS

% Private bath/shower: 30%

% Non-smoking: 100%

% Air conditioned: 0%

Car parking: Yes

Wheelchair access: No

Non-animal tested toiletries: Yes

Insecticides used? No

Pets welcome? Yes

Of animal origin: Farm animals, feather pillows, wool rugs

Nearby activities: Golf, bicycling, hiking, canoeing/kayaking, boating, snorkeling, scuba diving, water sports, horseback riding, beach, sightseeing tours, antique shops, museums, glass factory, gardens, historical ruins

Description: Private country house atmosphere. Good fresh local food. Three comfortable double bedrooms hosted by farming family on 58 acres. Quiet local-

ity, peaceful garden, lovely beaches, cliff walks, horseback riding by sea six miles, friendly pub, golf.

Forms of payment: *U.S. currency*—cash, travelers checks; *Local currency* —cash; VI

THE OLD FARMHOUSE

Greenane
Rathdrum
Co. Wicklow, Ireland
Phone: (353) 0404 46676

Proprietor: Caroline Buck
Category: Bed & Breakfast
Location: Mountain
Open all year? Yes
Price: Inexpensive
Special packages: Yes
Reader discount: Yes, inquire directly
Child discount: Yes

MEALS

Included: B
Offered: B, L, D
% Vegetarian: On request
% Vegan: On request
% Organic: 100%
Special diets: Yes
Nearby restaurants: Yes

ROOMS

% Private bath/shower: 100%
% Non-smoking: 100%
% Air conditioned: 0%

Pets welcome? No

Of animal origin: Farm animals, wool rugs

Nearby activities: Indoor pool, outdoor pool, tennis, golf, bicycling, hiking, canoeing/kayaking, horseback riding, nutrition classes, camping, beach, yoga, fitness classes, massage, educational lectures, sightseeing tours, nightclub, antique shops, museums, craft classes, organic gardening, Irish music

Description: Situated in the beautiful mountainous area of Glemulune, Co. Wicklow. En-suite rooms, large organic fruit and vegetable garden, largest herb garden in Co. Wicklow. Food all home-produced. Country wines (organic) always available, plus home-brewed beer. Can offer transport from airport or trains.

Forms of payment: *U.S. currency*—cash, travelers checks; *Local currency* —cash, travelers checks; AX, MC, VI

Car parking: Yes
Wheelchair access: Yes
Non-animal tested toiletries: Yes
Insecticides used? No

TIR NA N'OG

Ballinabarny
Greenane
Rathdrum
Co. Wicklow, Ireland
Phone: (353) 0404 46469

Proprietor: Anne Harpur

Category: B&B, retreat, self-catering

Location: Mountain

Open all year? Yes

Price: Inexpensive

Special packages: Yes

Reader discount: Yes, inquire directly

Child discount: Yes

MEALS

Included: B

Offered: B, L, D

% Vegetarian: 100%

% Vegan: On request

% Organic: 100%

Special diets: Yes

Nearby restaurants: Yes

ROOMS

% Private bath/shower: 100%

% Non-smoking: 100%

% Air conditioned: 0%

Car parking: Yes

Wheelchair access: No

Non-animal tested toiletries: Yes

Insecticides used? No

Pets welcome? Yes

Of animal origin: Wool rugs, down comforters, farm animals

Nearby activities: Indoor pool, outdoor pool, tennis, golf, bicycling, hiking, canoeing/kayaking, horseback riding, nutrition classes, camping, beach, yoga, fitness classes, massage, educational lectures, sightseeing tours, nightclub, antique shops, museums, meditation, counseling, Irish music

Description: Self-catering/B&B attic flat with spectacular views. Two bedrooms en-suite, sofa bed in small sitting room, kitchen downstairs, private entrance. Conservatory meditation cabin on grounds. Sleeps 4–6.

Forms of payment: *U.S. currency*—cash, travelers checks, personal checks; *Local currency*—cash, travelers checks

Belgium

France

Netherlands

Portugal

Spain

Western Europe

GRAINBOW

Consciencestraat 44
2018 Antwerpen, Belgium
Phone: (32) 03 230 13 82
Fax: (32) 03 281 21 81

Proprietor: Luc de Cuyper
Category: Outdoor adventure
Location: Varies
Open all year? Yes
Price: Moderate
Special packages: Yes
Reader discount: Yes;
 inquire directly
Child discount: Inquire

MEALS

Included: B, L, D
Offered: B, L, D
% Vegetarian: 95%
% Vegan: 85%
% Organic: As available
Special diets: Yes
Nearby restaurants: No
Comments: Belgian Bio-
 garantie certification label

ROOMS

% Private bath/shower: N/A
% Non-smoking: 0%
% Air conditioned: 0%

BELGIUM

Car parking: No
Wheelchair access: No
Non-animal tested toiletries: Yes
Insecticides used? No
Pets welcome? No
Of animal origin: Varies
Nearby activities: Hiking, cross-country
 skiing, yoga, massage, nutrition
 classes, dance, downhill skiing

Description: Grainbow is an organization supported by enthusiastic
trainers who value nature highly and consider humans and
the environment as one.
Activities we organize include
hiking, tours, walking, skiing,
yoga, massage, dance, natural
cooking, and natural healing.
Meals are mainly vegetarian
and vegan and organic ingredients are used whenever available. Accommodations depend
on the type of activity and
range from tents to large group
houses.

Forms of payment: *Local currency*—cash

IGNORAMUS

**Stationsstraat 121
B-3665 As, Belgium
Phone: (32) 089 65 70 34
Fax: (32) 089 65 72 34**

Proprietor: Egidius Musiek
Category: Hotel
Location: Quaint village
Open all year? Closed Jan. 2–16
Price: Moderate
Special packages: Yes
Reader discount: 10%
Child discount: Yes

MEALS

Included: B, L, D
Offered: B, L, D
% Vegetarian: 90%
% Vegan: 90%
% Organic: 95%
Special diets: Yes
Nearby restaurants: No

ROOMS

% Private bath/shower: 100%
% Non-smoking: 100%
% Air conditioned: 0%
Car parking: Yes
Wheelchair access: Yes
Non-animal tested toiletries: No
Insecticides used? No
Pets welcome? No
Of animal origin: None
Nearby activities: Indoor pool, outdoor pool, tennis, golf, bicycling, horseback riding, nutrition classes, yoga, exercise room, massage, juice fasting, educational lectures

Description: Hotel Ignoramus is a meeting place for people looking for rest and peacefully energizing surroundings. The hotel offers vegetarian and macrobiotic meals and a variety of alternative therapies and courses. Accommodations for groups with exercise and meditation rooms.

Forms of payment: *Local currency*—cash; AX, MC, VI, Diners Club

FRANCE

D'ASTROS

Le Pin
82340 Auvillar, France
Phone: (33) 63 95 95 20
Fax: (33) 63 95 93 55

Proprietor: David Boniface
Category: Guest house
Location: Rural
Open all year? Yes
Price: Inexpensive
Special packages: Yes
Reader discount: Yes; inquire directly
Child discount: Yes

MEALS

Included: B
Offered: B, L, D
% Vegetarian: 10%
% Vegan: 1%
% Organic: 5%
Special diets: Yes
Nearby restaurants: No
Comments: Picnic
    hampers available

ROOMS

% Private bath/shower:
    50%
% Non-smoking: 100%
% Air conditioned: 0%
Car parking: Yes
Wheelchair access: Yes
Non-animal tested toiletries: No
Insecticides used? Yes
Pets welcome? Yes
Of animal origin: Leather furniture,
    wool rugs, feather pillows
Nearby activities: Indoor pool, outdoor
    pool, tennis, golf, bicycling,
hiking, canoeing/kayaking,
boating, water sports, horse-
back riding, camping, beach,
sightseeing tours, gymnasium,
squash, nightclub, antique
shops, museums

Description: Conveniently located
    between Bordeaux and
    Toulouse, D'Astros is set in 3
    acres surrounded by fields, for-
    est, and fruit orchards. We have
    four comfortable family-sized
    bedrooms. Lunch and evening
    meals include both traditional

and vegetarian menus and picnic hampers can be arranged if
required. If you are looking for
a real French country-style holiday, this is for you. Picturesque
villages and fortified medieval
towns are to be found every-
where. It helps if you speak
French, but try a little Franglais
and the local people will love
you for it!

Forms of payment: *U.S. currency*—cash;
    Local currency—cash, travelers
    checks

LES SORBIERS *(Borderline Holidays)*

Rue Ramond
65120 Bareges
Hautes Pyrenees, France
Phone: (33) 62 92 68 95
Fax: (33) 62 92 66 93

Proprietor: Peter Derbyshire
Category: Guest house
Location: Mountain, quaint village
Open all year? Open Christmas to Easter and mid-May to October
Price: Inexpensive
Special packages: Yes
Reader discount: 10%
Child discount: Yes

MEALS

Included: B, D
Offered: B, D
% Vegetarian: 100%
% Vegan: 50%
% Organic: 50%
Special diets: Yes
Nearby restaurants: No

ROOMS

% Private bath/shower: 100%
% Non-smoking: 95%
% Air conditioned: 0%
Car parking: Yes
Wheelchair access: No
Non-animal tested toiletries: No
Insecticides used? No
Pets welcome? Yes
Of animal origin: Feather pillows
Nearby activities: Indoor pool, outdoor pool, tennis, bicycling, hiking, canoeing/kayaking, cross-country skiing, downhill skiing, horseback riding, camping, fitness classes, exercise room, massage, sightseeing tours, nightclub, antique shops, museums, spa baths

Description: At Les Sorbiers, we offer fine food in a comfortable and convivial setting. In summer we offer wildlife and walking holidays with local guides. The village is Napoleonic, the setting is breathtaking, and the welcome is warm.

Forms of payment: *U.S. currency*—travelers checks; *Local currency*—cash, travelers checks; MC, VI

DOMAINE DE MONTFLEURI

47250 Bouglon, France
Phone: (33) 53 20 61 30

Proprietor: Dominique Barron
Category: Bed & Breakfast

Location: Quaint village, lakefront, resort town, countryside

Open all year? Yes

Price: Inexpensive/Moderate

Special packages: Yes

Reader discount: No

Child discount: Yes

MEALS

Included: B

Offered: B, L, D

% Vegetarian: 100%

% Vegan: On request

% Organic: 75%

Special diets: Yes

Nearby restaurants: No

ROOMS

% Private bath/shower: 100%

% Non-smoking: 100%

% Air conditioned: 0%

Car parking: Yes

Wheelchair access: Yes

Non-animal tested toiletries: No

Insecticides used? No

Pets welcome? No

Of animal origin: Leather furniture, wool rugs

Nearby activities: Outdoor pool, tennis, golf, bicycling, hiking, canoeing/kayaking, boating, horseback riding, nutrition classes, yoga, sightseeing tours, antique shops, museums, chateaux

Description: The Domaine de Montfleuri is a handsome 18th century house standing on a sunny hilltop and surrounded by fragrant gardens, orchard, and park. This haven of peace offers superb views of the countryside. You will enjoy a warm welcome, comfortable accommodations, a beautiful swimming pool, a relaxing fire in the winter, and delicious vegetarian cuisine.

Forms of payment: *Local currency*—cash, travelers checks

LE BLE EN HERBE *(The Ripening Seed)*

Puissetier
23350 La Cellette, France
Phone: (33) 05 55 80 62 83

Proprietor: Maria Sperring

Category: Retreat

Location: Secluded rural hamlet

Open all year? Yes

Price: Moderate

Special packages: Yes

Reader discount: 5%

Child discount: Yes

MEALS

Included: B, L, D

Offered: B, L, D

% Vegetarian: 100%

% Vegan: 40%

% Organic: 90% in season

Special diets: Yes

Nearby restaurants: No

ROOMS

% Private bath/shower: 0%

% Non-smoking: 100%

% Air conditioned: 0%

Car parking: Yes

Wheelchair access: Yes

Non-animal tested toiletries: Yes

Insecticides used? No

Pets welcome? No

Of animal origin: Feather pillows,
wool rugs

Nearby activities: Outdoor pool, tennis, bicycling, hiking, canoeing/kayaking, cross-country skiing, horseback riding, camping, beach, yoga, massage, juice

LE BLE EN HERBE

fasting, educational lectures,
museums, antique shops,
gorges, rock formations

Description: Le Ble is a small international holistic retreat with 7-1/2 acres of beautiful organic gardens, fields, and woods. Located in rural central France, it is a place of enchantment and simplicity where a peaceful and nurturing atmosphere flows from living lightly on the Earth. Delicious vegetarian/vegan meals are lovingly prepared with produce fresh daily from our "Sun" garden.

Forms of payment: *U.S. currency*—cash; *Local currency*—cash, travelers checks

NATURE ET VIE

**8 Impasse Des Roitelets
Village de Kervam
56270 Ploemeur, France
Phone: (33) 97 82 85 20
Fax: (33) 97 82 84 91**

Proprietor: Merian
Category: Therapeutic fasting
Location: Beachfront, quaint village, resort town
Open all year? Yes
Price: Moderate
Special packages: No
Reader discount: 10%
Child discount: No

MEALS

Included: B, L, D
Offered: B, L, D
% Vegetarian: 100%
% Vegan: 100%
% Organic: 100%
Special diets: Yes
Nearby restaurants: No

ROOMS

% Private bath/shower: 50%
% Non-smoking: 100%
% Air conditioned: 50%
Car parking: Yes
Wheelchair access: No
Non-animal tested toiletries: Yes
Insecticides used? No
Pets welcome? Yes
Of animal origin: None
Nearby activities: Outdoor pool, tennis, golf, bicycling, hiking, canoeing/kayaking, boating,

snorkeling, scuba diving, water sports, horseback riding, nutrition classes, camping, beach, yoga, fitness classes, exercise room, massage, juice fasting, weight loss classes, educational lectures, training classes in vegetarianism

Description: Our concern is to conduct fasts, and we are the only establishment in France that offers strictly vegetarian natural foods. Please note: we do not take in people who do not do therapeutic fasting.

Forms of payment: *U.S. currency*—cash, travelers checks, personal checks; *Local currency*—cash, travelers checks

LE PLESSIS VEGETARIAN GUEST HOUSE

22350 Plumaudan
Brittany, France
Phone: (33) 96 86 00 44

Proprietor: Janine & Steve Judges
Category: Guest house
Location: Quaint village
Open all year? Yes
Price: Inexpensive
Special packages: Yes
Reader discount: 10% on 5–8 nights; 15% on 9+
Child discount: Yes
Comment: Self-catering cottage also available

MEALS
Included: B
Offered: B, L, D
% Vegetarian: 100%

% Vegan: On request
% Organic: 80%
Special diets: Yes
Nearby restaurants: No
Comments: Vegan food always available

ROOMS
% Private bath/shower: 60%
% Non-smoking: 100%
% Air conditioned: 0%
Car parking: Yes
Wheelchair access: No
Non-animal tested toiletries: No
Insecticides used? No
Pets welcome? No
Of animal origin: Feather pillows, wool rugs
Nearby activities: Indoor pool, outdoor pool, tennis, golf, bicycling, hiking, canoeing/kayaking, boating, horseback riding, camping, beach, nightclub, antique shops, museums
Description: Le Plessis is a charming old farmhouse in the beautiful Breton countryside. Close to the magnificent medieval fortress town of Dinan,

Merlin's Tomb and the Fountain of Youth, and the vast sandy beaches of the Côte d'Emeraude. Comfortable rooms, relaxed and friendly atmosphere, reasonable rates, and highly acclaimed vegetarian cuisine. Vegetarian proprietors.

Forms of payment: *Local currency*—cash, travelers checks; Eurocheck.

PAULIAC CHAMBRE D'HOTE

**Pauliac
Celles
24600 Riberac, France
Phone: (33) 53 91 97 45
Fax: (33) 53 90 43 46**

Proprietor: Jane Edwards
Category: Guest house
Location: Quaint village
Open all year? Yes
Price: Inexpensive
Special packages: Yes
Reader discount: 10%
Child discount: Yes

MEALS

Included: B, L, D
Offered: B, L, D
% Vegetarian: 100%
% Vegan: On request
% Organic: 50%
Special diets: Yes
Nearby restaurants: No

ROOMS

% Private bath/shower: 100%
% Non-smoking: 0%
% Air conditioned: 0%

Car parking: Yes
Wheelchair access: No
Non-animal tested toiletries: No
Insecticides used? No
Pets welcome? Yes
Of animal origin: Leather furniture, wool rugs, down comforters, feather pillows
Nearby activities: Outdoor pool, tennis, golf, bicycling, hiking, canoeing/kayaking, boating, snorkeling, horseback riding, camping, sightseeing tours, antique shops, museums
Description: Our 200-year-old guest house is set in wooded countryside, 8 kms from the Dordogne market town of Riberac. Over the years we have developed a reputation for good vegetarian food and comfortable accommodation. We are well-situated for visiting the famous

Dordogne prehistoric caves, chateaux, and the vineyards of Bordeaux.

Forms of payment: *U.S. currency*—cash, travelers checks; *Local currency* —cash, travelers checks

LE VERT BOCAGE

Hameau de Cornans
01190 St. Etienne sur Reyssouze,
France
Phone: (33) 85 30 97 27

Proprietor: Georges & Arlette
  Chervet
Category: Bed & Breakfast
Location: Countryside
Open all year? Yes
Price: Moderate
Special packages: No
Reader discount: No
Child discount: Yes

MEALS

Included: B, D
Offered: B, D
% Vegetarian: On request
% Vegan: Inquire
% Organic: 100%
Special diets: Inquire
Nearby restaurants: No

ROOMS

% Private bath/shower: 100%
% Non-smoking: 100%
% Air conditioned: 0%
Car parking: Yes
Wheelchair access: No
Non-animal tested toiletries: No
Insecticides used? No
Pets welcome? Yes
Of animal origin: Live caged ani-
  mals/birds, down com-
  forters, feather pillows
Nearby activities: Bicycling, hiking
Description: Far from highways
  and noise, Le Vert Bocage
  welcomes you to a real
country setting with a peaceful,
flowery environment. Five
unattached upstairs rooms each
have a bathroom with a shower
and can house from 10 to 15
people. Also a lounge with
greenery and an ornamental
pool. Dinner in the dining
room is by reservation (health
food lover's cuisine). Pensione
plan is available except in July
and August.

Forms of payment: *Local currency*—cash

S. E. CUISINE ET SANTE

Pont de Valentine
31800 Saint Gaudens, France
Phone: (33) 61 589 75 14
Fax: (33) 61 589 36 07

Proprietor: Rene Levy
Category: Macrobiotic center
Location: Mountain, quaint village,
  riverside
Open all year? Yes
Price: Inexpensive
Special packages: No
Reader discount: No
Child discount: Yes

MEALS

Included: B, L, D
Offered: B, L, D
% Vegetarian: 97%
% Vegan: 97%
% Organic: 80%
Special diets: Yes
Nearby restaurants: No
Comments: Afternoon tea served.
  Fish Friday lunch.

ROOMS

% Private bath/shower: 5%
% Non-smoking: 0%
% Air conditioned: 0%
Car parking: Yes
Wheelchair access: Yes
Non-animal tested toiletries: No
Insecticides used? No
Pets welcome? Yes
Of animal origin: None
Nearby activities: Indoor pool,
  outdoor pool, tennis,
  golf, canoeing/kayaking, cross-
  country skiing, downhill skiing, horseback riding, nutrition
  classes, camping, exercise
  room, massage, weight loss
  classes, educational lectures,
  antique shops, museums
Description: Our kitchens are open so
  you can become familiar with
  the preparation of basic macrobiotic cereal foods and original
  creations. Daily lectures give a
  complete introduction, including the yin-yang polarity prin-
  ciple and its applications in
  everyday life.
Forms of payment: *Local currency*—
  cash, travelers checks

VILLAGE VEGAN DE RABIES

E. et R. Zengaffinen
48240 St. Privat de Vallongue,
  France
Phone: (33) 66 45 01 27

Proprietor: E. & R. Zengaffinen
Category: Guest house
Location: Mountain, quaint village
Open all year? Yes

Price: Moderate
Special packages: No
Reader discount: No
Child discount: Yes

MEALS

Included: B, D
Offered: B, D
% Vegetarian: 100%
% Vegan: 100%
% Organic: 99%
Special diets: Inquire directly
Nearby restaurants: No

ROOMS

% Private bath/shower: 0%
% Non-smoking: 100%
% Air conditioned: 0%

Car parking: Yes

Wheelchair access: No

Non-animal tested toiletries: Yes

Insecticides used? No

Pets welcome? Yes

Of animal origin: None

Nearby activities: Bicycling, hiking, canoeing/kayaking, sightseeing tours

Description: A small fortified village located 900 meters up in the mountains. 100% vegan. Rent rooms or cottages and eat with the owners. Vegetables, bread, tofu, vegetable pate, and jelly are home-made and available for sale. Tours organized once a week.

Forms of payment: *Local currency*—cash

DOUCEUR HARMONIE

El-faitg
66230 Serralongue, France
Phone: (33) 68 39 62 56

Proprietor: N/A

Category: Commune

Location: Mountain, forest

Open all year? Yes

Price: Inexpensive

Special packages: No

Reader discount: 10%

Child discount: No

MEALS

Included: B, L, D

Offered: B, L, D

% Vegetarian: 100%

% Vegan: 98%

% Organic: 95%

Special diets: Yes

Nearby restaurants: No

ROOMS

% Private bath/shower: 0%

% Non-smoking: 100%

% Air conditioned: 0%

Car parking: Yes

Wheelchair access: No

Non-animal tested toiletries: Yes

Insecticides used? No

Pets welcome? No

Of animal origin: Wool rugs, farm animals, live caged animals/birds

Nearby activities: Hiking, spring pool, gardening

Description: Situated 850m above the sea, in the charm of "Pyrenees Orientalis," 21 hectares of garden and surrounding forest/

mountainside. Vegetarian and spiritual community consists currently of 5 adults and 2 children. We have a vision of a harmonious, gentle world, where love reigns and all beings live peacefully together.

Forms of payment: *Local currency*—cash

DOMAINE DE MAGOT

81330 Vabre, France
Phone: (33) 63 50 48 02
Fax: (33) 63 50 48 42

Proprietor: Erica Steinhauer
Category: Retreat
Location: Mountain
Open all year? Open summers; other seasons by arrangement
Price: Inexpensive/Moderate
Special packages: Yes
Reader discount: No
Child discount: Yes

MEALS

Included: B, L, D
Offered: B, L, D
% Vegetarian: 100%
% Vegan: 50%
% Organic: Varies
Special diets: Yes
Nearby restaurants: No

ROOMS

% Private bath/shower: 0%
% Non-smoking: 100%
% Air conditioned: 0%
Car parking: Yes
Wheelchair access: No
Non-animal tested toiletries: No

Insecticides used? No
Pets welcome? Yes
Of animal origin: Feather pillows, wool rugs, farm animals, down comforters
Nearby activities: Outdoor pool, tennis, bicycling, hiking, horseback riding, camping, sightseeing tours, nightclub
Description: Domaine de Magot is a wooded semi-wilderness of 80 acres in the Lanquedoc National Park in SW France. Unspoiled and carefully stewarded for decades. Organic, deep spring water, waterfall. A haven for wildlife and a "field hospital" for the world-weary. Deep ecology with humor. Comfortable farm house, tipis in the woods, simple, comfortable, and creative.
Forms of payment: *U.S. currency*—cash; *Local currency*—cash

LE MOULIN FOULON

**Aubry de Panthou
61120 Vimoutiers
Orne, France
Phone: (33) 0233 35 55 46**

Proprietor: Pamela Wheatley
Category: B&B, groups
Location: Countryside
Open all year? Yes
Price: Moderate
Special packages: No
Reader discount: 10% for first visit
Child discount: No

MEALS

Included: B, L, D
Offered: B, L, D
% Vegetarian: 100%
% Vegan: 20%
% Organic: 90%
Special diets: Yes
Nearby restaurants: Yes

ROOMS

% Private bath/shower: 20%
% Non-smoking: 100%
% Air conditioned: 0%
Car parking: Yes
Wheelchair access: No
Non-animal tested toiletries: No
Insecticides used? No
Pets welcome? No
Of animal origin: Farm animals, wool rugs
Nearby activities: Indoor pool, outdoor pool, tennis, golf, bicycling, hiking, canoeing/kayaking, boating, horseback riding, nutrition classes, camping, yoga, exercise room, massage, juice fasting, weight loss classes,

sightseeing tours, antique shops, museums

Description: Le Moulin Foulon is a beautiful 200-year-old Norman house in the heart of rolling dairy and apple countryside. Acclaimed for its exciting international vegetarian food, everything is home-made. One-day outings to Bayeux, Honfleur on the coast, Monet's garden at Giverny. Perfect venue for study groups—painting, writing, etc.

Forms of payment: *U.S. currency*—cash, travelers checks, personal checks; *Local currency*—cash, travelers checks

NETHERLANDS

Holland

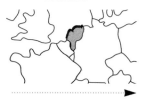

WESTERN EUROPE

HUIS AAN DE ROTS

Geulhemmerweg 32
Berg en Terblijt 6325 PK Netherlands
Phone: (31) 04360 41912
Fax: (31) 04360 42727

Proprietor: Mr. M. Berger
Category: Hotel
Location: Mountain,
    valley
Open all year? Yes
Price: Moderate
Special packages: Yes
Reader discount: No
Child discount: No

MEALS

Included: B
Offered: B, D
% Vegetarian: 30%
% Vegan: 15%
% Organic: 85%
Special diets: Yes
Nearby restaurants: No

ROOMS

% Private bath/shower: 10%
% Non-smoking: 100%
% Air conditioned: 0%
Car parking: Yes
Wheelchair access: No
Non-animal tested toiletries: Yes
Insecticides used? No
Pets welcome? Yes
Of animal origin: Farm animals
Nearby activities: Indoor pool, outdoor
    pool, tennis, bicycling, canoe-
    ing/kayaking, cross-country ski-
    ing, horseback riding, massage,
    sightseeing tours, antique
    shops

Description: We are a small, genteel
    hotel located in the Geul valley
    in the south of Holland. Our
    kitchen is healthy with vegan,
    ecological, and organic food.
    Our hotel is surrounded by for-
    est and situated next to the
    Dutch historical cave houses.

Opposite us floats the river
Geul with its old watermill
from Geulheim. The hotel has
a wildflower and herb garden
and a seasonal terrace.

Forms of payment: *U.S. currency*—cash;
    local currency—cash; MC, VI

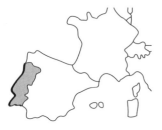

PORTUGAL

QUINTA DE SAO JOSE

Aldeia Galega
P2710 Sintra, Portugal
Phone: (351) 1961 8582
Fax: (351) 1922 0599

Proprietor: Stefanie Hillenbrand and
Paul Rosner
Category: Bed & Breakfast
Location: Quaint village
Open all year? Yes
Price: Moderate
Special packages: No
Reader discount: No
Child discount: Yes

MEALS

Included: B, L, D
Offered: B, L, D
% Vegetarian: 70%
% Vegan: 90%
% Organic: 70%
Special diets: Yes
Nearby restaurants: No
Comments: Packed
lunches offered

ROOMS

% Private bath/shower: 50%
% Non-smoking: 100%
% Air conditioned: 0%
Car parking: No
Wheelchair access: No
Non-animal tested toiletries: No
Insecticides used? No
Pets welcome? Yes
Of animal origin: Farm animals, cats
Nearby activities: Tennis, bicycling,
water sports, horseback riding,
camping, beach, yoga, massage,
sightseeing tours, nightclub,
antique shops, museums,
castles

Description: We are a German-
American couple with 2
children, 2 cats and 2 horses.
We live in a traditional farmhouse in a small village outside
the historic town of Sintra,
near Lisbon. We rent out two
rooms in our home and provide guests with vegetarian/
macrobiotic meals in a family
atmosphere.

Forms of payment: *U.S. currency*—cash,
travelers checks, personal
checks; *Local currency*—cash,
travelers checks

HOTEL DO PARQUE

Praca Da Galiza
4900 Viana Do Castelo, Portugal
Phone: (351) 058 828605
Fax: (351) 058 828612

Proprietor: Crispim Pedra
Category: Hotel
Location: Beachfront suburban, resort town
Open all year? Yes
Price: Moderate
Special packages: Yes
Reader discount: 10%
Child discount: Yes

MEALS

Included: B
Offered: B, L, D
% Vegetarian: 10%
% Vegan: 0%
% Organic: 30%
Special diets: Yes
Nearby restaurants: No

ROOMS

% Private bath/shower: 100%
% Non-smoking: 0%
% Air conditioned: 100%
Car parking: Yes
Wheelchair access: Yes
Non-animal tested toiletries: Yes
Insecticides used? No
Pets welcome? No
Of animal origin: Feather pillows
Nearby activities: Outdoor pool, tennis, bicycling, educational lectures
Description: 123 spacious rooms with full bathroom, hair dryer, air conditioner with in-room controls, color TV, individual chests, terrace above the pool, 3 musical bands, solarium on the 7th floor, restaurant with view and 300 seats on the 6th floor, 2 pools (one for children) with bar and large patio, banquet rooms, games, reading material, indoor garden, private park.

Forms of payment: *U.S. currency*—cash, travelers checks; *Local currency* —cash, travelers checks; AX, MC, VI, Discover

SPAIN

LA CASA ROSADA

P.O. Box 11
18400 Orgiva
Granada, Spain
Phone: *No phone yet. Write first.*

Proprietor: Camilla Drummond & Julia Steinson

Category: Self-catering

Location: Mountain, quaint village

Open all year? Yes

Price: Moderate

Special packages: No

Reader discount: 10%

Child discount: No

MEALS

Included: None

Offered: See comment

% Vegetarian: N/A

% Vegan: N/A

% Organic: N/A

Special diets: N/A

Nearby restaurants: Yes

Comments: Self catering, but vegetarian/ vegan cooks available on request

ROOMS

% Private bath/shower: 100%

% Non-smoking: 100%

% Air conditioned: 0%

Car parking: Yes

Wheelchair access: Yes

Non-animal tested toiletries: No

Insecticides used? No

Pets welcome? No

Of animal origin: Feather pillows, wool rugs

Nearby activities: Outdoor pool, golf, bicycling, hiking, boating, snorkeling, water sports, down-hill skiing, horseback riding, camping, beach, yoga, massage, sightseeing tours, nightclub

Description: This delightful country cottage with secluded garden and environmentally designed swimming pool is beautifully renovated and furnished. Solar powered, it is 1km from Orgiva, 35 minutes from sea, and surrounded by mountains. Nearby restaurants offer vegetarian meals and cooks are available to cook in your own home! Sleeps 4–6.

Forms of payment: *U.S. currency*—cash; *Local currency*—cash

MOLINO DEL SANTO S.L.

Bda Estacion S/N
29370 Benaojan
Malaga, Spain
Phone: (34) 5 216 7151
Fax: (34) 5 216 7327

Proprietor: Andy Chapell

Category: Hotel

Location: Mountain

Open all year? Open end of February
    until early December

Price: Moderate

Special packages: No

Reader discount: No

Child discount: Yes

MEALS

Included: None

Offered: B, L, D

% Vegetarian: 15%

% Vegan: 0%

% Organic: 10%

Special diets: Yes

Nearby restaurants: No

ROOMS

% Private bath/shower: 100%

% Non-smoking: 0%

% Air conditioned: 0%

Car parking: Yes

Wheelchair access: No

Non-animal tested toiletries: No

Insecticides used? Yes

Pets welcome? Inquire in
    advance

Of animal origin: Wool rugs

Nearby activities: Outdoor pool, bicy-
    cling, hiking, horseback riding

Description: A delightful small hotel
(12 rooms) converted from an old watermill. Situated alongside a mountain stream in the national park of Grazalema. We offer a very complete selection of walking routes that we have discovered ourselves. Food based on local produce whenever possible. Extremely friendly and helpful staff.

Forms of payment: *U.S. currency*—cash, travelers checks; *Local currency* —cash, travelers checks; AX, MC, VI, Diners Club

STAR CENTRE & VEGETARIAN RESTAURANT

C/Reyes Catolico 21
29640 Fuengirola
Malaga, Spain
Phone: (34) 95 2113001
Fax: (34) 95 2464248

Proprietor: Jerome Hall
Category: Alternative center
Location: Beachfront, quaint village, resort town
Open all year? Yes
Price: Inexpensive/Moderate
Special packages: Yes
Reader discount: 10%
Child discount: No

MEALS

Included: B, L, D
Offered: B, L, D
% Vegetarian: 100%
% Vegan: 100%
% Organic: 50%
Special diets: Yes
Nearby restaurants: No

ROOMS

% Private bath/shower: —
% Non-smoking: —
% Air conditioned: 50%
Car parking: No
Wheelchair access: Yes
Non-animal tested toiletries: No
Insecticides used? No
Pets welcome? Yes
Of animal origin: None
Nearby activities: Outdoor pool, hiking, tennis, golf, bicycling, boating, snorkeling, scuba diving, water sports, horseback riding, nutrition classes, camping, beach, yoga, fitness classes, exercise room, massage, weight loss classes, educational lectures, sightseeing tours, nightclub, antique shops

Description: Star Centre and Vegetarian Restaurant disseminates information on prophecies, earth changes, the importance of balanced food, healing, energy elevation, yoga, meditation, etc., offered by international teachers, healers, clairvoyants, and chanelers. It is situated in the resort town of Fuengirola, 50 yards from the beach and at the foot of the mountains.

Forms of payment: *U.S. currency*—cash, travelers checks; *Local currency* —cash, travelers checks

HOTEL DEL ALMIRANTE
(Collingwood House)

**Puerto de Mahon
07720 Es Castell
Menorca, Spain
Phone: (34) 971 362700
Fax: (34) 971 362704**

Proprietor: F.P. Montanari

Category: B&B, hotel

Location: Quaint village, resort town

Open all year? Open May 1 to October 31

Price: Moderate

Special packages: Yes

Reader discount: No

Child discount: Yes

MEALS

Included: B

Offered: B, L, D

% Vegetarian: 50%

% Vegan: 10%

% Organic: 50%

Special diets: Yes

Nearby restaurants: Yes

ROOMS

% Private bath/shower: 100%

% Non-smoking: 50%

% Air conditioned: 0%

Car parking: Yes

Wheelchair access: Yes

Non-animal tested toiletries: Yes

Insecticides used? Yes

Pets welcome? No

Of animal origin: None

Nearby activities: Outdoor pool, tennis, bicycling, hiking, boating, water sports, beach, sightseeing tours, nightclub, antique shops, museums

Description: This lovely Georgian House, situated on the south side of the Bay of Mahon, was once the home of Admiral Collingwood, friend of Nelson. Owner Paco Montanari has created a superb ambience, adorning its nooks with antiques and paintings, including a "Titian." Forty bedrooms, bar, restaurant, swimming pool, tennis court, parking.

Forms of payment: *U.S. currency*—cash, travelers checks; *Local currency* —cash, travelers checks

Austria

Denmark

Germany

Greece

Italy

Sweden

Switzerland

Northern and Central Europe

BIO LANDHAUS ARCHE

Fam. Tessmann
A-9372 Eberstein
Klagenfurt, Austria
Phone/Fax: (43) 4264 8120

Proprietor: Tessmann
Category: Hotel
Location: Mountain, quaint village
Open all year? Yes
Price: Moderate
Special packages: Yes
Reader discount: 10% in low season
Child discount: Yes

MEALS

Included: B, D
Offered: B, L, D
% Vegetarian: 100%
% Vegan: 40%
% Organic: 90%
Special diets: Yes
Nearby restaurants: Yes

ROOMS

% Private bath/shower: 100%
% Non-smoking: 100%
% Air conditioned: 0%
Car parking: Yes

AUSTRIA

Wheelchair access: Yes
Non-animal tested toiletries: Yes
Insecticides used? No
Pets welcome? Yes
Of animal origin: Wool rugs
Nearby activities: Hiking, cross-country skiing, downhill skiing, horseback riding, nutrition classes, massage, juice fasting, sightseeing tours
Description: Ours is a family operation in one of the sunniest regions of Austria. We are surrounded by unspoiled nature, crystal clear waters, fresh

mountain air, and people living connected with nature. Our vegetable based, high quality cuisine—winner of the "Green Chef's Hat" award—brings back to the table many culinary delights from plants that have been neglected. For health and recuperation!

Forms of payment: *U.S. currency*—cash, travelers checks, personal checks; *Local currency*—cash, travelers checks

BIO-HOTEL GOLDENE KRONE

Grazer Str. 1
A-8630 Mariazell, Austria
Phone: (43) 03882-2583
Fax: (43) 03882-25833

Proprietor: Alfred Enne
Category: B&B, hotel
Location: City center, mountain, quaint village, lakefront
Open all year? Yes
Price: Moderate
Special packages: No
Reader discount: 5%
Child discount: Yes

MEALS

Included: B, L, D
Offered: B, L, D
% Vegetarian: See comment
% Vegan: See comment
% Organic: Varies
Special diets: Yes
Nearby restaurants: No
Comments: 2–3 vegetarian and vegan dishes offered daily

ROOMS

% Private bath/shower: 100%
% Non-smoking: 20%
% Air conditioned: 0%
Car parking: Yes
Wheelchair access: Yes
Non-animal tested toiletries: Yes
Insecticides used? No
Pets welcome? Yes
Of animal origin: Feather pillows, dead mounted/stuffed animals, down comforters
Nearby activities: Indoor pool, outdoor pool, tennis, bicycling, hiking, boating, snorkeling, water sports, cross-country skiing, downhill skiing, horseback riding, massage, juice fasting, sightseeing tours, nightclub, antique shops, museums
Description: Old Styrian house with traditional character. Completely authentic furnishings and comfortable rooms. Styrian specialties and quality dishes are particularly delicious. 58 comfortable beds, telephone, and TV. Cafe, restaurant, social and TV room, library.
Forms of payment: *U.S. currency*—cash; *Local currency*—cash, travelers checks, AX, MC, VI

BIO-HOTEL ALPENROSE

Obermillstatt 84
A-9872 Millstatt, Austria
Phone: (43) 04766 2500
Fax: (43) 04766 3425

Proprietor: Alois Obweger
Category: Hotel
Location: Mountain, quaint village, lakefront
Open all year? Yes
Price: Moderate
Special packages: No
Reader discount: 10%
Child discount: Yes

MEALS

Included: B, D
Offered: B, D
% Vegetarian: 80%
% Vegan: 20%
% Organic: 100%
Special diets: Yes

Nearby restaurants: No

ROOMS

% Private bath/shower: 100%

% Non-smoking: 100%

% Air conditioned: 0%

Car parking: Yes

Wheelchair access: No

Non-animal tested toiletries: Yes

Insecticides used? No

Pets welcome? No

Of animal origin: None

Nearby activities: Outdoor pool, golf, bicycling, hiking, boating, water sports, cross-country skiing, horseback riding, nutrition classes, yoga, fitness classes, massage, juice fasting, sightseeing tours, museums

Description: The first Biohotel in Austria. A nature paradise for body, spirit, and soul, with a plenitude of comforts, organically organized, in the midst of greenery. Five-star treatment for the soul to luxuriate. A non-smoking hotel!

Forms of payment: *U.S. currency*—cash; *Local currency*—cash

GESUNDHEITSHOTEL FLORIAN

258 Am Bichlach
A-6370 Reith B/Kitzbuhl, Austria
Phone: (43) 05356 5633
Fax: (43) 5356 5242

Proprietor: Mr. Pointner

Category: Retreat, hotel

Location: Quaint village

Open all year? Inquire directly

Price: Moderate

Special packages: Yes

Reader discount: No

Child discount: Yes

MEALS

Included: B, L, D

Offered: B, L, D

% Vegetarian: 100%

% Vegan: On request

% Organic: 80%

Special diets: Yes

Nearby restaurants: Yes

ROOMS

% Private bath/shower: 100%

% Non-smoking: 100%

% Air conditioned: 0%

Car parking: Yes

Wheelchair access: Yes

Non-animal tested toiletries: Yes

Insecticides used? No

Pets welcome? Yes

Of animal origin: Wool rugs, down comforters

Nearby activities: Indoor pool, outdoor pool, tennis, golf, bicycling, hiking, boating, cross-country skiing, downhill skiing, horseback riding, nutrition classes, yoga, fitness classes, exercise room, massage, juice fasting, sightseeing tours, antique shops, museums

Description: Our family-owned health hotel is situated on a sunny hill, between the Kitzbuheler Alps and the Wilder Kaiser. Our beautiful environment is ideal for cycling, hiking, lake swimming, skiing, skating, and cross-country skiing. All meals are completely vegetarian and the house is smoke-free. The surrounding area of Reith offers the peace and quiet of virgin nature— walks in the peaceful mountains, climbing steep rockfaces, exploring dark romantic forests or sunny meadows filled with flowers.

Forms of payment: *U.S. currency*—cash, travelers checks; *Local currency* —cash, travelers checks; AX, MC, VI, Discover

PENSION HAUS LEO

**Am Rauchenberg
A-5092 St. Martin bei Lofer
Salzburg, Austria
Phone: (43) 06588 7065**

Proprietor: Rosmarie Kepplinger
Category: Pension
Location: Mountain
Open all year? Yes
Price: Inexpensive
Special packages: Yes
Reader discount: Yes; inquire directly
Child discount: Yes

MEALS

Included: B, D
Offered: B, D

% Vegetarian: 80%
% Vegan: 20%
% Organic: Varies
Special diets: Yes
Nearby restaurants: No

ROOMS

% Private bath/shower: 0%

% Non-smoking: 100%

% Air conditioned: 0%

Car parking: Yes

Wheelchair access: No

Non-animal tested toiletries: No

Insecticides used? No

Pets welcome? Yes

Of animal origin: Wool rugs, down comforters, feather pillows

Nearby activities: Outdoor pool, tennis, bicycling, hiking, canoeing/kayaking, cross-country skiing, downhill skiing, sightseeing tours

Description: A small cozy pension in a beautiful hiker's setting, with long trails and Alpine climbing in a snow-covered ski area. Quality meat-free fare.

Forms of payment: *U.S. currency*—cash; *Local currency*—cash; AX, VI

HOTEL BRISTOL

**Markarplatz 4
A-5024 Salzburg, Austria
Phone: (43) 662 873557
Fax: (43) 662 8735576**

Proprietor: Roswita Wurnitsch

Category: Hotel

Location: City center

Open all year? Open Easter to Janurary 2

Price: Expensive

Special packages: No

Reader discount: No

Child discount: Yes

MEALS

Included: B

Offered: B, L, D

% Vegetarian: See comment

% Vegan: See comment

% Organic: 20%

Special diets: Yes

Nearby restaurants: No

Comments: Vegetable or green salads on request

ROOMS

% Private bath/shower: 100%

% Non-smoking: 20%

% Air conditioned: 60%

Car parking: Yes

Wheelchair access: Yes

Non-animal tested toiletries: No

Insecticides used? No

Pets welcome? Yes

Of animal origin: Leather furniture, feather pillows, down comforters

Nearby activities: Indoor pool, tennis, golf, bicycling, canoeing/kayaking, hiking, water sports, cross-country and downhill skiing, horseback riding, massage, sightseeing tours, nightclub, antique shops, museums

Description: Traditional 5-star hotel in best part of town at the entrance to the Mirabellgardens and opposite Mozart's home. Rooms are individually furnished and charming, with marvelous views of the city or of Mirabellgardens. Very friendly and attentive service.

Forms of payment: *U.S. currency*—cash, travelers checks; *Local currency*—cash, travelers checks; AX, MC, VI

VITAL HOTEL ROYAL

Krinz 32
A-6100 Seefeld, Austria
Phone: (43) 05212 4431-0
Fax: (43) 5212 4431-450

Proprietor: Edoardo Crivelli

Category: Hotel

Location: Mountain, quaint village, lakefront

Open all year? Yes

Price: Moderate

Special packages: Yes

Reader discount: 10%

Child discount: Yes

MEALS

Included: B, D

Offered: B, L, D

% Vegetarian: 30%

% Vegan: 20%

% Organic: Varies

Special diets: Yes

Nearby restaurants: No

ROOMS

% Private bath/shower: 100%

% Non-smoking: 80%

% Air conditioned: 0%

Car parking: Yes

Wheelchair access: Yes

Non-animal tested toiletries: Yes

Insecticides used? No

Pets welcome? Yes

Of animal origin: Wool rugs, feather pillows, down comforters

Nearby activities: Indoor pool, outdoor pool, tennis, golf, bicycling, hiking, cross-country skiing, downhill skiing, horseback riding, nutrition classes, camping, yoga, fitness classes, exercise room, massage, juice fasting, educational lectures, weight loss classes, sightseeing tours, nightclub, antique shops

Description: Vital Hotel Royal operates in a symbiotic relationship with its environment. A luxurious trendsetter in gastronomy and hotel operation, it is also a center for holistic medicine and diagnosis.

Forms of payment: *U.S. currency*—cash, travelers checks; *Local currency*—cash, travelers checks; AX, MC, VI

DENMARK

CITY SLEEP-IN/KULTURGYNGEN

Haunegade 20
Arhus 8000, Denmark
Phone: (45) 86 19 20 55
Fax: (45) 86 19 18 11

Proprietor: N/A
Category: Hostel
Location: City center
Open all year? Yes
Price: Inexpensive
Special packages: Yes
Reader discount: No
Child discount: Yes

MEALS

Included: None
Offered: B, L, D
% Vegetarian: 100%
% Vegan: 0%
% Organic: 10%
Special diets: None
Nearby restaurants: No
Comments: Specials for groups only

ROOMS

% Private bath/shower: 33%
% Non-smoking: 100%
% Air conditioned: 0%
Car parking: No
Wheelchair access: Yes
Non-animal tested toiletries: No
Insecticides used? No
Pets welcome? No
Of animal origin: None
Nearby activities: Indoor
  pool, bicycling,
  camping, beach, fit-
  ness classes, exercise
  room, massage,
  weight loss classes,
educational lectures, sightsee-
  ing tours, nightclub, antique
  shops, museums

Description: Kulturgyngen is a cultural activity center situated in an
old factory building, with daily
activities run by young people.
Gyngen is a restaurant, cafe,
and gallery—cozy, healthy,
and cheap. Offers a variety of
events including music, poetry,
debate, ethnic arrangements,
and lots more. Musik Cafeen is
the hottest underground club
in the city, featuring live bands,
disco, and video shows. City
Sleep-In is a city center youth
hostel with the cheapest
accommodation.

Forms of payment: *Local currency*—cash

MARTINUS CENTER

Klintvej 69
Klint
Nykobing Sj 4500 Denmark
Phone: (45) 38 34 62 80
Fax: (45) 38 34 61 80

Proprietor: N/A
Category: Holistic educational center

Location: Beachfront, quaint village
Open all year? Open May to October
Price: Inexpensive
Special packages: Yes
Reader discount: No
Child discount: No

MEALS

Included: None
Offered: D
% Vegetarian: 100%
% Vegan: 50%
% Organic: 50%
Special diets: None
Nearby restaurants: Yes

ROOMS

% Private bath/shower: 5%
% Non-smoking: 100%
% Air conditioned: 0%
Car parking: Yes
Wheelchair access: Yes

Non-animal tested toiletries: Yes
Insecticides used? No
Pets welcome? No
Of animal origin: Wool rugs, down comforters, feather pillows
Nearby activities: Teaching about Martinus cosmology
Description: The Martinus Center is a center for the study of the work of the Danish writer Martinus. As Martinus considered vegetarianism the ideal form of nutrition, from both an ethical and a health point of view, vegetarianism is central to the center's ideology. Courses are available in English from March to November. Accommodations normally available only to course participants.
Forms of payment: *Local currency*—cash, travelers checks

SUNDGAARDEN

Slotsgade 10
Tranekaer 5953 Denmark
Phone: (45) 62 59 15 55
Fax: (45) 62 59 13 02

Proprietor: Rie Schmidt
Category: B&B, resort
Location: Quaint village
Open all year? Open March–Nov., Christmas, New Year
Price: Moderate
Special packages: Yes
Reader discount: 10%
Child discount: Yes

MEALS

Included: B, L, D
Offered: B, L, D
% Vegetarian: 100%
% Vegan: 100%
% Organic: 100%
Special diets: Yes
Nearby restaurants: No
Comments: Box lunch available

ROOMS

% Private bath/shower: 15%
% Non-smoking: 100%
% Air conditioned: 0%
Car parking: Yes

Wheelchair access:
  No
Non-animal tested
  toiletries: Yes
Insecticides used?
  No
Pets welcome? Yes
Of animal origin:
  Wool rugs
Nearby activities:
  Bicycling,
  horseback
  riding,
  beach, yoga,
  juice fast-
  ing, sight-
  seeing tours,
  museums

Description:
  Sundgaarden is a family-operat-
ed inn for those who prefer an
informal relaxed atmosphere.
Walk or bike the sights of
Langeland, swim at one of the
island's many beaches, or relax
in a hammock in a quiet corner
of the garden. Each and every
stay in our inn feels like a
health cure because of the varied food and hikes in clean
fresh air. For those who desire
them, juice fasting and a raw-
foods diet are also offered.

Forms of payment: *U.S. currency*—travelers checks; *Local currency*—
cash, travelers checks

GERMANY

WALDHAUS LANGE-ALTFELD

**Oberbremscheid
D-59889 Eslohe, Germany
Phone: (49) 029731 883**

Proprietor: Hellmuth Lange
Category: Pension
Location: Mountain, quaint village
Open all year? Closed Nov.–Feb.
Price: Moderate
Special packages: No
Reader discount: 10%
Child discount: Yes

MEALS

Included: B, L, D
Offered: B, L, D
% Vegetarian: 50%
% Vegan: 50%
% Organic: 100%
Special diets: Yes
Nearby restaurants: No

ROOMS

% Private bath/shower: 0%
% Non-smoking: 100%
% Air conditioned: 0%
Car parking: Yes
Wheelchair access: No
Non-animal tested toiletries: Yes
Insecticides used? No
Pets welcome? No
Of animal origin: Wool rugs, feather pillows
Nearby activities: Indoor pool, outdoor pool, tennis, bicycling, hiking, downhill skiing, horseback riding, sightseeing tours, museums
Description: This quiet setting provides solitude 450 meters up the forested southern slopes near the Winterberg in the Sauerland. Comfortably furnished. Has its own spring water source. Offers pure vegetarian fare and homemade bread from fresh ingredients.
Forms of payment: *U.S. currency*—cash, travelers checks; *Local currency*—cash

KURHOTEL LAUTERBAD

**Amselweg 5
72250 Freudenstadt-Lauterbad, Germany
Phone: (49) 07441 81006
Fax: (49) 07441 82688**

Proprietor: Heinzelmann-Schillinger
Category: Hotel
Location: Mountain, quaint village
Open all year? Yes
Price: Moderate
Special packages: Yes
Reader discount: 5%
Child discount: Yes

MEALS

Included: B, D
Offered: B, L, D
% Vegetarian: 40%
% Vegan: 10%
% Organic: 50%
Special diets: Yes
Nearby restaurants: No

ROOMS

% Private bath/shower: 100%
% Non-smoking: 50%
% Air conditioned: 0%
Car parking: Yes
Wheelchair access: Yes
Non-animal tested toiletries: No
Insecticides used? No
Pets welcome? Yes
Of animal origin: Leather furniture, feather pillows, wool rugs, down comforters
Nearby activities: Indoor pool, tennis, golf, bicycling, hiking, cross-country skiing, downhill skiing, horseback riding, nutrition classes, yoga, fitness classes, massage, juice fasting, sightseeing tours
Description: This health-oriented resort is an oasis of peace and quiet. Surrounded by evergreen forest, Lauterbad is smog-free and provides wide walking paths through beautiful landscapes. This Black Forest resort offers an indoor swimming pool, steam bath, sauna, solarium, gymnasium, cosmetic studio, massage, body-building with trainer, table tennis, dance evenings, bicycle rentals, 18-hole golf, horseback riding, a theater, and even a breakfast bar. Each room offers a shower or bath, WC, telephone, TV with cable, radio, and a balcony. The food is biologically grown in a greenhouse. Our restaurant offers a wide range of highly nutritious meals, including several tofu dishes and wheat-based vegetarian meals.

Forms of payment: *Local currency*—cash, travelers checks; MC, VI, Diners Club

GASTHAUS ZUR SCHNECKE

**Fam. Assenheimer
Ziegelstrasse 3
79400 Kandern, Germany
Phone/Fax: (49) 07626 8303**

Proprietor: Dietlinde Assenheimer
Category: Bed & Breakfast
Location: Mountain, quaint village
Open all year? Yes
Price: Moderate
Special packages: No
Reader discount: No
Child discount: No

MEALS

Included: B
Offered: B, L, D
% Vegetarian: 30%
% Vegan: 5%
% Organic: 70%
Special diets: Yes
Nearby restaurants: No

ROOMS

% Private bath/shower: 100%
% Non-smoking: 0%

% Air conditioned: 0%

Car parking: No

Wheelchair access: Yes

Non-animal tested toiletries: No

Insecticides used? No

Pets welcome? No

Of animal origin: Feather pillows, down comforters

Nearby activities: Outdoor pool, tennis, golf, bicycling, hiking, downhill skiing, horseback riding, camping, massage, sightseeing tours, antique shops, museums

Description: A friendly, family-oriented inn located where three countries come together: 15km from Basel (Switzerland), Strassbourg (France), and Freiburg (Germany). There are 13 a la carte dishes for vegetarians and the menu changes weekly.

Forms of payment: *Local currency*—cash, travelers checks; MC, VI

GASTHAUS ZUR SCHNECKE

GASTEHAUS BORSCH

Blumenstr. 11
D-5595 Lutzerath, Germany
Phone: (49) 02677 238
Fax: (49) 02677 540

Proprietor: Ursula Borsch

Category: Pension

Location: Mountain, quaint village, lakefront

Open all year? Closed in March

Price: Moderate

Special packages: No

Reader discount: No

Child discount: Yes

MEALS

Included: B, L, D

Offered: B, L, D

% Vegetarian: On request

% Vegan: On request

% Organic: 75%

Special diets: Yes

Nearby restaurants: Yes

ROOMS

% Private bath/shower: 100%

% Non-smoking: 0%

% Air conditioned: 0%

Car parking: Yes

Wheelchair access: No

Non-animal tested toiletries: No

Insecticides used? No

Pets welcome? Yes

Of animal origin: Feather pillows, wool rugs

Nearby activities: Indoor pool, outdoor pool, tennis, bicycling, hiking, water sports, nutrition classes, exercise room, massage, juice fasting, sightseeing tours, vacation programs

Description: Borsch Health Foods Guesthouse, a pension with special family-style service, is centrally located on a quiet side-street. Surrounded by greenery, it is modern, well-maintained, and offers a variety of leisure, recreational, and health-restoration opportunities.

Forms of payment: *U.S. currency*—cash; *Local currency*—cash

KINDER UND JUGENDHILFSWERK SALEM

Der Brunderschaft Salem
D-21369 Nahrendorf-Kovahl, Germany
Phone: (49) 058 55 242
Fax: (49) 058 55 1328

Proprietor: Mr. Olszewski
Location: Quaint village, woods
Category: Spa
Open all year? Yes
Price: Inexpensive
Special packages: No
Reader discount: 5%
Child discount: Yes

MEALS

Included: B, L, D
Offered: B, L, D
% Vegetarian: 100%
% Vegan: 90%
% Organic: 95%

Special diets: Yes
Nearby restaurants: No

ROOMS

% Private bath/shower: 0%
% Non-smoking: 100%
% Air conditioned: 0%
Car parking: Yes
Wheelchair access: Yes
Non-animal tested toiletries: Yes
Insecticides used? No
Pets welcome? No
Of animal origin: Feather pillows, wool rugs, farm animals

Nearby activities: Bicycling, hiking, horseback riding, nutrition classes, sightseeing tours, children's village

Description: Emphatically nature-friendly! Located in the well-forested and hilly (but not mountainous) Elbufer-Drawehn nature preserve. Our "Salem" guest house is part of the "Salem" children's village that is home to 5 children's village families. The children range from 3 to 20 years old. The village has a riding stable, a female riding teacher, and an enclosed riding area. We practice organic farming and gardening and serve natural foods. Guests from abroad are particularly welcome.

Forms of payment: *U.S. currency*—cash, travelers checks; *Local currency* —cash, travelers checks

GASTEHAUS HARMONIE

**D-97723
Thulba/Sudrhon, Germany
Phone: (49) 09736 503**

Proprietor: Gisela Schulz

Category: Pension

Location: Mountain, quaint village, lakefront

Open all year? Closed Nov. 15–Dec. 15

Price: Moderate

Special packages: Yes

Reader discount: 10% for 3 weeks+

Child discount: Yes

MEALS

Included: B, D

Offered: B, L, D

% Vegetarian: 100%

% Vegan: 50%

% Organic: 90%

Special diets: Yes

Nearby restaurants: No

ROOMS

% Private bath/shower: 80%

% Non-smoking: 100%

% Air conditioned: 0%

Car parking: Yes

Wheelchair access: No

Non-animal tested toiletries: Yes

Insecticides used? No

Pets welcome? Yes

Of animal origin: Wool rugs, down comforters, feather pillows

Nearby activities: Indoor pool, outdoor pool, tennis, golf, bicycling, hiking, cross-country skiing, downhill skiing, horseback riding, nutrition classes, camping, fitness classes, massage, juice fasting, sightseeing tours, nightclub, antique shops, museums, concerts, art exhibitions, health treatment centers, steamboat trips, carriage rides

Description: Harmonie is the right place for vegetarian guests, in an area of Bavaria with beautiful landscapes, healthy air, and clean water. This nature preserve is ideal for hiking and biking. World famous Spa Kissingen is only 12km away and the Frankfurt (am Main) airport is only 180km away. The food is tasty and 90% organic.

Forms of payment: *U.S. currency*—cash, travelers checks; *Local currency* —cash, travelers checks; Eurocheck

GREECE

Crete

HOLIDAY AZOGIRES

Azogires Near Paleochora
Crete, Greece
Phone: (44) 01789 267744
Fax: (44) 01789 267887 *(in the UK)*

Proprietor: Brian or Erna Holden

Category: Special interest activity and retreat holidays

Location: Quaint village, mountain, beachfront

Open all year? Inquire directly

Price: Moderate

Special packages: No

Reader discount: No

Child discount: Inquire directly

MEALS

Included: B, D

Offered: B, D

% Vegetarian: 100%

% Vegan: Inquire directly

% Organic: Varies

Special diets: Inquire directly

Nearby restaurants: Yes

Comments: Prices include breakfast every day, and dinner all but Friday/Saturday.

ROOMS

% Private bath/shower: 100%

% Non-smoking: None

% Air conditioned: None

Car parking: Yes

Wheelchair access: No

Non-animal tested toiletries: No

Insecticides used? No

Pets welcome? No

Of animal origin: Wool rugs

Nearby activities: Hiking, sightseeing

tours, nightclub, water sports, bicycling, boating, painting, talks on local history and folklore, film shows, tai chi lessons, nutrition classes, beach, archeological sites, Samaria Gorge

Description: Azogires is a small village high in the mountains above the beach resort of Paleochora in southwest Crete. Our one and two week theme/program holidays include discovery trips of southwest Crete, various personal development workshops, walking, painting, and much more. Our Spirit of Crete Holidays include excursions most mornings, talks and other entertainment in the evenings, and various daily programs to chose from, with afternoons free to spend on the beach, relaxing at the center, or exploring. For further details, write Holiday Azogires c/o Clifford Chambers, Stratford upon Avon CV37 8JF England.

Forms of payment: *Local currency*—cash, travelers checks

ITALY

GRAND HOTEL TERMES. R.L.

Via Roma 2
Castrocaro, Forli (Emilia Romagna)
47011 Italy
Phone: (39) 0543 767114
Fax: (39) 0543 768135

Proprietor: Dott. Ssa G. Poluzzi

Category: Hotel

Location: City center, resort town

Open all year? Open April to October

Price: Moderate

Special packages: No

Reader discount: 10%

Child discount: Yes

MEALS

Included: B

Offered: B, L, D

% Vegetarian: 30%

% Vegan: 70%

% Organic: 30%

Special diets: Yes

Nearby restaurants: Yes

ROOMS

% Private bath/shower: 90%

% Non-smoking: 0%

% Air conditioned: 0%

Car parking: Yes

Wheelchair access: Yes

Non-animal tested toiletries: No

Insecticides used? No

Pets welcome? Yes

Of animal origin: None

Nearby activities: Indoor pool, outdoor pool, tennis, golf, bicycling, hiking, fitness classes, exercise room, massage, weight loss

classes, educational lectures, sightseeing tours, nightclub

Description: The Grand Hotel in Castrocaro is a first-class historic hotel built in 1935 under Mussolini's government. It is situated in the superb park of the spa with over 30 hectares of tall trees, olympic swimming pool, mini-golf course, and children's playground. It offers 100 large rooms and apartments with private terrace, an elegant bar with verandas on the park. Facilities include a gourmet restaurant, a restaurant for those on special diets, billiards room, game room, solarium, gymnasium, and private parking with closed circuit TV. The private spa department offers special treatments with mud and sulfur or bromojodic waters for gynecological diseases and sterility, rheumatism, circulation problems, deafness, respiratory diseases, and skin problems.

Forms of payment: *U.S. currency*—cash, travelers checks; *Local currency* —cash, travelers checks; AX, MC, VI, Diners Club

AZIENDA AGRITURISTICA POGGIO AURORA

**Centro Di Vida Naturale
Via Boccognano 13
Fosdinovo 54035 Italy
Phone: (39) 0187 68732**

Proprietor: Dante Ivan Bernardini
Category: Tourist farm
Location: Hill
Open all year? Open April–Sept. 30
Price: Inexpensive
Special packages: Yes
Reader discount: No
Child discount: Yes

MEALS

Included: B, L, D
Offered: B, L, D
% Vegetarian: 70%
% Vegan: 30%
% Organic: 90%
Special diets: Yes
Nearby restaurants: No

ROOMS

% Private bath/shower: 0%
% Non-smoking: 90%
% Air conditioned: 0%
Car parking: Yes
Wheelchair access: No
Non-animal tested toiletries: Yes
Insecticides used? No
Pets welcome? No
Of animal origin: None
Nearby activities: Tennis, bicycling, hiking, boating, water sports, horseback riding, nutrition classes, camping, beach, yoga, exercise room, massage, juice fasting, educational lectures, sightseeing tours, antique shops, museums

Description: This old farmhouse among quiet woods offers small rooms with a view of the ocean. A serene and convivial atmosphere for people who love this earth. Fresh, life-giving food from our own organic gardens. A rich vegetarian diet with tasty macrobiotic touches. Music and poetry around the fire. Party times and tranquil walks allow people, together, to experience a harmonious dialogue between humankind and nature.

Forms of payment: *U.S. currency*—cash, travelers checks, personal checks; *Local currency*—cash, travelers checks

HOTEL MIRAMONTI

**Via Roma 84
Frabosa Soprana 12082 Italy
Phone: (39) 0174 244533
Fax: (39) 0174 244534**

Proprietor: ——
Category: Resort
Location: Mountain
Open all year? Inquire directly
Price: Inexpensive
Special packages: Yes
Reader discount: 10%
Child discount: Yes

MEALS

Included: None
Offered: B, L, D
% Vegetarian: 100%
% Vegan: 100%

% Organic: 60%

Special diets: Yes

Nearby restaurants: No

ROOMS

% Private bath/shower: 100%

% Non-smoking: 0%

% Air conditioned: 0%

Car parking: Yes

Wheelchair access: No

Non-animal tested toiletries: No

Insecticides used? No

Pets welcome? Yes

Of animal origin: Farm animals

Nearby activities: Tennis, bicycling, hiking, cross-country skiing, downhill skiing, horseback riding, exercise room, juice fasting, sightseeing tours, museums

Description: Restore body and spirit during your holidays enjoying traditional courtesy and hospitality of Piedmont. We offer much more than a usual holiday: a really healthy stay in all meanings. Hotel Miramonti is situated in an unspoiled and comfortable natural environment, amidst enchanting landscapes far from traffic, noise, and daily stress.

Forms of payment: *U.S. currency*—cash, travelers checks; *Local currency*—cash, travelers checks; MC, VI

LEONARDO DA VINCI— CASA PER VACANZE

Podere Pagliano
53010 Frosini (Siena)
Toscany, Italy
Phone/Fax: (39) 577 960122

Proprietor: Cielo E. Terra

Category: Hotel

Location: Mountain

Open all year? Open from end of March through October

Price: Moderate

Special packages: Yes

Reader discount: 10%

Child discount: Yes

MEALS

Included: B, L, D

Offered: B, L, D

% Vegetarian: 100%

% Vegan: 65%

% Organic: 20%

Special diets: Yes

Nearby restaurants: No

ROOMS

% Private bath/shower: 70%

% Non-smoking: 100%

% Air conditioned: 0%

Car parking: No

Wheelchair access: No

Non-animal tested toiletries: No

Insecticides used? No

Pets welcome? No

Of animal origin: None

Nearby activities: Outdoor pool, tennis, bicycling, hiking, horseback riding, nutrition classes, camping, beach, yoga, fitness classes, exercise room, massage, juice fasting, sightseeing tours, educational lectures, antique shops, museum, hot springs, lakes, monuments, seminars on therapy/meditation

Description: The hotel is surrounded by oak forests and very close to a green lake. It is a typical Toscany scenario: You will walk for hours and meet deer and wild boars. In a radius of 20 miles you will find Siena (shopping, culture, museums), several medieval castles and "borgos," vineyards, olive trees, rivers, and hot springs. The sea is a 90-minute drive away. The staff speaks English, German, French, and Spanish. Relaxation, delicious food, cozy space, massage, aurasoma, Feldenkrais method, and aromatherapy.

Forms of payment: *U.S. currency*—cash, travelers checks; *Local currency*—cash, travelers checks

CLUB PARADISE

Viale Italia 334
Pinarella
Cervia
Ravenna, Italy
Phone: (39) 0544 987 992
Fax: (39) 0544 987 871

Proprietor: Giovanni Moretti
Category: Self-catering residence
Location: Beachfront
Open all year? Open April-October
Price: Moderate
Special packages: No
Reader discount: 10%
Child discount: Yes

MEALS

Included: None
Offered: Self-catering
% Vegetarian: N/A
% Vegan: N/A
% Organic: N/A
Special diets: N/A
Nearby restaurants: Yes

ROOMS

% Private bath/shower: 100%
% Non-smoking: 0%
% Air conditioned: 0%
Car parking: Yes
Wheelchair access: Yes
Non-animal tested toiletries: No
Insecticides used? No
Pets welcome? Yes
Of animal origin: None
Nearby activities: Outdoor pool, tennis, golf, bicycling, hiking, canoeing/kayaking, boating, water sports, horseback riding, beach

Description: A new building adjacent to pine forest and ocean. Lots of space for enjoying a vacation. Single and double rooms with TV, phone, safe, cooking area. Private beach. Bicycles available, games for children.

Forms of payment: *U.S. currency*—cash, travelers checks, personal checks; *Local currency*—cash, travelers checks

HOTEL ANTONY

Via Titano 114
Pinarello
Cervia
Ravenna, Italy
Phone: (39) 0544 987412
Fax: (39) 0544 987871

Proprietor: Giovanni Moretti
Category: Hotel
Location: Beachfront
Open all year? Open April-September
Price: Moderate
Special packages: Yes
Reader discount: 10%
Child discount: Yes

MEALS

Included: B, L, D
Offered: B, L, D
% Vegetarian: 50%
% Vegan: 50%
% Organic: 50%
Special diets: Yes
Nearby restaurants: No

ROOMS

% Private bath/shower: 100%
% Non-smoking: 0%
% Air conditioned: 0%
Car parking: Yes
Wheelchair access: No
Non-animal tested toiletries: No
Insecticides used? No
Pets welcome? No
Of animal origin: None
Nearby activities: Tennis, golf, bicycling, hiking, canoeing/kayaking, boating, water sports, horseback riding, beach, juice fasting, nightclub

Description: Vacation in a youthful and happy environment where the atmosphere, novelty, buffets, and parties combine with a health-giving climate. Near the city center, ocean, and pine forest. All the rooms have a phone, room and maid service, and a balcony. Air-conditioned dining room, parking facility, elevator, TV room, bar with limited food service. Salad bar with every kind of fresh vegetable, both cooked and raw at every lunch and dinner. Extra virgin olive oil, homemade vinegar, sea salt, etc., show our love of tasty, pure, and wholesome food. Owner-managed hotel.

Forms of payment: *U.S. currency*—cash, travelers checks, personal checks; *Local currency*—cash, travelers checks

ALBERGO ROSY

Via Trebbia #8
Roseto degli Abruzzi 64026 Italy
Phone: 609-782-7310 (U.S.)
Phone/fax: (39) 085 899-2252 (It.)

Proprietor: Roseanna Martella
Category: Hotel
Location: Suburban, quaint village, resort town
Open all year? Open June-September
Price: Moderate
Special packages: Yes
Reader discount: Inquire directly
Child discount: Yes

MEALS

Included: B, L, D

Offered: B, L, D
% Vegetarian: 50%
% Vegan: On request
% Organic: 80%
Special diets: Yes
Nearby restaurants: No

ALBERGO ROSY

ROOMS

% Private bath/shower: 100%
% Non-smoking: 0%
% Air conditioned: 0%
Car parking: No
Wheelchair access: Yes
Non-animal tested toiletries: No
Insecticides used? No
Pets welcome? No
Of animal origin: Feather pillows
Nearby activities: Bicycling, hiking, boating, snorkeling, scuba diving, water sports, nutrition classes, camping, beach, yoga, massage, sightseeing tours, nightclub, antique shops, museums, medieval town

Description: Roseto degli Abruzzi is an enchanting sea-side resort on the Adriatic coast offering two miles of white sand, shady pines, and a charming promenade along the beach. Hotel Rosy offers homemade Abruzzese cooking, macrobiotic meals made with fresh produce directly from the farm, and local wines. Yoga on the beach every morning. Organized trips to the mountains and other special places are available.

Forms of payment: *U.S. currency*—cash; *Local currency*—cash

MOTRANO

**Societa Lila'aurora
53018 Sovicille
Siena, Italy
Phone: (39) 0577 311072**

Proprietor: Anselmi Anselmo
Category: Tourist farm
Location: Quaint village
Open all year? Yes
Price: Moderate
Special packages: Yes
Reader discount: No
Child discount: Yes

MEALS

Included: B, D
Offered: B, L, D
% Vegetarian: 50%
% Vegan: 50%

% Organic: 95%
Special diets: Yes
Nearby restaurants: No

ROOMS

% Private bath/shower: 80%
% Non-smoking: 100%
% Air conditioned: 0%
Car parking: Yes
Wheelchair access: No
Non-animal tested toiletries: No
Insecticides used? No
Pets welcome? Yes
Of animal origin: Farm animals
Nearby activities: Hiking, horseback riding, nutrition classes, yoga, educational lectures, sightseeing tours, craft shops

Description: Motrano is both a tourist farm operation and an art center that organizes activities on food/diet, contact with nature, and creativity. We hold classes in integral yoga, vegetarian cooking, botanicals, mushrooms, and horseback riding.

Forms of payment: *Local currency*—cash, travelers checks

SWEDEN

NORTHERN & CENTRAL EUROPE

MASESGARDEN

Grytnas 61
Leksand 793 92 Sweden
Phone: (46) 247 12231
Fax: (46) 247 12251

Proprietor: Christer Persson
Category: Spa
Location: Quaint village
Open all year? Yes
Price: Moderate
Special packages: Yes
Reader discount: No
Child discount: Yes

MEALS

Included: B, L, D
Offered: B, L, D
% Vegetarian: 100%
% Vegan: 90%
% Organic: 50%
Special diets: Yes
Nearby restaurants: No

ROOMS

% Private bath/shower: 90%
% Non-smoking: 100%
% Air conditioned: 0%
Car parking: Yes
Wheelchair access: No
Non-animal tested toiletries: No
Insecticides used? No
Pets welcome? No
Of animal origin: Leather furniture
Nearby activities: Indoor pool, bicycling, hiking, canoeing/kayaking, cross-country skiing, downhill skiing, nutrition classes, yoga, fitness classes, exercise room, massage, juice fasting, weight loss classes, educational lectures

Description: Situated close to Lake Siljan in the district of old traditions. The classic Swedish health farm.
Forms of payment: *U.S. currency*—cash, travelers checks; *Local currency*—cash, travelers checks; MC, VI

LEONARDO'S

Box 33
Silijansnas 790 34 Sweden
Phone: (46) 247 22495
Fax: (46) 247 23595

Proprietor: Christer Persson
Category: Spa
Location: Mountain
Open all year? Yes
Price: Moderate
Special packages: Yes
Reader discount: No
Child discount: Yes

MEALS

Included: B, L, D
Offered: B, L, D
% Vegetarian: 100%
% Vegan: 90%
% Organic: 50%
Special diets: Yes
Nearby restaurants: No

ROOMS

% Private bath/shower: 100%
% Non-smoking: 100%
% Air conditioned: 0%
Car parking: Yes
Wheelchair access: No
Non-animal tested toiletries: No
Insecticides used? No

Pets welcome? No

Of animal origin: Leather furniture

Nearby activities: Outdoor pool, bicy-cling, hiking, cross-country and downhill skiing, canoeing/kayaking, nutrition classes, yoga, fitness classes, exercise room, massage, juice fasting, educational lectures

Description: You stay from Thursday to Sunday and will join 18 hours of activities and lectures. Wonderful view over the countryside by Lake Siljan.

Forms of payment: *U.S. currency*—cash, travelers checks; *Local currency* —cash, travelers checks; MC, VI

TALLMOGARDEN

Box 48
Sunnansjo 77012 Sweden
Phone: (46) 240 690200
Fax: (46) 240 690235

Proprietor: ——

Category: Spa

Location: Quaint village

Open all year? Yes

Price: Moderate/Expensive

Special packages: No

Reader discount: No

Child discount: Yes

MEALS

Included: B, L, D

Offered: B, L, D

% Vegetarian: On request

% Vegan: On request

% Organic: Varies

Special diets: Yes

Nearby restaurants: No

ROOMS

% Private bath/shower: 0%

% Non-smoking: 100%

% Air conditioned: 0%

Car parking: Yes

Wheelchair access: Yes

Non-animal tested toiletries: No

Insecticides used? No

Pets welcome? No

Of animal origin: Leather furniture, wool rugs

Nearby activities: Indoor pool, golf, bicycling, canoeing/kayaking, boating, cross-country skiing, downhill skiing, nutrition classes, camping, beach, fitness classes, exercise room, massage, juice fasting, weight loss class-es, educational lectures, sight-seeing tours, antique shops, museums, wildlife excursions

Description: A well-known traditional health farm situated in an extremely beautiful country-side. Excellent vegetarian food. Produce from our own green-house. Wide choice of activities and relaxation training, spa and medical baths, massage, as well as skin and cosmetic treat-ments.

Forms of payment: *Local currency*—cash

SWITZERLAND

NORTHERN & CENTRAL EUROPE

BERGPENSION SONNMATT

Schwand
Ebnat-Kappel CH-9642 Switzerland
Phone: (41) 071 99 33 417

Proprietor: M. & S. Fischer
Category: Pension
Location: Mountain
Open all year? Yes
Price: Inexpensive/Moderate
Special packages: Yes
Reader discount: 3%
Child discount: Yes

MEALS

Included: B, L, D
Offered: B, L, D
% Vegetarian: 100%
% Vegan: 10%
% Organic: 80%
Special diets: Yes
Nearby restaurants: No

ROOMS

% Private bath/shower: 20%
% Non-smoking: 100%
% Air conditioned: 0%
Car parking: Yes
Wheelchair access: No
Non-animal tested toiletries: No
Insecticides used? No
Pets welcome? Yes
Of animal origin: Down comforters, wool rugs, feather pillows
Nearby activities: Indoor pool, outdoor pool, tennis, hiking, cross-country skiing, downhill skiing, juice fasting, weight loss classes, sightseeing tours, museums
Description: Homey pension away from heavily trafficked routes. 950 meters above sea level. Good rail connections through our own bus service. Tasty ovo-lacto vegetarian high-quality fare. Generous meals. Family atmosphere. We'll gladly pamper you.
Forms of payment: *Local currency*—cash

HITSCH-HUUS FANAS

CH-7215 Fanas
Graubunden, Switzerland
Phone: (41) 081 325 14 19
Fax: (41) 081 325 32 44

Proprietor: Rudolf Albonico
Category: Hotel
Location: Quaint village
Open all year? Yes
Price: Moderate
Special packages: No
Reader discount: 10% for cash
Child discount: Yes

MEALS

Included: B

Offered: B, L, D

% Vegetarian: On request

% Vegan: Inquire

% Organic: 90%

Special diets: Yes

Nearby restaurants: No

ROOMS

% Private bath/shower: 100%

% Non-smoking: 50%

% Air conditioned: 0%

Car parking: Yes

Wheelchair access: Yes

Non-animal tested toiletries: Yes

Insecticides used? No

Pets welcome? Yes

Of animal origin: Down comforters, feather pillows, farm animals

Nearby activities: Indoor pool, outdoor pool, tennis, golf, bicycling, hiking, canoeing/kayaking, boating, cross-country skiing, downhill skiing, horseback riding, nutrition classes, exercise room, sightseeing tours, antique shops, thermal bath, old mine, mountain climbing, museums

Description: The Hitsch-Huus is a tiny hotel in a small mountain village. Rooms with bath, balcony, minibar. Organic food, partially from our own farm and garden. Skiing, resorts Davos and Klosters, thermal bath Bad Ragaz, old town of Chur are nearby. 900 meters (3000 feet) above sea level. A sunny and quiet spot for enjoying yourself!

Forms of payment: U.S. currency—cash, travelers checks; Local currency —cash, travelers checks

HOTEL BALANCE

CH-1922 Les Granges VS, Switzerland
Phone: (41) 026 761 15 22
Fax: (41) 026 761 15 88

Proprietor: Eberle Roland

Category: Hotel

Location: Mountain, quaint village

Open all year? Closed November 1 and December 25

Price: Moderate

Special packages: No

Reader discount: No

Child discount: Yes

MEALS

Included: B, D

Offered: B, L, D

% Vegetarian: 100%

% Vegan: 90%

% Organic: 98%

Special diets: Yes

Nearby restaurants: No

ROOMS

% Private bath/shower: 30%

% Non-smoking: 100%

% Air conditioned: 0%

Car parking: Yes

Wheelchair access: No

Non-animal tested toiletries: No

Insecticides used? No

Pets welcome? Yes

Of animal origin: Wool rugs, feather pillows

Nearby activities: Outdoor pool, hiking, cross-country skiing, downhill skiing, yoga, massage, educational lectures, sightseeing tours, museums

Description: A vegetarian hotel with healthy and carefully prepared meals. All the food items we use are organic quality. The hotel is located at the highest point of a small peaceful village. You can enjoy a large magnificent garden, a pool heated by solar energy, a garden with aromatic plants, a sauna, a whirlpool, and a beautiful meditation room.

Forms of payment: *U.S. currency*—cash; *Local currency*—cash, travelers checks

FERIEN UND BILDUNGHAUS LINDENBUHL

CH-9043 Trogen, Switzerland
Phone: (41) 0713 441331

Proprietor: Margrit Hemmund
Category: Retreat, conference center
Location: Quaint village
Open all year? Yes
Price: Inexpensive
Special packages: No
Reader discount: No
Child discount: Yes

MEALS

Included: B, L, D
Offered: B, L, D
% Vegetarian: On request
% Vegan: On request
% Organic: 98%
Special diets: Yes
Nearby restaurants: Yes

ROOMS

% Private bath/shower: 2%

% Non-smoking: 100%
% Air conditioned: 0%
Car parking: Yes
Wheelchair access: No
Non-animal tested toiletries: No
Insecticides used? No
Pets welcome? Yes
Of animal origin: Down comforters, feather pillows
Nearby activities: Hiking

Description: Located in the gentle hills of the Appenzell District and offers groups of 10 to 20 persons an ideal spot for holding courses, meetings, workshops, parties or for simply enjoying stress-free vacations. The 200 year-old wooden building has character and 3 beautiful group activity rooms. Emphasis is on providing healthy and varying cuisine.

Forms of payment: *U.S. currency*—cash, travelers checks; *Local currency*—cash, travelers checks; Eurocard

HOTEL MARMOTTE

CH-3906 Saas-fee Wallis, Switzerland
Phone: (41) 028 57 28 52
Fax: (41) 028 57 19 87

Proprietor: Eva Dreier
Category: B&B, resort, hotel
Location: Mountain, resort town
Open all year? Open Dec. 1 to May 1 and June 20 to Oct. 15
Price: Inexpensive/ Moderate
Special packages: Yes
Reader discount: 10%
Child discount: Yes

MEALS

Included: B, D
Offered: B, D
% Vegetarian: On request
% Vegan: Inquire directly
% Organic: 30%
Special diets: Yes
Nearby restaurants: No

ROOMS

% Private bath/shower: 100%
% Non-smoking: 0%
% Air conditioned: 0%
Car parking: Yes
Wheelchair access: Yes
Non-animal tested toiletries: No
Insecticides used? No
Pets welcome? No
Of animal origin: Leather furniture, feather pillows

Nearby activities: Indoor pool, tennis, bicycling, hiking, cross-country skiing, downhill skiing, fitness classes, exercise room, massage, sightseeing tours, mountaineering, climbing

Description: Our pleasant and comfortable hotel is very quiet yet centrally located at the edge of the village center. It is specially suited for visitors seeking the comfort and first-class Swiss cuisine of a top hotel and also the individual, cozy atmosphere of a family enterprise.

Forms of payment: *U.S. currency*—cash, travelers checks; *Local currency* —cash, travelers checks

HOTEL UCLIVA

7158 Waltensburg/Vuorz, Switzerland
Phone: (41) 081 941 22 42
Fax: (41) 081 941 17 40

Proprietor: D. Saladino

Category: Hotel

Location: Mountain, quaint village

Open all year? Closed mid-December and end of October

Price: Moderate

Special packages: Yes

Reader discount: Yes; except high season

Child discount: Yes

MEALS

Included: B, D

Offered: B, L, D

% Vegetarian: 50%

% Vegan: On request

% Organic: 90%

Special diets: Yes

Nearby restaurants: No

ROOMS

% Private bath/shower: 100%

% Non-smoking: 95%

% Air conditioned: 0%

Car parking: Yes

Wheelchair access: Yes

Non-animal tested toiletries: Yes

Insecticides used? No

Pets welcome? Yes

Of animal origin: Wool rugs, down comforters, feather pillows

Nearby activities: Outdoor pool, tennis, bicycling, hiking, boating, downhill skiing, massage, sightseeing tours, museums, sauna

Description: Retreat and revive yourself at Ucliva, the first ecological hotel in the Graubunden (Grisons) Canton. Peace, mountain air, and beautiful paths for strolling and hiking. Child care and play area. Big, well-lit seminar rooms. Creative high-quality menu with organic, regional products. Sauna. Sunning terrace. All rooms have toilet and shower and are heated by wood fuel and solar energy. Attractive program of courses and vacation offerings.

Forms of payment: *U.S. currency*—cash, travelers checks; *Local currency*—cash, travelers checks

Australia

India

Israel

Sri Lanka

The Rest of
the World

VEGA GARDENS

**Holland Creek Rd.
Cudlee Creek S.A. 5232
Adelaide, Australia
Phone: (61) 08 8389 2372**

Proprietor: Rachel Thenisch
Category: Bed & Breakfast
Location: Quaint village
Open all year? Inquire directly
Price: Moderate
Special packages: No
Reader discount: 10%
Child discount: No

MEALS

Included: B
Offered: B, D
% Vegetarian: 100%
% Vegan: 100%
% Organic: 100%
Special diets: Yes
Nearby restaurants: No

ROOMS

% Private bath/shower: 100%
% Non-smoking: 100%
% Air conditioned: 100%
Car parking: Yes
Wheelchair access: No

Non-animal tested toiletries: No
Insecticides used? No
Pets welcome? No
Of animal origin: Wool rugs, down comforters
Nearby activities: Outdoor pool, tennis, golf
Description: Having been an animal liberationist for over 15 years now, I do not buy any more wool products, etc., but I still use what I bought before (woolen blankets for myself and downs for customers).
Forms of payment: *Local currency*—cash

CHENREZIG INSTITUTE

**Johnson Road
Eudlo 4554 Queensland, Australia
Phone: (61) 07 5445 0077
Fax: (61) 07 5445 0088**

Proprietor: N/A
Category: Retreat
Location: Rolling hills and forest
Open all year? Yes
Price: Moderate
Special packages: No
Reader discount: No
Child discount: Yes

MEALS

Included: B, L, D
Offered: B, L, D
% Vegetarian: 100%
% Vegan: 20%

AUSTRALIA

% Organic: 20%
Special diets: Yes
Nearby restaurants: No

ROOMS

% Private bath/shower: 10%
% Non-smoking: 100%
% Air conditioned: 0%
Car parking: Yes
Wheelchair access: No
Non-animal tested toiletries: No
Insecticides used? No
Pets welcome? No
Of animal origin: None

Nearby activities: Tibetan buddhist meditation and retreat center

Description: Chenrezig Institute is situated on 160 acres of subtropical forest and bushwalks with spectacular views over the hills to the sea on Queensland's Sunshine Coast. We offer an atmosphere of peace and tranquility, daily meditations, and regular teachings and courses on Tibetan Buddhist philosophy, psychology, and meditation.

Forms of payment: *Local currency*—cash; MC, VI

HIPPOCRATES HEALTH CENTRE

**Elaine Avenue
Mudgeeraba 4213
Gold Coast, Queensland, Australia
Phone: (61) 075 530 2860**

Proprietor: R. Bradley
Category: Retreat
Location: Mountain, foothills near ocean
Open all year? Yes
Price: Inexpensive
Special packages: Yes
Reader discount: Contact for details
Child discount: Yes

MEALS

Included: B, L, D
Offered: B, L, D
% Vegetarian: 100%
% Vegan: 100%

% Organic: 90%
Special diets: Yes
Nearby restaurants: No

ROOMS

% Private bath/shower: 100%
% Non-smoking: 100%
% Air conditioned: 0%
Car parking: Yes
Wheelchair access: Yes
Non-animal tested toiletries: Yes
Insecticides used? No
Pets welcome? No
Of animal origin: None
Nearby activities: Outdoor pool, tennis, nutrition classes, yoga, fitness classes, massage, juice fasting, weight loss classes, educational lectures

Description: The Hippocrates self-help and self-improvement program focuses on your nutritional, physical, mental, and emotional balance and harmony. Our time-tested health education program fosters your internal cleansing, regeneration, revitalization, and rejuvenation for health, vigor, longevity, and youthful slimness. Dr. Ann Wigmore's Wheatgrass and Living Foods Program—which excludes bread, flesh, dairy products and all processed and cooked foods—has shown hundreds of thousands of people around the world, since 1960, that ideal health is natural for all of us.

Forms of payment: *U.S. currency*—cash, travelers checks; *Local currency* —cash, travelers checks; MC, VI

HOPEWOOD HEALTH CENTER

**103 Greendale Rd
Wallacia 2745
New South Wales, Australia
Phone: (61) 047 738401
Fax: (61) 047 738735**

Proprietor: Sharon Beavon

Category: Retreat

Location: Mountain, riverfront, bushland

Open all year? Yes

Price: Moderate

Special packages: Yes

Reader discount: Inquire directly

Child discount: No

MEALS

Included: B, L, D

Offered: B, L, D

% Vegetarian: 100%

% Vegan: See comments

% Organic: 50%

Special diets: Yes

Nearby restaurants: No

Comments: Smorgasbord-style meals: guest can choose vegan items

ROOMS

% Private bath/shower: 60%

% Non-smoking: 100%

% Air conditioned: 50%

Car parking: Yes

Wheelchair access: Yes

Non-animal tested toiletries: No

Insecticides used? —

Pets welcome? No

Of animal origin: Wool rugs

Nearby activities: Outdoor pool, tennis, golf, bicycling, hiking, canoeing/kayaking, horseback riding, nutrition classes, yoga, fitness classes, exercise room, massage, juice fasting, weight loss classes, educational lectures, sightseeing tours, antique shops, museums, stress management and healthy lifestyle seminars, beauty treatment facilities, tai chi, line dancing, aqua aerobics classes

Description: Come to Hopewood for a holiday, or to enjoy a personal health program. Nestled in the foothills of the Blue Mountains, 68 kilometers from Sydney, this comfortable guest house is an ideal retreat from the stresses of modern living. Hopewood has over 35 years experience in providing a natural health alternative with our unique combination of qualified naturopaths, masseurs, and beauticians. Flexible range of accommodation packages.

Forms of payment: *Local currency*—cash, travelers checks, MC, VI

INDIA

HOTEL SWAGATH

75 Hospital Rd.
Balepet Cross
Bangalore 560 053 India
Phone: (91) 80 2877200 or
(91) 80 2870007

Proprietor: T.K. Duraiswamy
Category: Hotel
Location: City center
Open all year? Yes
Price: Moderate
Special packages: Yes
Reader discount: 10%
Child discount: Yes

MEALS

Included: None
Offered: B, L, D
% Vegetarian: 100%
% Vegan: 95%
% Organic: Varies
Special diets: Yes
Nearby restaurants: Yes

ROOMS

% Private bath/shower: 100%
% Non-smoking: 100%
% Air conditioned: 40%
Car parking: Yes
Wheelchair access: No
Non-animal tested toiletries: Yes
Insecticides used? Yes
Pets welcome? No
Of animal origin: Wool rugs
Nearby activities: Indoor pool, outdoor pool, tennis, golf, bicycling, boating, horseback riding, nutrition classes, camping, yoga, fitness classes, exercise room, massage, juice fasting, weight loss classes, educational lectures, sightseeing tours, nightclub, antique shops, museums

Description: An all-vegetarian hotel. The room, the furnishing, the food, the entire atmosphere is ideal for vegetarians and vegans.

Forms of payment: *Local currency*—cash, travelers checks; MC, VI

XENDRY HEALTH BEACH RESORT

Xendry
Loliem
Canacona (Goa) 403728 India
Phone: (91) 0834 735955
Fax: (91) 0834 735544

Proprietor: Dr. Manu Shah
Category: Resort, spa
Location: Beachfront
Open all year? Yes
Price: Moderate
Special packages: Yes
Reader discount: No
Child discount: Yes

MEALS

Included: B, L, D
Offered: B, L, D
% Vegetarian: 100%
% Vegan: 100%
% Organic: Varies
Special diets: Yes
Nearby restaurants: No

ROOMS

% Private bath/shower: 100%

% Non-smoking: 100%

% Air conditioned: 0%

Car parking: Yes

Wheelchair access: No

Non-animal tested toiletries: Yes

Insecticides used? No

Pets welcome? No

Of animal origin: None

Nearby activities: Outdoor pool, bicycling, hiking, nutrition classes, beach, yoga, fitness classes, exercise room, massage, juice fasting, weight loss classes, educational lectures, sightseeing tours

Description: This unique health/ beach resort offers specialized cranial osteopathy, acupuncture, naturopathy, living food diet, reflexology, yoga, meditation, and other alternative therapies for rejuvenation and relaxation of mind and body. Situated in an unpolluted natural setting by the Arabian Sea, complete with forests for a truly healthful holiday.

Forms of payment: *U.S. currency*—cash, travelers checks; *Local currency* —cash, travelers checks

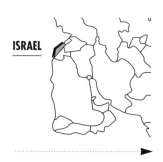

ISRAEL

MOSHAV AMIRIM

**Bikat Beit Hakarem
Carmel 20115 Israel
Phone: (972) 6-980946**

Proprietor: Mordechai Stutt
Category: Bed & Breakfast, cottages
Location: Mountain, quaint village, resort town
Open all year? Yes
Price: Moderate
Special packages: Yes
Reader discount: 10%
Child discount: Yes

MEALS

Included: See comments
Offered: B, L, D
% Vegetarian: 100%
% Vegan: 80%
% Organic: As available
Special diets: Yes
Nearby restaurants: No
Comments: Can choose half-board or full board

ROOMS

% Private bath/shower: 100%
% Non-smoking: 0%
% Air conditioned: 100%
Car parking: Yes
Wheelchair access: Yes
Non-animal tested toiletries: Yes
Insecticides used? No

Pets welcome? Yes
Of animal origin: None
Nearby activities: Outdoor pool, hiking, canoeing/kayaking, downhill skiing, horseback riding, nutrition classes, yoga, fitness classes, massage, juice fasting, weight loss classes, sightseeing tours, nightclub, antique shops, museums
Description: Far from the city's noise and surrounded by nature. Spectacular magnificent view from 800 meters above the Sea of Galilee. Amirim is the only

vegetarian village in Israel with bed and breakfast accommodations. We offer a swimming pool in the summer, a tea house, movies, lectures, Israeli folk dancing, nature walks, jeep tours, a synagogue, a library, and a sculpture garden. Meals are primarily vegan.
Forms of payment: *U.S. currency*—cash, travelers checks

SOUTH CEYLON RESTAURANT & LODGING

Yadehimulla Rd.
Unawatuna, Sri Lanka
Phone: (94) 09 2628

Proprietor: —
Category: Hotel
Location: Quaint village
Open all year? Yes
Price: Moderate
Special packages: Yes
Reader discount: No
Child discount: No

MEALS

Included: B, L, D
Offered: B, L, D
% Vegetarian: 75%
% Vegan: 25%
% Organic: Varies
Special diets: Yes
Nearby restaurants: No

ROOMS

% Private bath/shower: 0%
% Non-smoking: 0%
% Air conditioned: 0%
Car parking: Yes
Wheelchair access: No
Non-animal tested toiletries: No
Insecticides used? No
Pets welcome? No
Of animal origin: None
Nearby activities: Beach, massage, nightclub, antique shops, handicraft, jewelry shop

Description: This is the only vegetarian restaurant in Sri Lanka at present. We intend to open a same type of restaurant at Thiranagama close to Hikkaduwa during the course of next year.

Forms of payment: *U.S. currency*—cash, personal checks; *Local currency*—cash

Other Destinations

THE FOLLOWING organizations offer tours to various countries for vegetarians and vegans:

Green Tortoise Adventure Travel (p. 34)
494 Broadway, San Francisco, CA 94133
(Trips to Mexico and Central America)

Vegi Ventures Holidays (p. 164)
Castle Cottage, Castle Square, Castle Acre, Norfolk, England PE32 2AJ (Trips to Greece, Peru, and Bali)

Wild Explorer Holidays (p. 186)
Skye Environmental Centre, Broadford, Isle of Sky, Scotland (Trips to Russia)

Sea Quest Expeditions, Zoetic Research (p. 49)
P.O. Box 2424, Friday Harbor, WA 98250 (Trips to Mexico)

Laughing Heart Adventures (p. 40)
P.O. Box 669, Willow Creek, CA 92086
(Trips to Belize and Mexico)

Hawk, I'm Your Sister (p. 67)
Box 9109, Santa Fe, NM 87504
(Trips to Mexico, Russia, Bahamas, and Peru)

Her Wild Song (p. 78)
P.O. Box 515, Brunswick, ME 04011 (Trips to Canada)

Yasodhara Ashram Society (p. 22)
Box 9, Kootenay Bay, BC, Canada V0B 1X0 (Trips to Mexico)

Green Hotels

GREEN HOTELS ASSOCIATION is a membership organization comprised of hotels throughout the world. Members are committed to encouraging, promoting, and supporting ecological consciousness in the hospitality industry. "Green" hotels emphasize water conservation through the use of low-flow sink aerators and showerheads and by encouraging guests to re-use towels and linens. They are committed to conserving energy through the use of fluorescent lighting and thinner off-white vinyl-backed lampshades. They use environmentally friendly products such as bulk dispensers for amenities and non-toxic, phosphate-free cleaning solutions. They also participate in recycling programs. Many of these hotels recognize vegetarian and vegan diets.

One money-and-energy-saving feature is a towel rack with a sign that says, "Please decide for yourself. Towels on the rack mean 'I'll use it again.' Towels on the floor mean 'Please exchange.'" The thought here is to reduce the huge amount of unnecessary laundering of hotel towels, which uses large amounts of water, detergent, cleansers, and other solutions detrimental to our habitat. Similar sheet-changing cards can be left on your pillow in the morning to indicate whether sheets need changing or will be used again. (Ordinarily hotel sheets are changed daily.)

For a listing of Green Hotel Asociation member hotels, contact Patricia Griffin at P.O. Box 420212, Houston, TX 77242-0212. Phone 713-789-8889. Fax 713-789-9786.

Index to Cities

WALES

Your Feedback

IF YOU KNOW of any good lodging facilities not in this book that put special emphasis on vegetarianism or cater thoughtfully to vegetarian travelers, please complete the form on the following page and mail it back to us. Photocopy as many copies of this form as you need.

If you can send us a brochure or additional literature from the establishment, that would be very helpful as well.

Mail to Jed & Susan Civic, c/o Larson Publications, 4936 NYS Route 414, Burdett, NY 14818 USA.

Your

Name _____

Address _____

_____

City, ST & Zip _____

Telephone number _____

Establishment

Name _____

Address _____

_____

Country _____

Phone _____

Fax _____

E-mail _____

Your comments about this establishment:

_____

_____

_____

_____

_____

_____

_____

Mail to Jed & Susan Civic
c/o Larson Publications, 4936 NYS Route 414, Burdett, NY 14818 USA.

NAME _____

ADDRESS _____

_____

_____

PHONE _____

_____

_____

_____

_____

_____

_____

_____

NAME _____

ADDRESS _____

_____

_____

PHONE _____

_____

_____

_____

_____

_____

_____

_____

NAME _____

ADDRESS _____

_____

_____

PHONE _____

_____

_____

_____

_____

_____

_____

_____

NAME _____

ADDRESS _____

_____

_____

PHONE _____

_____

_____

_____

_____

_____

_____

_____

NAME

ADDRESS

PHONE

NAME

ADDRESS

PHONE

NAME

ADDRESS

PHONE

NAME

ADDRESS

PHONE

NAME _____

ADDRESS _____

_____

_____

PHONE _____

_____

_____

_____

_____

_____

_____

NAME _____

ADDRESS _____

_____

_____

PHONE _____

_____

_____

_____

_____

_____

_____

_____

NAME _____

ADDRESS _____

_____

_____

PHONE _____

_____

_____

_____

_____

_____

_____

NAME _____

ADDRESS _____

_____

_____

PHONE _____

_____

_____

_____

_____

_____

_____

NAME

ADDRESS

PHONE

NAME

ADDRESS

PHONE

NAME

ADDRESS

PHONE

NAME

ADDRESS

PHONE